HERACLES AND EURIPIDEAN TRAGEDY

Euripides' *Heracles* is an extraordinary play of great complexity, exploring the co-existence of both positive and negative aspects of the eponymous hero. Euripides treats Heracles' ambivalence by showing his uncertain position after the completion of his labours and turns him into a tragic hero by dramatizing his development from the invincible hero of the labours to the courageous bearer of suffering. This book offers a comprehensive reading of *Heracles* examining it in the contexts of Euripidean dramaturgy, Greek drama and fifth-century Athenian society. It shows that the play, which raises profound questions on divinity and human values, deserves to have a prominent place in every discussion about Euripides and about Greek tragedy. Tracing some of Euripides' most spectacular writing in terms of emotional and intellectual effect, and discussing questions of narrative, rhetoric, stagecraft and audience reception, this work is required reading for all students and scholars of Euripides.

THALIA PAPADOPOULOU is Lecturer in Greek at the University of Ioannina.

CAMBRIDGE CLASSICAL STUDIES

HERACLES AND EURIPIDEAN TRAGEDY

THALIA PAPADOPOULOU
University of Ioannina

CAMBRIDGE
UNIVERSITY PRESS

CAMBRIDGE UNIVERSITY PRESS
Cambridge, New York, Melbourne, Madrid, Cape Town, Singapore, São Paulo

CAMBRIDGE UNIVERSITY PRESS
The Edinburgh Building, Cambridge CB2 2RU, UK
Published in the United States of America by Cambridge University Press, New York

www.cambridge.org
Information on this title: www.cambridge.org/9780521851268

© Faculty of Classics, University of Cambridge 2005

First published 2005

Printed in the United Kingdom at the University Press, Cambridge

A catalogue record for this book is available from the British Library

ISBN-13 978-0-521-85126-8 hardback
ISBN-10 0-521-85126-2 hardback

CONTENTS

ACKNOWLEDGMENTS

This book is a revised version of my Cambridge Ph.D. thesis. I should like to express my gratitude to the Greek State Scholarship Foundation for awarding me a Scholarship-by-examination, without which I would not have undertaken graduate work. For financial assistance I am also grateful to the A. G. Leventis Foundation for a supplementary grant towards College fees. I would also like to thank the Cambridge Faculty of Classics for the Laurence Studentship, as well as the University of Cambridge for an Award from the Jebb Fund. I am also grateful to the Faculty of Classics and Newnham College for providing me with a unique environment for research and social life, as well as for being generous in giving me many conference grants.

My interest in Greek tragedy originated in my happy under-graduate years at the University of Thessaloniki, and in Antonios Kapsomenos' thought provoking lectures on Aeschylus, and continued in my equally happy graduate years at Cambridge. My greatest debt I owe to my Supervisor, Pat Easterling, and it is a great pleasure to express my love and thanks. Words fail to express how much I am indebted to her for her exemplary teaching and unfailing sup-port. I am immensely grateful to her for her consistent concern, encouragement and help during my M.Phil. and Ph.D. as well as during the revision of my doctoral thesis for publication.

I would also like to thank my Ph.D. examiners, James Diggle and Christopher Collard, for making useful comments on the thesis and for recommending it to Cambridge University Press. I am very grateful to Professor Diggle also for his constant support and kindness during my graduate years at Cambridge. The editors of the Cambridge Classical Studies series, Richard Hunter and Michael Reeve, have helped considerably in reshaping the work and I would like to thank them for their suggestions.

I also wish to thank the staff of Cambridge University Press, especially Michael Sharp and Linda Woodward, for overseeing the production of the book.

Thanks also go to Ewen Bowie and Stephen Harrison for a lectureship at Corpus Christi College, Oxford, in 2000–1, as well as to the interview committee of Wolfson College, Oxford, for a Junior Research Fellowship during the same period; on both occasions I benefited a great deal from the research environment and the friendly atmosphere. I am also grateful to the staff members of the Department of Classics, University of Crete, and especially to Michael Paschalis, for a temporary lectureship during 2001–2, which enabled me to continue my work under the most pleasant circumstances.

In 2001 I was elected to a lectureship at the University of Ioannina and it is with pleasure that I thank all colleagues who welcomed me to the Classics department; special gratitude is owed to Soteroula Constantinidou, Magda Strouggari and Gerasimoula Zographou for their unfailing kindness. But my greatest thanks are due to two people in the department who believed in me, and I am very grateful to them for their constant concern and support: Mary Mantziou and I. N. Perysinakis have had a profound influence on me and I could never thank them enough.

Finally, I am grateful to many friends, especially Natasha Neogi, Katia Caldari, Nikos Charalabopoulos, Tim Duff, Evelyn Fong, Stavros Frangoulidis, Emily Greenwood, Evangelos Karakasis, Ashwini Kshirsagar, Ismene Lada-Richards, Sue Mullin-Meissner, Noriko Yasumura, Dimitris Yatromanolakis and Misun Yun, for providing me with the most welcome context of *philia* during various periods of my work. Special thanks go to my sister Kiki, her husband George and my grandmother Thalia for their understanding, affection and moral support; and, above all, to my parents, Charalambos Papadopoulos and Maria De Filippo, to whom this book is dedicated with love and gratitude for everything.

ABBREVIATIONS

NOTE: The Euripidean text is cited from the standard edition by J. Diggle in the Oxford Classical Texts (3 vols., 1981–94). Fragments of Aeschylus and Sophocles are cited from the editions of Radt in *TrGF* (see below), while those of Euripides are cited, unless otherwise stated, from A. Nauck, *Tragicorum Graecorum Fragmenta*, 2nd edn, Leipzig 1889, with a *Supplementum* by B. Snell, Hildesheim 1964. Names of authors and their works are generally abbreviated as in *OCD*[3] (= *The Oxford Classical Dictionary*, eds. S. Hornblower and A. Spawforth, 3rd edn, Oxford 1996).

Bernabé, *PEG*	A. Bernabé, *Poetae epici Graeci*, 1, Leipzig 1988.
Davies	M. Davies, *Epicorum Graecorum fragmenta*. Göttingen 1988.
Diggle	J. Diggle (ed.), *Tragicorum Graecorum Fragmenta Selecta*. Oxford 1998.
DK	H. Diels and W. Kranz, *Fragmente der Vorsokratiker*, 6th edn, Berlin 1952.
FGrH	F. Jacoby, *Fragmente der griechischen Historiker*. Berlin and Leiden 1923–58.
K–A	R. Kassel and C. Austin, *Poetae comici Graeci*, vol. 1. Berlin 2001.
Kambitsis	J. Kambitsis (ed.), *Euripides: Antiope*. Athens 1972.
LIMC	*Lexicon iconographicum mythologiae classicae*. Zurich and Munich 1981–97.
LSJ	H. G. Liddell, R. Scott, H. Stuart Jones, R. Mc Kenzie, *A Greek–English Lexicon*, 9th edn, Oxford 1940.

PMG	D. L. Page, *Poetae melici Graeci*. Oxford 1962.
PMGF	M. Davies, *Poetarum melicorum Graecorum fragmenta*. Oxford 1991.
TrGF	B. Snell, R. Kannicht and S. L. Radt, *Tragicorum Graecorum fragmenta*. Göttingen 1971–85.

INTRODUCTION: HERACLES IN PERSPECTIVE

This is a study of Euripides' *Heracles*, a play which has given rise to a wide range of responses on the part of the critics, from condemnation to admiration.[1] In some ways, of course, the tradition of interpretation of a particular play stays consistent over a long period, because all commentators and critics use previous readings, but their manner of reading is also informed by changes in their cultural environment. At the same time, the study of tragedy, set against the larger framework of the humanities, is continuously enriched by trends in literary criticism.[2] The underestimated subtlety and the critical history of the play justify writing a whole book on *Heracles*. To begin with, this is a play of great significance in examinations of other Euripidean dramas, especially in discussions of themes such as heroic ethics, madness and the role of the gods. But, above all, it is a drama which deserves a full and fresh treatment in its own right because it represents some of Euripides' most spectacular writing, in terms of emotional and intellectual effect, structure, narrative, rhetoric, stagecraft and audience reception.

Most studies during the nineteenth and twentieth centuries focused on the unity of the play, either questioning or defending it.[3] Wilamowitz[4] devoted his imposing study of Greek tragedy to

---

[1] Cf. 'broken backed' (Murray 1946: 112); 'the most tragic of all the dramas of Euripides' (Bates 1930: 105); 'the structure of the play is very simple. Neither the course of events nor the interplay of characters provides anything dramatically notable' (Vellacott 1963: 14); 'an extraordinary play, innovative in its treatment of the myth, bold in its dramatic structure, and filled with affecting human pathos' (Halleran 1988: vii); 'the most underrated of all Greek tragedies' (Walton 1977: xviii); 'one of the greatest Euripidean tragedies' (Reinhardt 2003: 23); 'masterpiece' (Hall 2003: vii).

[2] For these issues, see e.g. Segal 1986a; Michelini 1987: 3–51; Goldhill 1997. For tendencies in Euripidean scholarship, see the collections of essays in Burian 1985; Cropp et al. 2000; Mossman 2003.

[3] See in brief Bond 1981: xvii–xxvi.   [4] Wilamowitz ²1895.

this particular play, and his approach proved to be influential for at least a couple of generations. The question of unity was essential to Wilamowitz, and one way to defend it was his theory that Heracles does not suddenly go mad but already shows signs of madness on his first appearance on stage. The emerging science of psychology during the nineteenth century probably influenced the 'megalomaniac' theory, according to which the strains of the labours were the cause of Heracles' madness. In Wilamowitz's view, which suppressed Heracles' panhellenic status, the hero in the play was the Dorian hero *par excellence*, whose main characteristic was manly courage.[5]

The unity and structure of the play remained the focus of research for many decades after Wilamowitz's work. The treatment of myth and the arrangement of the plot have been variously examined,[6] and issues such as the eccentricities of the plot or the dramatic ironies became the focus of critical analysis, which showed an increasing interest in generic definition; hence, although *Heracles* is a tragedy, it was credited with elements which distanced it from what was considered 'a true tragedy'.[7] All these approaches have in general treated *Heracles* as a literary work. On the other hand, there were also studies which examined the play as a source for historical information and sought to establish a direct correspondence between the text and contemporary events.[8] A more elaborate approach to the political meaning of the play was made in the eighties, under the impact of studies which emphasized *polis* consciousness and the relation between myth and *polis*,[9] and the focus shifted to an evaluation of some aspects of the play against the background of Athenian democracy.[10]

---

[5] See Bond 1981: xxxii.
[6] See esp. Kitto [3]1961[first published in 1939]; Grube 1941; Conacher 1967; Burnett 1971; Michelini 1987: 231–42; Barlow 1993; Barlow 1996.
[7] See Michelini 1987: 27 on the approach by Conacher (1967). For generic distinctions with regard to tragedy, cf. Kitto [3]1961. For a recent evaluation of tragedy and genre terminology, see Mastronarde 2000.
[8] Cf. Parmentier and Grégoire 1923: 12–15 on *Heracles*. Cf. more generally Delebecque 1951; Zuntz 1955; Goossens 1962; more recently Vickers 1995.
[9] Cf. the influential work by Vernant and Vidal-Naquet 1988.
[10] Cf. Foley 1985; Michelini 1987.

The presentation of Heracles, the question of his madness, and the role of the gods, have been central issues in every discussion of the play and have often led to contradictory approaches. For example, the Euripidean Heracles has been viewed at one extreme as an essentially flawed figure[11] and at the other as an idealized character.[12] His madness has been taken as divinely imposed[13] but modern categories such as manic depression have also been used to describe it.[14] And although the religious universe of the play seems to consist in vindictive anthropomorphic gods, several critics have argued that Euripides, via Heracles, undermines their divine status, expresses strong disbelief to the point of erasing them, and introduces a new notion of divinity.[15]

Although the play has attracted plenty of critical attention, either in its own right or in discussions of other plays, most studies have focused on individual issues or examined the play from a specific angle. The most interesting of these contributions is the chapter on *Heracles* by Foley,[16] which examines the sacrificial metaphor in the play, showing how the archaic poetic tradition about Heracles is made relevant to Athenian democratic society. Anthropology and literary criticism are here fruitfully combined and illuminate aspects of Euripides' dramatic technique.

My own approach in this book aims at offering a comprehensive reading of the play, which will explore the literary and cultural background as well as the subtleties of Euripides' dramatic technique, by examining it in the contexts of Euripidean dramaturgy, of Greek tragedy more generally and of fifth-century Athenian society. At the same time I try to illuminate some aspects of Heracles as a mythical hero. My aim is to show that Euripides' *Heracles* is an extraordinary play, of great complexity, which raises profound questions about divinity and human values. The discussion offers a fresh evaluation of central themes in the play and of Heracles as a tragic hero, bringing out what makes him so exceptional: the co-existence of

---

[11] E.g. Burnett 1971.   [12] E.g. Yunis 1988.   [13] E.g. Bond 1981.
[14] E.g. Barlow 1996.   [15] For an overview, see Lawrence 1998.   [16] Foley 1985.

3

both positive and negative aspects in his behaviour, to a degree unmatched by any other figure in Greek tragedy. Of course, both aspects are well known from the literary tradition; but the important thing is the subtle way in which Euripides evokes for his audience different sides of Heracles within a single play. In chapter 1, for example, I use narratological criteria to show how the bold structure of the play hints at the complexity of Heracles. This complexity is corroborated by an examination of the ritual elements which also point in the same direction. Overall, a thorough investigation helps to demonstrate that the figure of Heracles and the play as a whole are more complex than many critics have thought. At this point it will be helpful to give a brief outline of Heracles in tradition, as it is against this background that the presentation of the Euripidean Heracles will be examined.

Heracles was an important figure in literature, art and cult throughout Greek and Roman antiquity and this fascination in him has persisted in many later cultures.[17] An investigation of all the various adaptations of the hero throughout the centuries is in itself a Herculean task.[18] What is important is that so many periods found in Heracles elements which they could appropriate and redefine according to their own ideologies and concerns. An aspect of Heracles which is evident in every examination of him is his fundamental ambivalence,[19] a fact which may explain both the fascination which he has exerted through the centuries and the often contradictory ways in which he has been presented.

Heracles' double-sidedness starts from his own semi-divine self as the son of Zeus. He is both mortal and immortal, and he is also worshipped both as a hero and as a god. The

---

[17] Cf. esp. Galinsky 1972; Effe 1980; Vollkommer 1988; Boardman et al. 1988 and 1990; Farnell 1921: 910–1000; Jourdain-Annequin 1989; Bonnet and Jourdain-Annequin 1992; Mastrocinque 1993.

[18] The best study of the adaptations of Heracles remains that by Galinsky 1972.

[19] For a concise account of Heracles' ambivalence in both Greece and Rome, see Fitch 1987: 15–20. On Heracles' ambivalent aspects, see also Kirk 1977. Cf. Loraux 1990 and 1995: 116–39, who adds to Heracles' contradictions, as listed by Kirk, that between virile and feminine (on Heracles' similarity with Dionysus in this respect, see Lada-Richards 1999: 18–25).

4

ambivalence of his status in cult is well summarized in Pindar's reference to him as ἥρως θεός (*Nem.* 3.22). There is the same contradiction in representations of his heroic valour. On the one hand he is the civilizer of mankind, the epitome of excellence. On the other hand, he is the transgressive warrior, a representative of excess. Thus in Homer he is mentioned as a powerful hero and dearest to Zeus (*Il.* 18.115–21), but he is also the godless and abominable man who dared to attack the gods (*Il.* 5.403–4). He is a hero of supreme valour, whom Odysseus admits he could not rival (*Od.* 8.223–5), but he is a flawed hero, who does not hesitate to challenge the gods and to violate the law of hospitality (*Od.* 8.223–5; 21.11–41).

In particular, his murder of his guest Iphitus is one of the darkest episodes in Heracles' life; in this respect it is interesting that in post-Homeric tradition there was also another version introduced, according to which Heracles' murder of Iphitus was the result of madness,[20] like the attack of madness during which the hero killed his family. This version of the story of Iphitus' murder, which uses madness to exonerate Heracles from responsibility, is a telling example of the tendency to cleanse him of his negative aspects, a tendency which was in accord with the gradual moralization and intellectualization of the hero that developed especially from the fifth century onwards.

The idea of Heracles as a culture hero takes shape in Hesiod, and his labours outline his civilizing role in accord with Zeus's beneficent role in the world. On the other hand, attacks on the credibility of his supernatural exploits, especially under Ionian rationalizing influence in the sixth century BC, also challenged the validity of his *arete,* 'virtue' or 'excellence'. This *arete* was also brought into question by the lyric poets, preoccupied with inner experience rather than with exterior exploits. It was especially the gradual 'internalization' of Heracles which led the way to his treatment by the philosophers as an example of virtue. Bacchylides has a prominent role in this process, shown

---

[20] Schol. Pind. *Isthm.* 4.104g (Dr.) on the account by Herodorus (*FGrH* 32); Apoll. *Bibl.* 2.6.2; Tzetz. *Chil.* II, 36.425.

by his famous portrayal of an emotional Heracles who feels compassion and weeps for the fate of Meleager (5.155–8).

The tension between the positive and the threatening sides of Heracles continues in every period in antiquity. Thus, Stesichorus attempted to suppress Heracles' transgressive aspect, whereas Panyassis revived it.[21] Similarly, the image of an intellectualized Heracles, which is usually associated with the sophist Prodicus[22] and which developed in both philosophy and rhetoric from the fifth century onwards, is quite distinct from Heracles in Apollonius Rhodius' *Argonautica*, which revives him as the hero who is second to none in might, but whose *arete*, based on physical strength, seems out of context, and who is eventually removed from the epic by being left behind by the Argo when he has gone to look for Hylas (1.1257–1362). In general, the notion that Heracles' power was excessive is evident in attempts to suppress it. Thus Pisander called Heracles 'the justest of homicides' (fr. 10 Bernabé, *PEG*), for his violence was directed against evil-doers.

Pindar too,[23] for whom Heracles became the ideal ethical hero, constantly stressed that Heracles was doing a service to mankind in ridding it of evil creatures who violated human and divine laws (e.g. *Nem.* 1.62–6; *Ol.* 10.34), and he also rejected the stories of Heracles' hubristic attacks on the gods (*Ol.* 9.30–41). Even in favourable approaches to Heracles, there is a tendency to define his *arete* not in terms of his physical strength but in terms of his spiritual qualities. Thus Isocrates praises Heracles not for his external achievements, but for qualities such as his wisdom or justice (5.109–14). Accordingly, although his labours are of course important, it is at the same time recognized that there are other challenges that the hero can face, challenges which have nothing to do with fights against monsters, but with circumstances in human life. *Heracles* is a

---

[21] See Galinsky 1972: 20–1, 25.
[22] Prodicus' famous fable 'The Choice of Heracles', where the hero prefers the hard path of virtue to the easy path of vice, and undertakes the labours out of free choice rather than under constraint, is paraphrased in Xen. *Mem.* 2.1.21–34. On this see Kuntz 1994.
[23] On the tendency to justify Heracles' violence in Pisander, Stesichorus and Pindar, see Gentili 1977.

prime and early example of the process whereby Heracles finds himself confronted by circumstances more difficult than his labours.

Heracles is the most popular character of satyr-play after Silenus and the satyrs themselves, and his predominant role is that of fighting evil-doers. Satyr-drama, with its fairy-tale like settings and characters, was the most suitable for accommodating Heracles, who often transgressed the borders between civilization and wildness as well as between humanity and bestiality. The excess of his behaviour, whether good or bad, was suitable for comedy, too. It is usually his insatiable appetite and excessive drinking, which mingle with his traditional role as the mighty hero and the punisher of the wicked, that make Heracles comic. Thus in Aristophanes' *Birds* he is determined to throttle whoever objects to the gods, only to change his mind at the smell of food (1574–90).

Compared to the frequency of Heracles' appearances in satyr-drama and comedy, the relatively infrequent presentations of him in tragedy have often been explained in terms of his comic associations or of the nature of his exploits, which would not be suitable in tragedy.[24] His ambivalent status, too, which shares in both humanity and divinity, may have made tragic treatments of Heracles problematic. The belief that whatever misfortunes he experienced, he was eventually rewarded with immortality may have accounted for the rarity of his appearances as the protagonist in tragedy. He appears in the role of a saviour in *Prometheus Unbound*, Sophocles' *Athamas*, Euripides' *Alcestis* and *Auge* and [Euripides'] *Peirithous*, while in *Philoctetes* this role takes on a new dimension as there he has divine status and appears as a *deus ex machina* in order to help Philoctetes and to carry out Zeus's will. The deified status of Heracles is also presented in *Heraclidae* (857–8; 869–72), where, though he does not appear, his divine intervention is reported by the Messenger.

---

[24] On Heracles in Athenian drama, see Conradie 1958; Woodford 1966: 49–115; Galinsky 1972: 40–100. On Heracles' relatively rare presence in tragedy as opposed to comedy and satyr-drama, see Silk 1993. On the tragic Heracles, see also Nesselrath 1997.

It is only in two extant tragedies, that is, *Trachiniae* and *Heracles,* that Heracles is at the centre of the drama as the suffering hero. *Trachiniae* presents him near the end of his heroic career and dramatizes the way in which he responds to his suffering. In *Trachiniae,* Heracles is the 'best of men' (811), but at the same time his valour is darkened with his portrayal as lustful and vengeful in his sack of Oechalia, as deceitful in his murder of Iphitus and as inflexible in his relationship with both his wife and son.

Like *Trachiniae, Heracles*[25] presents the hero at the end of his heroic career and also dramatizes the relation of Heracles with his family. The familiarity of the audience with previous portrayals of the hero is crucial for guiding the reception of Heracles in this particular play. Heracles is now portrayed as a more humanized and domesticated hero, until the onset of madness violently reverses this image and turns him into the murderer of his own family. The play thus brings to the fore the question of Heracles' *arete* with regard both to his heroic career in the past and to his familial and civic present. The relation between past and present is problematized in the play, as is also the role of the gods and the relation between them and humans. The themes raised throughout the play concerning the status of heroic excellence and the status of divinity and humanity are taken forward to their redefinition in a new context, into which Heracles can finally be safely integrated, and which also evokes for the Athenian audience familiar ideas concerning their own distinctive qualities as Athenians.

Ritual and violence, madness and the gods, *arete* and the image of Athens are central units comprising a number of important themes. Each of the next three chapters elaborates on a different thematic unit, and together they constitute a reading of the Euripidean play.

---

[25] On the relative dating of these two plays, see Easterling 1982: 19–23 and Bond 1981: xxx–xxxii respectively. Easterling 1982: 23 suggests a date between 457 and 430 BC for *Trachiniae,* while Bond 1981: xxxi argues for a date between 415 and 406 BC for *Heracles.* In his OCT edition of *Heracles,* 116, Diggle suggests a date around 415 BC for *Heracles.*

RITUAL AND VIOLENCE

Introduction

In the previous section I showed how the literary tradition from Homer onwards provides conflicting views about the mythological figure of Heracles. In particular, I pointed out that what seems to be constantly brought to the fore is a sense of an extreme ambivalence concerning the nature of Heracles' *arete*, 'virtue' or 'excellence'. On the one hand he is portrayed as the invincible hero and civilizer of mankind, an exemplar of virtue; on the other hand he is presented as the megalomaniac and hubristic conqueror, a representative of excess. In this chapter I will argue that Euripides exploits the dynamics of this ambivalence for his own dramatic purposes. What is missing in previous approaches to *Heracles* is an understanding of the central role of Heracles' ambivalence. The question is not whether Heracles is innocent or hubristic; what matters is the interplay between his virtue and his excess. The use of ritual[1] in the play makes a good starting point, particularly as the onset of Heracles' madness is set in a sacrificial context.

---

[1] On ritual and literature in general, see esp. Hardin 1983. The study of ritual and tragedy has focused on the sacrificial origins of the tragic genre (cf. Burkert 1966; Guépin 1968) and on sacrificial structures and themes in the plays (cf. Zeitlin 1965 and 1966; Seidensticker 1979; Foley 1985; Vidal-Naquet 1988; Lloyd-Jones 1998; Krummen 1998; Henrichs 2000; Gibert 2003), while comprehensive accounts of the function of different rituals have also been given and the association between ritual action and theatrical action has been explored (cf. Easterling 1988 and 1993a; Jouanna 1992; Seaford 1994; Rehm 1994; Lada-Richards 1997 and 1998; Tzanetou 2000). See also Sourvinou-Inwood 2003 for an examination of the ritual context as well as the deployment of ritual in Greek tragedy.

Ritual and ambivalence

In *Heracles* ritual has an ever-present and multi-dimensional role: supplication, *makarismos*, victory-song, hero-cult, all have their place in this tragedy.[2] But the aspect which dominates, and which acquires the major function to the point of becoming, arguably, the subject of the play,[3] is that of purification by means of sacrifice; in this respect, the dramatic action culminates in the event which determines everything else and around which everything else revolves, i.e. the catastrophic perversion of a purificatory sacrificial procedure, which results in a series of 'sacrificial' deaths. This development is significant not only because of the inherently problematic character of 'reversal' and all its connotations in tragedy, but also, in a broader sense, because sacrificial death is evidently a recurrent topic in Euripidean tragedies and indeed inextricably interwoven with their thematic concerns.[4]

With this in mind let us now examine the inversion of Heracles' purificatory sacrificial act, which lies at the core of the drama and constitutes the climax of the sacrificial imagery. In *Heracles*, the imposition of madness upon the hero, which results in the unintentional murder of his wife and children, is foreshadowed in the extraordinary scene between Iris and Lyssa, in an ascending order, i.e. from the general outline of the divine plan given by Iris and her exhortation to her unwilling companion (822–40), to the description by Lyssa of the nature of the forthcoming madness (861–6, in future tenses), until the direct presentation of the onset of madness (867–70, in present tenses), which is followed by the prediction of the subsequent stages of madness (871, in future tenses).

Although the scene between Iris and Lyssa sets in motion the off-stage action which is subsequently verified in the Messenger's long *rhesis*,[5] it does not provide any reference at

---

[2] See Sourvinou-Inwood 2003: 361–77.

[3] Cf. Girard 1977: 40.   [4] See Foley 1985: 21.

[5] As de Jong 1991: 165 n. 116 remarks, there are three symptoms, i.e. shaking of the head, groaning and irregular breathing, which were mentioned by Lyssa but are not reported by the Messenger.

all either to the ritual moment or to the ritual setting. The emphasis is all on the symptoms of Heracles' wild disorder: shaking his head and rolling his eyes, breathing uncontrollably and bellowing like a bull (867–70). In fact, the ritual context is introduced for the first time at the beginning of the Messenger's *rhesis*, in the form of an *ekphrasis* (922–30):

ἱερὰ μὲν ἦν πάροιθεν ἐσχάρας Διὸς
καθάρσι' οἴκων, γῆς ἄνακτ' ἐπεὶ κτανὼν
⟨ἐξέβαλε⟩ τῶνδε δωμάτων Ἡρακλέης·
χορὸς δὲ καλλίμορφος εἱστήκει τέκνων
πατήρ τε Μεγάρα τ', ἐν κύκλωι δ' ἤδη κανοῦν
εἵλικτο βωμοῦ, φθέγμα δ' ὅσιον εἴχομεν.
μέλλων δὲ δαλὸν χειρὶ δεξιᾶι φέρειν,
ἐς χέρνιβ' ὡς βάψειεν,' Ἀλκμήνης τόκος
ἔστη σιωπῆι.

Offerings were set in front of Zeus's altar to purify the house after Heracles had killed the king and ⟨flung⟩ his body outside the palace. The children stood there in a graceful cluster with Megara and Heracles' father. The basket had just been passed in a circle round the altar and we were reverently keeping silent. Then, just as he was about to bring a torch in his right hand to dip in the holy water, Alcmena's son stopped and stood silent[6]

The emphasis on the ritual context[7] is evident later on in the play too, when Heracles, having just learned from Amphitryon about his horrible crimes, asks at what point madness attacked him; Amphitryon answers by giving both the ritual moment and the ritual setting (1144–5):

Ηρ. ποῦ δ' οἶστρος ἡμᾶς ἔλαβε; ποῦ διώλεσεν;
Αμ. ὅτ' ἀμφὶ βωμὸν χεῖρας ἡγνίζου πυρί.

Heracles: Where did the attack take me? Where did it destroy me?
Amphitryon: By the altar when you were purifying your hands at the fire.

The exact nature of the ritual initiated by Heracles is commonly now taken to consist in a purification by means of a sacrificial procedure with animal victims rather than by means of fire.[8] This purification is intended to cleanse both the house

---

[6] Translations from *Heracles* will be quoted throughout from Barlow 1996.
[7] Cf. Girard 1977: 40.
[8] See the discussion in Foley 1985: 153 n. 11.

(923: καθάρσι'οἴκων, 'to purify the house') and Heracles
himself (940: ἁγνιῶ χέρας, 'I shall cleanse my hands'; 1145:
χεῖρας ἡγνίζου, 'you were purifying your hands') from the
murder of Lycus. The expression ἐσχάρας Διὸς, 'Zeus's
altar', in line 922 refers to that of Ζεὺς Ἑρκεῖος,[9] which is
different from the altar at which Heracles' family had taken
refuge; that was the altar of Ζεὺς Σωτήρ, instituted by Heracles
in celebration of his triumphs (47–9). The reference to the altar of
Ζεὺς Ἑρκεῖος is dramatically effective because of its symbolism,
that is, its association with family. Rehm[10] gives examples
illustrating the symbolism of this altar: its pollution by
Eurydice in *Antigone*, an act which signals the death of the
family, and of course the *locus classicus* in the epic tradition for
the destruction of a family, i.e. the murder of Priam at the altar
of the same god.

In *Heracles* then, the reference is more than apt, since the
purificatory animal sacrifice intended to take place at this altar
ultimately results in the perverted sacrifice of the family
around it; in other words, the *locus* of domestic cult and
familial cohesion, besides being a dramatic image of the solidarity of the family group before sacrifice, is suddenly turned
into the *locus* of an outrageous familial annihilation. The
powerful contrast via the symbolism of the altar could not be
more striking.The altar of Zeus was certainly the most appropriate for the performance of this ritual procedure. As Parker[11]
remarks: 'the god at whose altar murderers sought purification
was Zeus; he acquired this function, which fell to him naturally
as god of suppliants, when he performed for Ixion the first of
all such rites'.

Apart from *Heracles*, the violent disruption of a sacrifice at a
critical moment of the dramatic action also appears in four
other extant tragedies. In *Trachiniae* (749–806) Heracles' offering
of a hecatomb is suddenly interrupted, when the ritual fire
which the hero lights to purify himself from the blood he
spilt during his labours activates the poison in his robe,
which consumes him. The imposing sacrifice eventually 'turns

[9] See Bond 1981 ad loc.   [10] Rehm 1994: 66 and n. 25.   [11] Parker 1983: 139.

12

out to be a sacrifice in which the sacrificer himself becomes the victim: Heracles is going to be burned on the pyre on Mt Oeta instead of conducting the hecatomb at Cape Cenaeum'.[12] Segal[13] elaborates on the way in which the spread of violence in all directions unites the destructiveness of the present sacrifice with Heracles' lust and with the centaur's instructions; the transformation of the sacrificer into the sacrificial victim, that is, the inversion of the roles between human and animal during the sacrifice, ultimately marks the fusion of Heracles with Nessus, his bestial double. The differences are effaced: the lust and bestiality of both are eventually united literally through the blood of Nessus on the robe which devours Heracles' flesh. Thus, the sacrifice, which is given a prominent role in the drama, becomes the scene in which, as Segal (1990a: 22) remarks, 'the violence hidden within humans breaks forth into its clearest, most terrible form. At this point, humanity is converted into its bestial opposite and double. The result is chaos for both the house and city, until (in this play at least) another sacrificial act and a purer fire, now for a self-chosen death, intimate a movement in the opposite direction.'

Girard[14] attributes the failure of Heracles' purificatory ritual in *Heracles* to 'a special sort of impurity' that 'clings to the warrior returning to his homeland', owing to 'the contagious nature of the violence encountered by the warrior in battle'.[15] Foley[16] corroborates Girard's observation, by referring to Douglas'[17] analysis of impurity as a characteristic of transitional states; however, Foley thinks that such a view is applicable only to the Sophoclean play, which portrays a violent hero, and not to *Heracles*, which presents, according to her view, a constantly modest Heracles. I shall discuss later

---

[12] Easterling 1982: 6.   [13] Segal 1990a; see also Segal 1995a: 58–9.
[14] Girard 1977: 40–2.
[15] On the ambivalence associated with the ancient warrior in general, see Dumézil 1969 (89–94 on Heracles). See also Konstan 1999: 85–7, who discusses the inherently dangerous nature of the warrior and the anxiety that the military violence will turn into domestic violence using examples from tragedy (the Euripidean Heracles), philosophy (the guardians in Plato's *Republic*) and comedy (the soldier in Menander's *The Shorn Girl*).
[16] Foley 1985: 159 and n. 24.   [17] Douglas 1966.

in this chapter the relation between the failure of the purificatory ritual in *Heracles* and the nature of Heracles' *arete*.

In Euripides' *Electra* (774–855) the sacrifice of a bull which is conducted by the usurper and adulterer Aegisthus turns into his own 'sacrificial' death at the hands of Orestes. The murder of Aegisthus is evidently pictured as a 'sacrifice' corresponding to the archetypal sacrificial murder in Greek tragedy, that of Agamemnon (*Ag.* 1118; 1433; 1504).[18] In Euripides' play, the presentation of the abrupt reversal of the role between sacrificer and sacrificed within a context of an outrageous violation of ritual propriety and norms casts a shadow over the otherwise justified revenge upon Aegisthus, and provides insight into central themes that the play raises.[19] The emphasis on the justifiability of a killing on the one hand, and the ritual outrage within which this killing occurs on the other, shows the problematic character of the exacted revenge, and this kind of juxtaposition will also prove to be of fundamental significance in *Heracles*, a tragedy which shares many patterns with *Electra*.[20]

In *Andromache* (1100–60) Neoptolemus, while he is engaged in sacrificial rites before his prayer to Apollo in Delphi, falls victim to the murderous ambush arranged against him by Orestes. Whether viewed, as it usually has been, as an attack on Delphi and Orestes, or as an example of the disastrous aftermath of war on victors and vanquished alike,[21] the prolonged description of Neoptolemus' murder emphasizes the ritual framework in a manner similar to Euripides' *Electra*. It is worth noting here that there are three common denominators underlying *Electra* and *Andromache*, just as there are similar issues in the case of *Heracles*: (a) the ritual framework, (b) the use of treachery (δόλος), (c) the ambivalent status of Orestes.

---

[18] See Cropp 1988 on Eur. *El.* 774–858.
[19] See further Easterling 1988: 101–9; Cropp 1988: 154. On ritual aspects in the play, see also Zeitlin 1970; Mirto 1980.
[20] Cf. Matthiessen 1964: 74–8; 161–3; Cropp 1988: xxxviii.
[21] See Stevens 1971: 1–15, for a discussion of the interpretations suggested. Stevens concludes that the aftermath of war is the major theme of the play. *Contra* his view, see e.g. Lloyd 1994, who notes that this theme is not distinctive of *Andromache* alone, since it appears in a number of Euripidean tragedies.

Finally, the disruption of a sacrifice in *Helen* (1526–1610) is slightly different from the previous examples in that here a sacrifice turns into a murder, which, however, is not that of the sacrificer. The sacrifice of a bull by Menelaus is followed by the massacre of the fifty men of Theoclymenus; this sacrifice, which constitutes the core of a deceptive escape-plot and leads to an outrageous escalation of violence, cannot be separated from the preoccupation of this tragedy with the deceptive character of appearances and with the play between illusion and reality.[22] Furthermore, the proliferation of excessive violence, whereby the Greeks are the agents and the barbarians the victims, degrades the Greeks, since their change of status from victims to agents is accompanied by a demonstration of a sort of violence that surpasses the violence of the barbarians.

As for the implications of such an inversion, we need only think of the central distinction, in the fifth century BC, between 'Greek' and 'barbarian', a distinction which plays a fundamental role in the system of moral values and in the definition of the category 'Greek'.[23] And we may easily recall how Euripides often exploits the ambiguities of this distinction for his own dramatic purposes. To mention two telling examples: in *Trojan Women*, the Trojan (that is, 'barbarian') Andromache accuses the Greeks of 'inventing atrocities worthy of barbarians' in killing her child (764–5), while in *Iphigenia among the Taurians*, Iphigenia comments on the Taurians' (that is, the barbarians') practice of sacrificing foreigners to the goddess Artemis that they, being murderers themselves, attribute their own violence to the gods (389–91); but her remark is of course deeply ironic, since it evokes the attempted sacrifice of herself to the same goddess by the Greeks.

The examples mentioned above concerned the violent disruption of a ritual procedure and its possible implications for the interpretation of each tragedy. To them we may also add examples where the ambivalence of some ritual action is

---

[22] On these issues, see esp. Segal 1986b; on deception in the play, see also Downing 1990.

[23] See Hall 1989.

dramatically exploited in order to highlight issues raised in each tragedy. We find it in some cases of human sacrifice,[24] a practice which, as Hughes notes,[25] 'flourished nowhere in Greece so much as in Athens upon the tragic stage'. The sacrifice of Iphigenia is one such case, and the substitution of a deer for a human victim by Artemis, not mentioned of course in the *Oresteia* for obvious dramatic reasons, is the prerequisite for the plot in *Iphigenia among the Taurians*, while in *Iphigenia at Aulis* the sacrifice, which takes on the character of a self-sacrifice, eventually becomes that of a deer substituted for Iphigenia, as we learn from the Messenger's report.[26] In *Iphigenia at Aulis* in particular, the sacrifice holds the central position, and articulates issues such as the role of the divine or human responsibility, while the disruption of the prepared human sacrifice by the substitution of an animal for a human victim in the end puts these issues in a new context and redefines them.

In *Phoenissae*, the Teiresias–Menoeceus episode introduces both another cause and another solution to the Theban crisis. But the suggested solution, that is, the ritual which starts as a proposed human sacrifice and ends as a self-sacrifice, that of Menoeceus,[27] turns out to be ineffective as a solution,[28] and this 'failure' shifts the focus to another issue. Menoeceus' sacrifice is set against the fratricide, which is separated from the civic context and reduced to a fight for personal power, since it reveals that self-interest is carefully disguised under the cover of love for the city. Since the action of the two brothers seems to ignore what Menoeceus does, and emphasizes Oedipus' curse as the cause and the mutual killing as the 'solution', it is left more than uncertain at the end of the play

---

[24] On human sacrifice particularly in Euripides, see O' Connor-Visser 1987; cf. O' Bryhim 2000. On human sacrifice in ancient Greece generally, see Henrichs 1981; Hughes 1991; Bonnechère 1994; Georgoudi 1999.

[25] Hughes 1991: 189.

[26] It should be noted, with regard to Euripides' *Iphigenia at Aulis,* that it has been questioned whether the closing scene with the animal substitution is Euripidean; whatever view we take of Aelian's fragment (Ael. *NA* 7.39 = Eur. *IA* fr. 1 Diggle = Eur. fr. 857 N), lines 1578 to the end of the play are treated as post-Euripidean by Diggle (OCT edition) and others. On this issue, see also Aretz 1999: 110.

[27] This character is considered to be a Euripidean invention; see Mastronarde 1994: 28–9.

[28] O' Connor-Visser 1987: 73–98 and 179 sees in Menoeceus a clear solution to the crisis.

whether Menoeceus' death was a crucial factor or not. What characterizes *Phoenissae* is its 'open' form of dramatic composition, which was observed by the writers of two of the ancient hypotheses of the play.[29] πολυπρόσωπον, 'with a large cast' and παραπληρωματικόν, 'overfull',[30] refer to Euripides' deviation from the traditional technique and to his innovative experimentation with the multiplication of characters and events; in other words, his abandonment of the usual concentration on one central character and on the development of one central action. It is, in fact, this peripheral and episodic function of characters and events that reduces the Menoeceus episode to a single scene among many others, and undermines the connection and the contribution of Menoeceus' sacrifice to the development of the plot and the salvation of Thebes.

The sacrificial death of Polyxena in *Hecuba* is comparable, not only because the motivation of her sacrifice becomes complex, as in the case of the sacrifice of Iphigenia, an issue which aptly and ironically questions the distinction between sacrifice and murder, but also, in a very practical sense, because Polyxena's sacrifice does not achieve its desired and expected effect. The Greeks believe that Achilles restrains the favourable winds which will carry the ships back to Greece, and that their offer of a virgin's blood to him as he demanded will satisfy his sense of honour and will secure for them, in return, the trip homeward. But nothing suggests that the winds change after the sacrifice of Polyxena, which seems to imply that Polyxena's sacrifice remains in essence entirely ineffective. The 'failure' of this sacrifice, this time not through disruption but through ineffectiveness, is of primary importance in the play. The desired effect for the Greeks, the change of the winds, is accomplished only *after* Hecuba's 'sacrificial' revenge upon Polymestor. This is a subject which, as Mitchell-Boyask[31] remarks in his article on sacrifice and revenge in this play, links the two halves of the play and shows how closely intertwined the events of this tragedy are.

[29] See Mastronarde 1994: 3 and n. 1.   [30] See Craik 1988: 58.
[31] Mitchell-Boyask 1993. Cf. Michelakis 2002: 58–83.

So far I have discussed some examples of sacrificial rituals. With regard to purificatory ritual proper, we may also mention the Aeschylean Orestes and his purification, which remains ineffective.[32] Ambivalence may of course be attributed to other rituals as well. Easterling[33] mentions a telling example in her discussion of the ritual in *Trojan Women*: Hecuba, over the body of the dead Astyanax, wonders whether the decking of the corpse has any significance at all for the dead; it seems rather like an empty pretension for the living. But despite her doubtful words about the ritual, it is important that Hecuba still performs the ritual action.[34]

To return to *Heracles*, the significance that Euripides attaches to the ritual context within which Heracles is attacked by madness is further emphasized by the very introduction of a purificatory ritual which is not dramatically necessary, since the murder of Lycus is undoubtedly presented as a justified killing which the simplest ritual could purify.[35] At this point, however, it may also be remarked that the simplicity, in general, with which the blood of a villain can be cleansed by means of a purificatory ritual seems to take on, momentarily at least, another dimension in the play. In the madness scene, which is narrated by the Messenger, Heracles is reported to have said the following:

Πάτερ, τί θύω πρὶν κτανεῖν Εὐρυσθέα
καθάρσιον πῦρ καὶ πόνους διπλοῦς ἔχω;
ἔργον μιᾶς μοι χειρὸς εὖ θέσθαι τάδε.
ὅταν δ᾿ ἐνέγκω δεῦρο κρᾶτ᾿ Εὐρυσθέως
ἐπὶ τοῖσι νῦν θανοῦσιν ἁγνιῶ χέρας. (936–40)

Why am I offering cleansing fire, father, before I kill Eurystheus? Why double the labour? A single blow can arrange things as I want them. When I have brought Eurystheus' head back here, then I shall cleanse my hands for those who have just been killed.

---

[32] On Orestes' purification, see Taplin 1977: 382–3; Garvie 1986 on Aesch. *Cho.* 1059–60; Sommerstein 1989 on Aesch. *Eum.* 237; Podlecki 1989 on Aesch. *Eum.* 238 ff.

[33] See Easterling 1993a: 19 and n. 19.

[34] For mourners' similar attitudes to ritual in modern Greece, see Danforth 1982.

[35] On 'justified homicide' and purification, see Parker 1983: Appendices 5 and 6.

Now, these are said to be the words of Heracles when 'he was no longer himself' (ὁ δ᾽ οὐκέθ᾽ αὐτὸς ἦν, 931) and had already started to have the physical symptoms of madness (932–4). But this stage is obviously described as an initial phase of his madness, in the sense that Heracles still recognizes Amphitryon as his father and does not mistake him for another person as he will do shortly. At all events, it is interesting that Heracles' reported words, which convey his perspective on the function of ritual, seem to give this function an ironic touch. What Heracles says is that there is no need to perform the purificatory ritual for the murder of his recent victims now; it is better to kill Eurystheus too and then simply perform a single purification for both killings.[36] Why should he bother to spend time and effort in two activities when he can well combine them in a single blow (938)? Similarly when he is in the process of his murders he will kill both his third child and his wife with one and the same arrow (1000).

Heracles' words, to be sure, and his wish to rush into another action, may be said to be in accord with what Amphitryon said of him earlier, when he was in his right mind. Heracles at that point was eager to take revenge on his enemies, to rush into killing, and Amphitryon had to warn him not to be too precipitate (586). It is not strange, after all, for Heracles, a man of action, to be described as being precipitate. However, there is more to be read in his words; it seems that there is a play here with the whole notion of ritual in a way which does not of course negate its importance (the ritual will still be performed) but ultimately undermines its very function; some sort of 'ritual economy' is introduced, that is, one single purification is chosen in order to save the trouble of having to perform two separate ones (for the killings during the labours and for the murder of Eurystheus). The performance of the ritual acts is said to be a 'labour' and described with the word πόνους (937), a word which properly conveys this meaning but is also the standard term for denoting Heracles' heroic labours in

---

[36] Cf. Higgins 1984: 100: 'a notion for ritual economy'. On the possible criticism, in this passage, of the formal nature of this ritual act, see Adkins 1960: 90 n. h.

general.[37] The implication may then be that the performance of a purificatory ritual is as painstaking as the performance of a heroic labour, and consequently that Heracles could save himself one such labour.

The reading of a comic touch at this particular dramatic point may of course be argued to be entirely out of place in a scene which depicts madness and its implications, in a scene, that is, which shows Heracles, a stricken victim himself, carrying out terrible murders in his delusion.[38] However, Heracles' words are said by the Messenger to be spoken with mad laughter (935). On the other hand, Heracles' strange behaviour thereafter perplexes the attendants and causes different reactions on their part: διπλοῦς δ᾽ ὀπαδοῖς ἦν γέλως φόβος θ᾽ ὁμοῦ, 'the servants began to laugh and tremble both at once', 950. Laughter and fear, in fact, well summarize the conglomerate of comic appearance and horrible reality.

To return now to the violent disruption of Heracles' purification, the failure of what may be regarded as the simplest ritual comes as a surprise when we bear in mind that the more justified the murder the simpler the purificatory ritual. Indeed, it may also be argued that the purification which fails in the play contrasts with the many[39] purifications that Heracles successfully underwent in order to cleanse himself of the murders he committed during his violent career – Heracles, the Greek hero *par excellence* and also, as Pisander of Rhodes (fr. 10 Bernabé, *PEG*) called him, the 'justest of homicides'. Be that as it may, the fact remains that although the purification started by Heracles in the play may indicate his piety, yet the negation and reversal of what is in fact the easiest purificatory ritual renders it deeply problematic and inevitably raises the question of how it is to be interpreted.

[37] E.g. Soph. *Phil.* 1419; Eur. *Alc.* 481; Eur. *HF* 22; 575.
[38] For a similar reading of Eur. *HF* 1380–1, where Heracles imagines his weapons rebuking him, and its comic overtones, see Kirkpatrick and Dunn 2002. For the presence of comic elements in Greek tragedy, see Seidensticker 1982. For a more sceptical approach to this issue in Euripidean scholarship, see more recently Gregory 2000.
[39] For an account see Parker 1983: 381–3.

Thus, the issue is precisely what may be the significance of this ritual and of its failure for our reading of the play. The only extensive literary study to use the sacrificial ritual as the key theme for the interpretation of the play is that of Foley.[40] Whereas Foley emphasizes the Euripidean presentation of an ideal Heracles throughout *Heracles*, I focus instead on the hero's ambivalence. In what follows I try to outline a different approach to the sacrificial ritual of the play, and suggest an alternative 'reading' of the ritual crisis and of its relation to the play's thematic concerns.

Although the well-established structuralist view of sacrifice as the demarcation of boundaries between the divine, human and bestial realms[41] would naturally lead to the assumption that the failure of a sacrifice might hint at the possibility of a transgression of the boundaries that separate these realms,[42] Foley denies the possibility of any transgression of the cosmic boundaries by the hero and argues that Euripides hints at a Girardian identity of divine and communal violence, in which case the failure of the ritual of purification symbolizes the inability of a community ridden by *stasis* to reintegrate the hero. Girard, however, as Foley herself acknowledges (159 n. 23), did not interpret the failure of the sacrificial ritual in this way, but emphasized instead Heracles' own pollution, i.e. his impurity and his violence, which was so extreme that it could no longer be contained by the ritual: 'the blood shed in the

---

[40] Foley 1985.

[41] See the Introduction of Foley 1985: *passim,* and esp. 35: 'sacrifice comes to be understood in the symbolic system of Greek thought as a way of marking out the special precinct of the human, of setting men apart from the immortal gods with their imperishable food (nectar and ambrosia) and from the beasts, who eat raw food. Whereas beasts kill each other with impunity, man imposes taboos on the killing of fellow humans and eats no meat of domestic animals without previously sacrificing and cooking it. By delineating sharply the boundaries and differences between god and man, sacrifice, like Greek popular wisdom, serves to keep its participants strictly within the limits of the human', and 37: 'sacrifice thus becomes a part of the definition of the human in Greek culture'.

[42] Sacrifice shares with the Attic theatre the delineation of boundaries in the *cosmos*; cf. Meagher 1989: 64–5. On the interplay between order and transgression in the theatre of Dionysus, see Goldhill 1990. On the relation of the views expressed by Goldhill and those expressed by Brelich in some of his studies, see Aronen 1992.

course of the terrible labors and in the city itself finally turned the hero's head. Instead of drawing off the violence and allowing it to ebb away, the rites brought a veritable flood of violence down on the victim. The sacrificial rites were no longer able to accomplish their task; they swelled the surging tide of impure violence instead of channeling it.'[43]

Foley's explanation of the failure of the sacrificial ritual is based upon her conviction, repeatedly noted in her study, that Heracles in this play is a model of modesty, who falls victim to Hera's hostility (identified with the indifference of the Thebans, according to her 'Girardian' interpretation). Critics[44] who believe in the 'idealized' portrayal of Heracles seem to have been reacting against the kind of approach that saw the existence of some sin or fault within Heracles as a plausible cause of his madness.[45] The association of madness with punishment is made in Iris' final words:

ὡς ἂν πορεύσας δι' Ἀχερούσιον πόρον
τὸν καλλίπαιδα στέφανον αὐθέντηι φόνωι
γνῶι μὲν τὸν "Ηρας οἷός ἐστ' αὐτῶι χόλος,
μάθηι δὲ τὸν ἐμόν· ἢ θεοὶ μὲν οὐδαμοῦ,
τὰ θνητὰ δ' ἔσται μεγάλα, μὴ δόντος δίκην. (838–42)

so that when by his own murderous hand he has made his crown of lovely children cross the river of Death, he may recognise the nature of Hera's anger, and learn mine. Otherwise the gods are worth nothing and men shall prevail, if Heracles does not pay the penalty.

The interest of this passage, however, lies rather in the deliberate overdetermination of the causation of Heracles' madness, as the theme of divine anger underlines both a

[43] Girard 1977: 40.
[44] Yunis 1988, writing after Foley, reflects the same approach: '[Heracles] has been portrayed throughout as a man of unblemished virtue' (150); cf. the introductions in the commentaries by Barlow 1996 and Mirto 1997.
[45] This is mainly an old view, variously expressed by critics, which stresses the inherent danger of Heracles' elevation above the human level especially after his return from Hades; cf. Sheppard 1916: 72–9; Mullens 1939: 165; Grube 1941: 252–6; Kitto ³1961: 245; Burnett 1971: ch. 7; Rivier ²1975: 201; Pike 1978; Shelton 1979: 109; more recently Bárberi-Squarotti 1993.

sense of capriciousness and a sense of justice. In his article entitled 'Bafflement in Greek Tragedy', Buxton[46] discusses how certain scenes, actions, events, in tragedy are baffling to the extent of becoming inexplicable. The reason, as Buxton argues, is that the dramatist provides either too few clues or too much, often conflicting, information. Euripides' *Heracles* is a very good example of the latter tendency. What is important to bear in mind is that in the case of overdetermination, as here, we cannot isolate one piece of information at the expense of another. The overflow of information cannot be ignored, but should always be taken into consideration, and it seems that this is what is missing from the approaches of the critics of *Heracles* so far.

The provision of many versions or of conflicting information, it should be added, plays an important role in this tragedy, and this fact may provide significant clues, particularly as the interpretation and re-interpretation of events and their causes is a recurrent feature of this play. To mention one example from the prologue, Amphitryon, while referring to Heracles' labours, gives more than one possible reason for them (17–21). The provision, as early as the prologue, of multiple reasons for the undertaking of the labours is a device which sets the pattern of the dramatic technique of this play, exploiting to the full the dynamics of ambiguity.

Let us now return to the function of ritual, and more specifically to the relation between pollution and purification.[47] Pollution is associated with the confusion of boundaries between opposite categories, and ritual with a process of re-establishing the collapsed boundaries.[48] Human community makes a distinction between good (sacrificial) and bad (non-sacrificial) violence, while tragedy brings humans very close to a realization of their own violence, but the distinction between sacrificial and non-sacrificial violence, as Girard has pointed

---

[46] Buxton 1988; see also Buxton 1994: 151.
[47] On this issue, see esp. Moulinier 1952; Douglas 1966; Turner 1969; Girard 1977; Parker 1983.
[48] Turner 1969.

out, 'is anything but exact; it is even arbitrary. At times the difference threatens to disappear entirely. There is no such thing as "pure" violence.'[49]

In *Heracles*, the identification of Heracles with pure excellence is reinforced by his presentation in the role of the exterminator of all the representatives of evil. The annihilation of the bad by the good functions on two levels, which represent both the dramatic past and the dramatic present of the play. The dramatic past refers to Heracles' labours, during which the hero undertook the task of eliminating the monstrous creatures of the earth. The character of this undertaking as symbolizing the polarity between good and bad, and the annihilation of the bad by the good, in fact bears a considerable similarity to the function of purification, and in this respect it is not surprising that Heracles' labours were taken to be a sort of purification. In the play, which abounds in references to these labours and to their civilizing character (e.g. 20–5, 225–6, 359–435, 1270–8), this purificatory nature of Heracles' exploits is directly raised at 225–6: ποντίων καθαρμάτων | χέρσου τ᾽, 'his clearing of land and sea' (cf. *Trach.* 1012).[50] Heracles also had the standard associations of 'cleanser', 'civilizer' and 'averter of evil'.[51] Thus, the failure of Heracles' own purification in the play becomes even more problematic for the audience when considered against the background of these standard associations of the hero.

If the identification of Heracles with virtue in the dramatic past occurs in the destruction of evil during his heroic labours, then the annihilation of the bad by the good in the dramatic present of the play occurs in the murder of Lycus. It is striking that the presentation of Lycus and its possible significance have hardly attracted the interest of critics. An interesting exception is Foley's perceptive analysis, which tries to link

[49] Girard 1977: 40. Despite some reservations (cf. Gordon 1979; Drew Griffith 1993), Girard's anthropological theory has been influential for classical studies; see esp. *Helios* 1990.
[50] For the association between purification and elimination of evils, see Parker 1983: 211.
[51] On this, see Galinsky 1972: *passim*.

Lycus with the tradition of poetic invective.[52] Although the presentation of Lycus as unquestionably evil may at first give the impression that Euripides showed no interest in the characterization of this figure, yet it seems more probable that Euripides actually created a character (Lycus seems to be a Euripidean invention) who would represent pure wickedness only to emphasize its opposite pole,[53] i.e. Heracles as the representative of pure virtue. This of course suggests the building of an extreme polarity on the part of the playwright between the two opposite qualities, where the deliberate devaluation of the bad promotes the idealization of the good; however, it seems that this polarity is built by Euripides only to be demolished, so that the confusion between good and bad as the core of Heracles' constantly emphasized duality, which begins from his parentage[54] and is revealed in his violence/valour, is always in focus.

One notable point is the parallelism drawn between Heracles and Lycus, which may have been underlined by the same actor taking both parts: Heracles holding a torch (928) and Lycus as 'torch in hand' (240–6); rejection of supplication by both; arrival of Heracles the rescuer instead of Lycus the killer, and the subsequent turning of Heracles into a killer. Porter[55] uses these similarities in support of his argument that the unity of the play depends on multiple structural parallels. Since, however, his approach is strictly concerned with the issues of structure and unity, he does not deal with the potential *significance* that the parallel between Heracles and Lycus may have in the play. In fact, an examination of the parallelism in the presentation of Heracles and Lycus does not simply reveal a sense of unity in a 'loosely structured' tragedy (a view which

---

[52] Foley 1985: 180–2. Also, for the association of Lycus ('Wolf') with tyranny, see e.g. Pachet 1972: 540–1 (for the use, in general, of the wolf and its connotations in the political vocabulary of antiquity, see Kunstler 1991). For Lycus in the play as the symbol of a world gone wrong, see Baudy 1993.

[53] Cf. Yunis 1988: 151: 'Heracles' piety has been especially prominent in contrast to the thoroughly impious Lycus.'

[54] For the significance of the dual parentage of Heracles, see Gregory 1977 and 1991: 121–54; Mirto 1997: 15–27; cf. also Ferguson 1969: *passim*; Padilla 1994: *passim*.

[55] Porter 1987: 104–6.

is in any case questionable) but seems indeed to suggest the collapse of the created polarity between these two figures and to prompt an interest, in turn, in the meaning of this collapse for the interpretation of the play as a whole.[56] We need to look more closely at the examples which seem to establish a parallelism between Heracles and Lycus in relation to ritual.[57]

Both characters attempt to violate supplication twice; Lycus' plans are thwarted by his murder, while both of Heracles' violations are carried out, one resulting in murder. In the case of Lycus, the first attempted violation appears in the long supplication scene of the first part of the play (240–6). Lycus' second attempted violation is directed against the 'mock' supplication of Megara (with her children), which constitutes a part of the plan to lure Lycus into the palace, so that he is murdered by Heracles (712–25). In the case of Heracles, both violations of the supplications appear in the madness scene, which is narrated by the Messenger. In the first instance, Heracles, while his father tries to understand what is happening to his son, thinks in his madness that Amphitryon is Eurystheus' father touching his hand in supplication for his own son (965–9). The second violation results in the murder of the son of Heracles, whom Heracles mistakes for Eurystheus' son (984–94).

Another possible parallelism between Heracles and Lycus may be traced in the elaborate use of sacrificial imagery, which starts in the long supplication scene of the first part of the play and is repeated in the madness scene. The description by Megara of Lycus' attempted murder of Heracles' family in sacrificial terms, i.e. the odd application of the terms ἱερεύς, σφαγεύς, θύματα, which are normally used to describe the

---

[56] On violence as a linking element between Heracles and Lycus in the play, see Chalk 1962: 16; Baudy 1993: *passim*.

[57] It has been suggested (Ruck 1976: 57 and n. 14; Porter 1987: 90 and 106) that Heracles' and Lycus' physical similarity on stage (they are both mentioned as having blond hair: 233; 362) would be enhanced if Lycus ('the wolf') was presented wearing a wolf-skin, to correspond with Heracles wearing the lion-skin. We may recall Dolon in [Euripides'] *Rhesus*, who was disguised as a wolf (209). However, in the case of the Euripidean Lycus there is no evidence in the text to support such an assumption. For more examples of the parallelism between the two characters in both Euripides and Seneca, see Papadopoulou 2004.

sacrifice of animals, to the description of a slaughter of human beings, ironically stresses the outrage of the imminent act, when this is envisaged as a perverted sacrifice:

εἶέν· τίς ἱερεύς, τίς σφαγεὺς τῶν δυσπότμων;
[ἢ τῆς ταλαίνης τῆς ἐμῆς ψυχῆς φονεύς;]
ἕτοιμ' ἄγειν τὰ θύματ' εἰς Ἅιδου τάδε. (451–3)

Well then. Who is the priest, who the slaughterer of these ill-fated children [or the murderer of my own unhappy existence]? The sacrificial victims are ready here for you to lead off to their deaths.

The anomalous situation in which Heracles' family is trapped because of Lycus' attempted murder is also stressed by the initiation of part of a death ritual for Heracles' children, i.e. the dressing of the dead with funeral garments and the crowning of their heads with funeral wreaths. The realization of this part of the death ritual was of course the result of Lycus' concession to Megara's entreaty to dress her children for their death (327–35). The presentation of the living children in funeral adornments forms a remarkably effective visual reminder of the anomalous and problematic character of the situation, and is also repeatedly noted in the dramatic discourse (442–3, 525–6,[58] 548–9,[59] 562, 702–3).

Lycus' attempted murder of Heracles' family, viewed as a perverted sacrifice, is presented in relation not only to a problematic death ritual but also to the inversion of two wedding *makarismoi*, the former (with reference to the children) in anticipation, the latter (with regard to Megara) in retrospect. Both reversals are noted by Megara (480–4 and 492–3). Both these inverted wedding *makarismoi* are given emphasis, while their association under the light of imminent death suggestively alludes to their transformation into a single funeral

---

[58] Here the contradiction of the living in funeral adornments is obvious and causes surprise to Heracles, who is unaware of the situation. On costume as visual metaphor indicating change of state, see Arnott 1989: 171–2. For a reading of the imagery of (both Heracles' and his family's) costuming throughout the play and its association with character delineation, see Worman 1999.

[59] Here the plural ἐνήμμεθα, 'we are wearing', indicates the whole family, although only the dressing of the children in funeral clothes has been mentioned so far. See Bond 1981 ad loc.

makarismos, since *makarismos* is applicable both to the newly wed and to the recently deceased.[60]

The description, in the case of Lycus, of the nexus of abnormal rituals contributes to the play's emphasis upon Lycus' wickedness. On the other hand, the murder of the three children by Heracles himself is described, in the Messenger's *rhesis*, in terms of a perverted sacrifice. Let us have a closer look:

(...) δεύτερον δὲ παῖδ' ἑλὼν
χωρεῖ τρίτον θῦμ' ὡς ἐπισφάξων δυοῖν. (994–5)

Now that he had caught the second son, he advanced to add a third sacrifice of slaughter to the two others.

The use of the terms θῦμα and ἐπισφάξων, terms which have standard ritual connotations,[61] clearly recalls Megara's use of τὰ θύματ', 'the sacrificial victims' (453) and σφαγεύς, 'slaughterer' (451), to refer to the imminent murder of her children by Lycus. Surprisingly, it was not until recently that this passage was interpreted in a way which showed Heracles' problematic attitude towards those whom, during his delusion, he considers to be his victims. As de Jong[62] acutely remarks with reference to the use of the words θῦμα and ἐπισφάξων at 995: 'whose blasphemy is it? Certainly not of the speaker, the Messenger. The final ὡς + participle-clause must be interpreted as expressing Heracles' focalization, and we are dealing not so much with conscious blasphemy, as with another manifestation of his delusion: he considers his killing of "Eurystheus' son" as a justified sacrifice on the altar of vengeance.'

The introduction of Heracles' perspective with regard to his attitude towards murder and sacrifice is of course crucial. The use of sacrificial terminology, the introduction of a character's perspective and the reception of these two elements by the audience constitute a fundamental framework, the careful examination of which can provide useful insight into the interpretation of Greek tragedy in general. In his article 'Greek

---

[60] Marriage and funeral motifs are often interrelated in Greek tragedy, starting from Aeschylus' *Oresteia*. On this issue see Rehm 1994; see also Giannakis 1998.
[61] Casabona 1966: *passim*.   [62] de Jong 1991: 169–70.

Tragedy and Sacrificial Ritual', Burkert[63] noted that the plot of many Greek tragedies includes a human sacrifice, and went on to make the following remark (116): 'What is more general and more important: any sort of killing in tragedy may be termed θύειν as early as Aeschylus and the intoxication of killing is called βακχεύειν. In earlier choral lyric, these metaphors do not occur.'

To Burkert's remark we may add the observation made by Casabona[64] that in Greek tragedy the use of terminology with clear sacrificial associations (his example is the term θύειν, 'sacrifice') to refer to the perspective of a character indicates that this character regards the act, that is the killing, as legitimate, as a proper sacrifice. One of the many telling examples adduced by Casabona to prove his point is *Orestes*, where there is a range of terms used to describe the murder of Clytemnestra, that is θύειν, 'sacrifice', κτείνειν, 'slaughter', φονεύειν 'murder'. The selection of a term by each character reveals this character's attitude towards the status of Clytemnestra's killing. Thus, Tyndareus, who considers the killing an outrageous murder and sees no justification in it whatsoever, uses exclusively the terms κτείνειν and φονεύειν. Orestes uses the terminology of κτείνειν, 'slaughter' (546), when he concedes that his act was in a sense impious, but when he says that his act is indeed also pious if viewed as an avenging of his father, then he uses the terminology of θύειν, 'sacrifice'.

But what is particularly significant is the way the spectator/reader receives the character's use of sacrificial terminology. This practice of describing a murder in sacrificial terms brings emphatically into focus the problematic nature of the character's attitude, as well as the whole issue of the ironies and ambiguities which accompany such an attitude.[65]

To return now to the example from *Heracles*, it is clear that the sacrificial terminology used at 994–5, if it indeed indicates Heracles' own perspective on the murder he is committing,

[63] Burkert 1966.   [64] Casabona 1966: 75–80.
[65] For examples from tragedy of a description of a killing as a sacrifice, see briefly Guépin 1968: 1–5.

reveals that he considers the murder to be a proper sacrifice, with all the implications that such an attitude will have for the reception by the spectator/reader. At the same time, this interpretation stresses the fact that the madness scene presents Heracles' murders both as they appear in dramatic reality, i.e. as killings of his family, and as they appear in Heracles' delusions, i.e. as killings of his enemies.

Possession is 'an extreme form of alienation, in which the subject totally absorbs the desires of another', as Girard[66] puts it, and Heracles is indeed presented as afflicted with madness, yet his violence against those he considers to be his enemies during the madness scene is not alien to his habitual behaviour; rather, it follows the typical patterns of his own valour, as in the case of his famous contests.[67] 'The bad seems good to whomever a god leads to disaster', says the Chorus in *Antigone* (621–2); this change in the perception of good and bad seems to be the one essential thing that has to be imposed on Heracles, since the carrying out of the act follows his familiar routes. It is Heracles' excessive violence which brings (to use Lévi-Strauss's terms) the 'raw' into the 'cooked', that is, the wild into the civilized.[68] It is the transgression or rather the confusion of the boundary between 'wild' and 'civilized' which becomes all the more effective by means of a dramatic 'fusion' of Heracles' past and present in his behaviour under the influence of Lyssa.

Let us take our point here a bit further. As Turner[69] observed, liminality occurs in many contexts, one of which is the state of solitude away from society. In being away from Thebes and indeed in the wild during the whole duration of his contests, Heracles was in such a state. On the other hand, Heracles' eventual incorporation into society upon his return

---

[66] Girard 1977: 165.

[67] Cf. Barlow 1993, who argues that Euripides in the play juxtaposes three sequences of Heracles' violent action in an ascending order of horror (that is, during his labours; against Lycus; against his family).

[68] For a discussion of some aspects of the spatial dimension of the play, see Rehm 2000 and 2002: 100–13; 339–43.

[69] Turner 1974a: 52–3; see also Turner 1974b: *passim*; cf. Leach 1976: 71–5.

to Thebes, a process which in terms of a 'rite of passage'[70] may be regarded as 'reintegration', becomes problematic, and this is emphatically manifested in the fact that it is negated, since it is accompanied by his atrocious murders. We have seen the negation of Heracles' reintegration in the failure of his purificatory ritual; purification is, after all, a rite which removes pollution and aims at the reincorporation of the polluted person into his community.[71]

But we also clearly see the problematic nature of the 'reintegration' of the liminal hero in the examples which show that his liminality does not end upon his arrival at Thebes. I shall mention more examples in my discussion of revenge and violence in the next section. For the time being, it suffices to draw attention to the linking of Heracles' dramatic past (contests) and dramatic present (killing of Lycus) by the use of hunt imagery to describe both. The hunt imagery, which as Bárberi-Squarotti[72] points out is commonly associated with violence and the wild, is used by the Chorus in their singing of Heracles' contests (cf. 151–8), notably his killing of the Nemean lion (359–63), of the Centaurs (364–7), of the golden hind, which he devotes to Artemis, the goddess of hunting (375–9), and of Cycnus (389–93), while even the fight against the Amazons takes on images from hunting (cf. ἄγρας, 415). In the dramatic present, the hunt imagery continues in the murder of Lycus, when Amphitryon describes Lycus as an animal which is hunted down by means of nets (728–31).

The disappearance of a difference between the two types of violence (beneficent and disastrous) is a key issue in *Heracles*. It is particularly significant that this tragedy questions the traditional association of Heracles exclusively with virtue, and hints at the confusion of good and bad in his violence and valour. Thus, it is not the excess of violence, but rather the actual confusion between good and evil that the play illustrates by exploiting the dynamics of ritual. In this respect, a close examination of the interplay and of the failure of the polarity

---

[70] Cf. van Gennep 1960.   [71] Cf. Jameson 1988: 974.
[72] Bárberi-Squarotti 1993.

between good and bad in the play can indeed challenge in turn the 'polarity' of many critical approaches to the play, which focus on one pole of an assumed polarity, namely, Heracles' innocence-virtue (e.g. Foley 1985) vs Heracles' *hubris*-evil (e.g. Burnett 1971); the existence of this polarity, however, seems to be exactly what this tragedy negates. In other words, the question is not whether we are presented with an exemplary hero throughout the play or whether, on the contrary, his faults overshadow his virtues; rather, it is important to understand that both sides of Heracles can be 'read' in a single portrayal. It is the interplay between Heracles' virtue and excess that constitutes the essence of his ambivalence.

The primary thematic concern of the play with the relation between the categories good and bad is illustrated in the second stasimon, where the elderly Chorus sing in praise of Heracles;[73] the emphasis of the whole ode on good and bad is evident in the abundance of moralizing maxims, on such themes as youth and old age (637–54), wealth (642–8), wisdom (655–72), excellence (658–70).[74] But it is especially the second stanza of this stasimon which explicitly raises the question of both the distinction and the confusion between good and evil. The Chorus express their longing that a second youth might be given to the virtuous, as a reward, which might also serve as a clear distinction between good and evil men, since, at the present time, confusion about good and bad prevails:

εἰ δὲ θεοῖς ἦν ξύνεσις
καὶ σοφία κατ' ἄνδρας,
δίδυμον ἂν ἥβαν ἔφερον,
φανερὸν χαρακτῆρ' ἀρετᾶς
ὅσοισιν μέτα, καὶ θανόντες
εἰς αὐγὰς πάλιν ἁλίου
δισσοὺς ἂν ἔβαν διαύλους,
ἁ δυσγένεια δ' ἁπλοῦν ἂν
εἶχε ζόας βίοτον,

---

[73] The image of the swan, which is used with regard to the Chorus, is an apt symbol of both age and song (692–4, cf. 679 and 110). On this image, see Bond 1981 ad loc.; Assaël 1996; cf. Hose 1990: 90–1.

[74] See Barlow 1996: 152, where she also comments on the connections between the stanzas of this seemingly thematically disparate ode. Cf. Hose 1991: 37–40.

καὶ τῶιδ' ἂν τούς τε κακοὺς ἦν
γνῶναι καὶ τοὺς ἀγαθούς,
ἴσον ἅτ' ἐν νεφέλαισιν ἄ-
στρων ναύταις ἀριθμὸς πέλει.
νῦν δ' οὐδεὶς ὅρος ἐκ θεῶν
χρηστοῖς οὐδὲ κακοῖς σαφής,
ἀλλ' εἱλισσόμενός τις αἰ-
ὼν πλοῦτον μόνον αὔξει. (655–72)

If the gods had understanding and wisdom as men conceive it, men would
have obtained a second youth as a clear mark of the goodness of certain
people, and such men, after dying, would return to the light of the sun again
and complete a double course, whereas the meaner folk would have a single
term of life. In this way it would be possible to distinguish good men from
bad just as amid the clouds there are always a number of stars for the sailors
to count. At the moment there is no clear definition by the gods of the good
and bad, and as a man's lifetime unfolds it increases only his wealth.

Although this stasimon, the famous encomium of Heracles'
ἀρετή, has been much studied, until now there has been no
attempt to assess the significance of this stanza in raising an
issue which might prove to be a central theme in the play.
Critics have exclusively focused upon the distinction between
good and bad, ignoring the explicit reference to the confusion
of these two categories. Yunis[75] simply notes the mention of
the confusion between good and evil, without commenting
upon its potential significance. The distinction between good
and bad has been interpreted as the rhetorical *sine qua non* for
the Chorus' praise of Heracles' ἀρετή.[76]

Although Heracles is not mentioned, it is obvious that the
content of this stanza is relevant to him and that it actually
derives its meaning from an evaluation of his case. We may
also recall in this context, that is, with regard to the acquisition
of a second youth, that it was a datum of the myth that
Heracles eventually married Hebe, the personification of

---

[75] Yunis 1988: 147.
[76] Cf. Bond 1981: 232: 'the insistence in stanza 2 on distinguishing the good from the
bad is appropriate for the Chorus as *laudator boni*, and prepares for the encomium
in stanzas 3 and 4'; Foley 1985: 184: 'The elders of the Chorus establish themselves
as competent *laudatores*, worthy to praise the hero through their ability to distinguish good from bad.'

youth.[77] Since Heracles has returned safe from Hades, he has indeed acquired the 'second term of life' (662: δισσοὺς ... διαύλους) which should, according to the formulation of the Chorus' expression, be considered as a reward for his virtue and as a distinction of this virtue from other people's evil; Heracles' undoubted goodness, after all, is the object of the Chorus' praise in the next two stanzas. However, although Heracles is the visible proof for the fulfilment of the Chorus' words, the way the expression is structured, in an unreal conditional clause, leaves us with a hypothesis doomed to be left unfulfilled. The impact of this contradiction is skilfully to question and undermine the validity of the identification of Heracles with pure virtue.

The Chorus may of course be using Heracles' case as an *exemplum* in order to generalize and ask why a second youth and a second life are not given to *all* good people, in the same way as has happened with Heracles, the model of goodness.[78] However, even if we accept an underlying exemplarity instead of a simple allusion to Heracles, such an exemplarity would still be trapped within the context of non-fulfilment and would consequently be rendered problematic. The non-realizable character of the Chorus' expression is followed by their affirmation of the prevailing confusion between goodness and evil: νῦν δ᾽ οὐδεὶς ὅρος ἐκ θεῶν | χρηστοῖς οὐδὲ κακοῖς σαφής, 'at the moment there is no clear definition by the gods of good and bad' (669–70), where the meaning 'definition' of the term ὅρος 'is not far removed from the original "landmark", "boundary line" ';[79] definition is based upon distinction and requires precision (i.e what is good and what is bad) to avoid confusion.

Revenge[80] and transgression

So far I have discussed pollution and purification, within the context of the ritual crisis in the play, in terms of a polarity

---

[77] Cf. Bond 1981 on Eur. *HF* 637–54. See also Scodel 1980a.
[78] Bond 1981: 232.   [79] Bond 1981 on Eur. *HF* 669 f.
[80] A version of this section on revenge in *Heracles* appears in Papadopoulou 2001a.

between 'good' and 'bad' violence. I argued that this polarity informs the presentation of Heracles, and concluded that Heracles' ambivalence is implied in the failure of this polarity; I also concluded that this failure is matched in the parallelism between Heracles and Lycus in the play, and I stressed how the sacrificial vocabulary which is used casts a shadow over Heracles' action against his enemy. Heracles' action, which is described as a sacrifice, consists in fact in violent revenge against his enemy. The notions of sacrifice and revenge are often closely intertwined in Greek literature, perhaps because both represent responses to powerful emotional needs. Both seek to impose a kind of order on violence, but they are threatened by the tendency of violence to become uncontrollable.

Vengeance killing described in ritual language is found already in Homer (see p. 41 below on *Iliad* 18) but appears most frequently in Greek tragedy. Orestes is an obvious case, and there is a telling example in *Hecuba*, where Hecuba has this to say about the Greeks' preparations for the sacrifice of her daughter Polyxena:

πότερα τὸ χρή σφ᾽ ἐπήγαγ᾽ ἀνθρωποσφαγεῖν
πρὸς τύμβον, ἔνθα βουθυτεῖν μᾶλλον πρέπει;
ἢ τοὺς κτανόντας ἀνταποκτεῖναι θέλων
ἐς τήνδ᾽ Ἀχιλλεὺς ἐνδίκως τείνει φόνον; (260–3)

Was it necessity that led them to human sacrifice at a tomb where offering oxen is more fitting? Or is Achilles justified in aiming death at her, from a wish to retaliate by killing those who killed himself?[81]

The presentation of an act of revenge as a sacrifice already makes this act problematic. In what follows, I shall focus on the theme of revenge in *Heracles* in order to show how an investigation of this theme and of its implications further contributes to the reception of Heracles as an ambivalent hero. This is one of the most keenly contested issues in the interpretation of Greek tragedy: while some critics discuss an act of revenge in negative terms, others counterargue that such views reflect a modern ideological system and not that of the original

---

[81] Translation from Collard 1991.

audience. Burnett's[82] recent book on revenge in Greek tragedy
is particularly useful in trying to cleanse the discussion of
Platonic and later (still prevailing) influences and trends,
which view revenge with some uneasiness, and instead to situ-
ate the topic within the specific historical and cultural context
of the original audience. But Burnett's clear-cut distinctions
between what was acceptable to the original audience and what
not, what was justified and what not, and so on, risk ignoring
what even the original audience may have recognized as
ambiguous.

Revenge is a central theme in *Heracles*, if we agree that it is
revenge that motivates Heracles' murder of the tyrant Lycus,
when he is still sane, and revenge that is also behind his
imagined attack against 'Eurystheus' and 'Eurystheus'' family,
which results in his murder of wife and children during the
madness scene. Revenge is retributive, and its reciprocal character is emphatically presented in the play.[83] But such a presentation of it is liable to make the spectator/reader think that
revenge is also mimetic in that the victim who becomes the
avenger gets involved in a reciprocal process which eventually
reduces him/her to an image of the 'other'. The mimetic character of Hecuba's revenge in *Hecuba*, which emphasizes the
similarities between avenger and victim, is a telling example
from Euripides.[84] Similarly, it may be argued that it is precisely
the mimetic character of revenge that underlies the parallelism
implied in *Heracles* between Heracles and Lycus. This parallelism culminates, and thus becomes more evident one may say,
when Heracles, by killing his wife and children, brings to
completion what Lycus attempted but failed to do.

[82] Burnett 1998. Cf. Papadopoulou 2001d.
[83] Cf. ll. 38–43; 166–9; 209–12; 215–16; 727–8.
[84] See esp. Mitchell-Boyask 1993 and his response to the discussions by Nussbaum
1986; Michelini 1987; Segal 1990b; Zeitlin 1996. On other approaches to revenge in
Hecuba, see Meridor 1983; Gregory 1991: 107–11 and 1999: xxxiv; Mossman 1995:
164–203; Hartigan 1997; Burnett 1998: 157–76. Collard 1991 (26, 32) seems to offer
the most balanced approach to the issue, as he takes into account the ancient
context, but also admits that the play eventually leaves the audience with more
questions than answers.

Another aspect of revenge, which is in fact related to both its retributive and its mimetic character, is its transgression of normality,[85] whereby uncontrollable rage finds release in revenge.[86] Heracles' revenge on Lycus may be said to show signs of excess.[87] To begin with, Heracles mentions decapitation and exposure of his victim:[88]

ἐγὼ δέ, νῦν γὰρ τῆς ἐμῆς ἔργον χερός,
πρῶτον μὲν εἶμι καὶ κατασκάψω δόμους
καινῶν τυράννων, κρᾶτα δ' ἀνόσιον τεμὼν
ῥίψω κυνῶν ἕλκημα· (565–8)

As for me – it's for my hand to act now – first I shall go and raze to the ground[89] the palace of this new king, I shall cut off his unholy head and throw it to the dogs to tear at.

Heracles' threats to abuse and to expose the corpse of his enemy[90] are reminiscent of another threatened revenge, in Euripides' *Electra*, where Orestes, after the murder of Aegisthus, invites Electra to abuse the corpse (895–8). The problematic character of such a threatened revenge[91] (cf. Soph. *El.* 1487–90) is raised in Electra's initial reaction, that is, her hesitation to abuse the dead (900–4), and will be

<hr/>

85 On this issue and on the ambivalent character of revenge see Hallett and Hallett 1980.
86 On attempts at anger control in classical antiquity, see Harris 2001. On aggression as an aspect of human nature, cf. Burkert 1966; Girard 1977. For a more recent approach, cf. Foley 1985: 50–1.
87 For the different view that Heracles' threatened violence against Lycus and the Thebans is not at all problematic, see e.g. Kamerbeek 1966; Michelini 1987: 263: 'Heracles is a warrior; and it is his business to kill'; more recently Barlow 1996. For the contrary view, see e.g. Burnett 1971: 165–6.
88 Denial of burial to enemies was not unheard of for an Athenian audience; it was for example a penalty for serious criminals at Athens. However, in literature abuse of a corpse was usually presented as reprehensible. On these issues see e.g. Rosivach 1983; Griffith 1999.
89 On the associations of κατασκαφή, 'razing to the ground' of a convicted criminal's house as a punishment in antiquity, see Connor 1985.
90 As Bond 1981 remarks on Eur. *HF* 568: 'Lycus' head will be not merely "food for dogs" (κυσίν); it will be "dog-food" (κυνῶν), a more contemptuous expression.' For the motif of throwing an enemy's body to the dogs and its significance, see Wilkins 1993 on Eur. *Heracl.* 1050–1, with passages and bibliography.
91 Contrast Hom. *Od.* 3.258–61 and 309–10, where we learn, in Nestor's words, that Aegisthus' corpse was buried by Orestes, instead of being exposed to the birds and dogs as it actually deserved. Cf. Cropp 1988 on Eur. *El.* 896–8, who, however, plays down the seriousness of the threat in *Electra* and reduces it to a rhetorical device.

recalled, too, at the end of the play, when Castor determines that Aegisthus' corpse will be finally buried and that it will be the citizens of Argos who will perform the burial (1276–7). In both the examples from the Euripidean *Heracles* and *Electra*, what is described is an act of revenge, the violent character of which, no matter how justified it may be considered to be, is ultimately an outrage not very different from the behaviour of savage barbarians.[92] On the other hand, the burial of the dead was thought to be a panhellenic rule, as Adrastus points out in Euripides' *Suppliants* (524–7), while the exposure of corpses and the refusal of burial is a theme the problematic character of which is treated in several tragedies (e.g. *Antigone*). In *Heracles* the problematic character is suggested especially if one considers the emphasis given, by contrast, to the burial of Heracles' own children and the importance of the funerary rites at the end of the play (1360–5, 1389–92,[93] 1419).

When Heracles announces his intention to cut off the head of his enemy, he is placing himself on the same level of savagery as some of the villains he eliminated during his purificatory/civilizing career. One such villain, Cycnus, is actually mentioned in the play, as the object of the fifth of Heracles' labours (389–93).[94] The assimilation by Heracles of the outrageous acts of those whom he eliminated in order to purify the

---

[92] Cf. Eur. *IT* 72–6; 1428–30. In Aesch. *Eum.* 186–7, too, decapitation is the first example of barbaric cruelties mentioned by Apollo. See Sommerstein 1989 on Aesch. *Eum.* 186–90, where he also mentions decapitation as a Persian (barbaric) punishment in Aesch. *Pers.* 369–71. In the *Iliad* too, where the disfigurement of the fallen enemy in the context of battle is not rare (cf. Segal 1971; Vernant 1991a), decapitation as a form of outrage is rather rare and seems horrific. In fact, it is worth mentioning that the scholiast on an Iliadic passage (schol. B. *Il.* 13.203) describes decapitation as savage and not a Greek practice: ὠμὸν καὶ οὐχ ἑλληνικόν.

[93] In this passage Heracles, in a series of three imperatives (κείρασθε, 'cut your hair', συμπενθήσατ᾽, 'mourn with me', ἔλθετ᾽, 'come'), invites the whole land of Cadmus and the people of Thebes to engage in the rites for the dead. Heracles' words are apt, as they give the sense both of solidarity and of propriety in the performance of the rites. In this respect we may also wonder about the function of similar rites at the end of other plays with violent deaths. In *Bacchae* for example, where the body of Pentheus has been dismembered, it is difficult to imagine that the carrying of Pentheus' corpse is not to be followed by proper rites. On this issue, see Easterling 1987; cf. Segal 2000.

[94] As Bond 1981 comments about Cycnus on Eur. *HF* 389–93: 'He cut off his victims' heads to build a temple from their skulls (ΣPind. *Ol.* 10.19b); this gives point to

earth from evil is in fact a clear indication of the mimetic
character of revenge/punishment as I discussed it above; in
other words, the avenger turns momentarily into his 'other'.
Of course, one might remark that the Chorus do not expand on
Heracles' murder of this villain and do not describe his crimes.
But this is not necessary, since the mere mention of Cycnus and
his murder by Heracles is enough to evoke all the details for an
informed audience.[95]

Perhaps the most telling example of the identification
between Heracles and the opponents he fights against during
his labours is *Trachiniae*. I have already discussed, at the
beginning of this chapter, the way in which the violent disruption of Heracles' sacrifice brings to the fore the thematic concerns of this tragedy with the inversion of the categories
'human' and 'beast' and ultimately with the fusion between
Heracles and his bestial enemies. The most concrete example in
the play is the description, in the first stasimon (497–530), of
the duel between Heracles and the river-god Achelous; a fight
in which the two opponents, as the Chorus say in the epode,
mingle to the point of becoming almost indistinguishable from
each other (517–22). This is one of several ways in which
Heracles' attitude becomes hard to separate from that of his
monstrous opponents.[96]

In this respect, it is also worth considering the evidence
provided by satyr-drama. It was in this genre after all that
Heracles appeared very frequently, and particularly in the
Euripidean satyr-play, where Heracles seems to have been
introduced even into plays where the myth treated by the
dramatist was not traditionally associated with this hero.[97]

ξεινοδαΐκταν (391). It is a habit attributed to Antaeus – also inhibited by Heracles
(Pind. *Isth.* 4.70 Snell) – Diomedes (see on 380–8) and other "legendary evil-doers";
see Dodds on *Ba* 1214.'
[95] Cf. the assimilation by Hercules of Busiris' attitude in Seneca's *Hercules Furens*
(483–4), for which see Papadopoulou 2004. The example of Busiris is telling because
it is unanimously taken by critics as a manifestation of Hercules' civilizing role (cf.
Piccaluga 1968: 149–55; Laurens 1986; Durand 1986: 107–32; van Straaten 1995:
46–9).
[96] See e.g. Elliott-Sorum 1978.
[97] On the satyr-plays where Heracles featured, see Sutton 1980: 154; for a discussion of
Heracles in satyr-drama and of his popularity with Euripides, see Hourmouziades
²1984: 117–64.

Two of Heracles' standard associations in the satyr-drama are his gluttony and his role as the fighter against monsters and villains.[98] What is important for our discussion here is that although there is a clear juxtaposition between Heracles and his 'evil' opponents, nevertheless he often behaves like them, the reason being perhaps the comic effect of such contradiction.[99]

To return to *Heracles*, Heracles' threatened revenge against Lycus, when he is sane, will find its equivalent in his treatment of Eurystheus at the initial stage of his madness as narrated by the Messenger and quoted at p. 18 above.

The similarity between Heracles' threats against Lycus on the one hand and against Eurystheus on the other shows that Heracles follows familiar patterns of behaviour whether in sanity or in madness;[100] revenge, as I noted above, transgresses the boundaries between normality and excess, rationality and madness.

Moreover, Heracles' threat to cut off Eurystheus' head may not be without significance, that is, it may sound more possible, given the story that Eurystheus' head was indeed buried separately from the rest of his body.[101] Heracles also intends to bring the head of Eurystheus back to the town, as Agave brings

[98] Cf. Sutton 1980: 154. For Heracles' role as the representative of good and the fighter against evil in Euripidean satyr-plays, see Hourmouziades [2]1984: 124.

[99] See Hourmouziades [2]1984: 168–9 (cf. his discussion of the similarities of Heracles in Euripides' *Syleus* and *Alcestis* with Polyphemus in Euripides' *Cyclops* at 134–9).

[100] But this continuity has also been taken by several critics (beginning with Wilamowitz, who later renounced it) as an indication that Heracles was mad from the time he appeared onstage. This view has long been refuted. Cf. Burnett 1971: 168–70, esp. n. 20: 'The likeness between the two crimes has inspired the curious theory that Heracles has been mad from the beginning; so Wilamowitz, Verrall, Grube, and Dodds (. . .) However, the madness quite plainly begins at line 931 (. . .) What has confused the critics is the gods' usual tact, for they have chosen to destroy Heracles in a fashion that is suitable to him. Violence has always been a part of Heracles' mixed nature (. . .) and Euripides has shown Heracles' own "sane" violence in the killing of Lycus and in its double, the fantasy killing of Eurystheus.'

[101] See Kearns 1989: 49; 164. In Eur. *Heracl.* 1050–1 Alcmene proposes to throw Eurystheus to the dogs, while there is no threatened outrage to his head; a later source, however, Apollodorus (*Bibl.* 2.8.1), mentions that Hyllus cut Eurystheus' head off and sent it to Alcmene, who then further outraged the head by gouging out the eyes (Wilkins 1993 on Eur. *Heracl.* 1050–1; cf. also Seaford 1994: 128 n. 119).

the head of Pentheus in *Bacchae* and (perhaps) Orestes brings the head of Aegisthus in Euripides' *Electra*.[102]

Heracles' revenge is designed to recall the Homeric Achilles.[103] It is reminiscent of the excess in Achilles' determination to abuse Hector's body (*Il.* 18.334–5, 23.20–1, 182–3) and to sacrifice twelve Trojan captives (*Il.* 18.336–7, 23.181–2).[104] The excess in Achilles' case is evident in the gods' reactions: Thetis wonders why her son's grief over the death of Patroclus is so uncontrollable (*Il.* 24.128–37), while Zeus expresses his disapproval of the fact that Achilles continues the disfigurement of the corpse of Hector, and describes Achilles' state as madness (φρεσὶ μαινομένηισιν, *Il.* 24.114). Similarly Apollo had said earlier that Achilles was not in his right senses but behaved like a wild animal, in fact like a lion (*Il.* 24.39–43).

The similarity between Heracles and Achilles is also evoked when Heracles utters his threats against the Thebans who did not oppose Lycus:

(...) Καδμείων δ' ὅσους
κακοὺς ἐφηῦρον εὖ παθόντας ἐξ ἐμοῦ
τῶι καλλινίκωι τῶιδ' ὅπλωι χειρώσομαι,
τοὺς δὲ πτερωτοῖς διαφορῶν τοξεύμασιν

---

[102] It should be noted that in Euripides' *Electra* it is not clear whether Orestes has actually severed Aegisthus' head from the rest of the corpse. For a comprehensive account of the views held by various scholars on this issue, see Cropp 1988 on Eur. *El.* 855–7; against the view that Orestes brings the severed head, see more recently Burnett 1998: 236 n. 40. For other instances of the association between decapitation of an enemy and hubristic behaviour, cf. [Euripides'] *Rhesus,* a drama which re-writes the Doloneia from *Iliad* 10 (for a more sceptical view on their exact relation see Fenik 1964). For iconography, see Lissarrague 1980; on Dolon, see Williams 1986. On Dolon's appearance, cf. Reinhardt 1961: 247; Hainsworth 1993 on Hom. *Il.* 10.334–5; Bond 1996: 260. On the symbolism of wearing animal-skin (wolf-skin in Dolon's case, lion-skin in Heracles' case) see e.g. Vernant 1991b: 38. Cf. the Plutarchan Lysander, who ridiculed those who argued that the descendants of Heracles should not wage war by deceit, saying that 'ὅπου γὰρ ἡ λεοντῆ μὴ ἀφικνεῖται, προσραπτέον ἐκεῖ τὴν ἀλωπεκῆν', 'where the lion-skin does not come, there one must sew on a fox-skin' (Plut. *Lys.* vii.4).

[103] For the Homeric Achilles as a paradigmatic hero for the double nature of heroism (both outstanding and terrible), see Goldhill 1991: 16–18; for the Homeric Achilles as a hero who foreshadows the heroes of tragedy, especially those of Sophocles, cf. Knox 1964: *passim*; Rutherford 1982: 146.

[104] The sacrifice of the captives is accompanied by a (rare) comment of disapproval on the part of the narrator (23.176). For a discussion of this slaughter as a ritual act, see Hughes 1991: 49–55.

νεκρῶν ἅπαντ᾽ ᾽Ισμηνὸν ἐμπλήσω φόνου,
Δίρκης τε νᾶμα λευκὸν αἱμαχθήσεται. (568–73)

Those of the Thebans whom I have found to be treacherous in spite of being
well treated by me, these I shall overcome with my conquering club.
Dispersing others with my winged arrows, I shall fill the whole of the river
Ismenus with bloody corpses and the clear stream of Dirce shall run red
with gore.

Heracles' threat, in particular, to fill the river Ismenus with
the carnage of corpses and to redden the stream of Dirce is
reminiscent of Achilles' slaughter of the Trojans who took
refuge in the river Scamander in *Iliad* 21. There too the water
turned red with the blood of the slaughtered victims
(ἐρυθαίνετο δ᾽ αἵματι ὕδωρ, *Il.* 21.21), and Scamander appeared
to Achilles and asked him, in vain, to desist (*Il.* 21.218–21).

It was the excess of the killings and Achilles' contemptuous-
ness that caused the river-god's anger, an anger which resulted
in Scamander's pursuit of Achilles over the plain. Achilles'
slaughter of the Trojans in Scamander is part of his revenge
for the death of Patroclus; his achievement represents at the
same time supreme valour and arrogant transgression. In a
rather similar manner Heracles seems to represent absolute
strength, the uncontrollable use of which becomes threatening.

If Heracles' threats are viewed against this background, then
their problematic character comes to the fore. We may recall how
the Chorus, after Lycus' murder, invoke the entire city of Thebes
to join in celebrations for Heracles' achievement and invite Dirce
and Ismenus to join 'Heracles' victorious contest' (781–9). In
fact, it may be argued that the Chorus' invocation of Dirce and
Ismenus in this laudatory context is darkened if considered in
relation to Heracles' threats that precede (568–73).[105]

The passage where these threats are uttered (568–73, quoted
above) calls for further discussion. It is evident that Heracles'
revenge will be excessive, in the sense that it will not differentiate between guilty and innocent; Heracles will not confine
his revenge to the people who have betrayed him in not

[105] Cf. Burnett 1971: 167.

reciprocating his benefactions. Bond[106] comments: 'Innocent persons will suffer, but that is not unusual, and is perhaps intended.' Bond's underplaying of the problematic nature of Heracles' revenge is difficult to sustain, even conceding a degree of force to some critics' view[107] that the violence of a justified revenge would have been received by a typical fifth-century audience with more tolerance.

At this point we should note that the text does not provide a detailed description of Heracles' revenge against Lycus and Thebes, apart from mentioning the murder of Lycus, but only hints at the question whether Heracles' threats to cut off Lycus' head and throw it to the dogs, as well as to kill the Thebans who did not defend his family against Lycus, are accomplished before the initiation of the purificatory ritual. The beginning of the Messenger's speech mentions the murder of Lycus and the flinging of his corpse outside the palace (923–4). As for the revenge against the Thebans, this, according to Amphitryon's instructions (604–5), would follow the murder of Lycus, but we are not told whether or not it did.

In terms of dramatic effect it is the very refusal of the text to give a clear answer and the consequent openness of the issue that actually draw attention to whether Heracles carried out his threats and inevitably generate assumptions. In other words, if the audience are invited to think that Heracles' threats were fulfilled, then the impression of Heracles' excess in his revenge is brought to the fore.[108] With regard to Heracles' threats it is also worth quoting Luschnig,[109] who seems to me to come closer to the possible effect of the scene upon the audience: 'In unedited life, a man may well threaten more

---

[106] Bond 1981 on Eur. *HF* 568–73.   [107] E.g. Burnett 1998.

[108] Cf. Bond 1981 on Eur. *HF* 604: 'It is wrong to assume that Heracles forgets about the perfidious Thebans. The killing of Lycus is to come first (πρίν); only that is referred to at 923. But the vehemence of 568–73 coupled with 940 τοῖσι νῦν θανοῦσιν, "those who have just been killed" and 966 οὔ τί που φόνος σ' ἐβάκχευσεν νεκρῶν | οὓς ἄρτι καίνεις;, "surely the blood of those you have just been killing has not made you mad?", suggest that Heracles carries out his plan of mass vengeance after killing Lycus. However, one is better off without any assumptions at all about this.'

[109] Luschnig 1988: 102.

than he means to do, more than he is capable of doing. But the same cannot be said of an economical tragedy. It is less true of Heracles. (...) Are we not being told in no uncertain terms that there is nothing that Heracles cannot do? He could make Dirce run with blood. These threats are evidence of the man's superhuman violence that turns out also to be sub-human.'

Heracles' threats, when he was sane, against the Thebans who did not help his family against Lycus will be recalled later in the play in a way which suggests (like the parallel we saw between Heracles' threats to cut off Lycus' and Eurystheus' heads) the continuity between the killings that Heracles commits in sanity and in madness.[110]

In particular, Athena's sudden intervention,[111] which prevents Heracles from committing patricide, puts an end to his violence; by interrupting Heracles' action,[112] this divine intervention also prevents the audience from knowing the course that Heracles' violent outburst would have followed if it had not been interrupted. However, Amphitryon provides some hints which refer to Heracles' uncontrollable violence when he alerts the Chorus:

<Αμ.> οὐκ ἀτρεμαῖα θρῆνον αἰ-
    άξετ᾽, ὦ γέροντες;
    ἢ δέσμ᾽ ἀνεγειρόμενος χαλάσας ἀπολεῖ πόλιν,
    ἀπὸ δὲ πατέρα, μέλαθρά τε καταρρήξει. (1053–7)

<Amphitryon>: Old friends, will you not lament more softly? Otherwise when he wakes he will break his bonds and destroy the city, and destroy his father and tear down the house.

Again, when Amphitryon notices that Heracles is waking, he fears that he will attack the whole city (1081–6). What Amphitryon fears never takes place, but the description of the possible continuation of the action is apt, because it

[110] Another parallel which could be mentioned is that the potential destruction of the palace (envisaged by Amphitryon, 1056) is the equivalent of Heracles' threat to raze to the ground the palace of the new king, that is Lycus (566–7).
[111] Athena's intervention is discussed at the end of the next chapter.
[112] Heracles' interrupted action is categorized as 'blind vengeance plot' in Burnett 1973.

suggests that violent action is so habitual with Heracles that it can be predictable.[113]

To sum up, whether in madness or in sanity, what is given emphasis is the conflation of good and evil in Heracles' violence. An act described as justified revenge (against Lycus or against Eurystheus) and as an attack of the good against the bad is rendered deeply problematic when the good shows signs of excess.

I turn now to a related topic, the assimilation by Heracles of his opponents' behaviour, which also hints at the hero's transgression of the border between humans and beasts. I discussed for example how this transgression was treated by Sophocles in his *Trachiniae*. In *Heracles* there are also indications of this transgression; the phraseology used is a metaphor which points to the liminal status of Heracles between humans and beasts. We find this metaphor at 870 (δεινὰ μυκᾶται, 'he bellows terribly'), at 962 (δεινὰ δ' Εὐρυσθεῖ βρέμων, 'he shouted terrible threats against Eurystheus'), and also at 1212 if the reading of the manuscript βρόμον, 'roaring' is maintained instead of Reiske's correction δρόμον, 'race'. As Bond[114] comments on 1212, although Reiske's correction 'brings in a whole complex of madman/horse images (...) Nevertheless βρόμον should be kept. A roaring is a more exquisite image than a race course. λέοντος ἀγρίου θυμόν has prepared us for it, and it is not strictly a metaphor. Heracles the θυμολέων has been making loud animal noises which have proclaimed the onset of madness: 870 δεινὰ μυκᾶται (preceded by ταῦρος ὣς ἐς ἐμβολήν, cf. λέοντος here), 962 δεινά ... βρέμων. No wonder Amphitryon thinks first of this terrible noise when he fears a recurrence.'[115]

Heracles also seems to have transgressed the other metaphysical border, that between humanity and divinity. The references to him by both the Chorus and the characters imply that

---

[113] Cf. ll. 1210–11, where Amphitryon comments on Heracles' wild nature.

[114] Bond 1981.

[115] For the terms used to denote Heracles' 'wildness' we may also compare Soph. *OT* 1265 (δεινὰ βρυχηθεὶς τάλας, 'terribly roaring, poor man') and *Aj.* 322 (ὑπεστέναζε ταῦρος ὣς βρυχώμενος, 'he was moaning low like a bellowing bull').

Heracles has acquired a near-divine status, as a natural consequence of his semi-divine nature. As Amphitryon remarks, Heracles joined battle with the gods against the giants and celebrated the glorious victory with them (177–80; cf. 1190–4).

The Chorus sing the second stasimon in honour of Heracles; this ode is usually taken to be not only an *enkomion*,[116] but also a *paian*.[117] The fourth stanza draws a parallel between Heracles and Apollo, when the Chorus say that, as Apollo is celebrated with *paians*, Heracles is also worthy of the same honour, since his exploits have bestowed on him a reputation which by far exceeds that of his divine birth. The association between Heracles and Apollo after Heracles' opportune arrival, which saves his family from imminent death, may have some relation to their sharing the epithet ἀλεξίκακος, i.e. 'averter of evils'. Heracles' potential power to help his family even while he is in Hades is earlier suggested by Megara's appeal to him for help, at a time when she considers him to be dead: ἄρηξον, ἐλθέ· καὶ σκιὰ φάνηθί μοι. | ἅλις γὰρ ἐλθὼν κἂν ὄναρ γένοιο σύ, 'come, help us! Even as a shadow appear to me! It would be enough if you were to come even as a dream' (494–5). Although this seems to be a desperate appeal, the text may at the same time be hinting at a 'heroization' of Heracles; if this is a possible reading, then this reference parallels the establishment, at the end of the play, of a hero-cult for Heracles after his death (1331–3). Support for this reading may be offered by Amphitryon's phrase σὺ μὲν τὰ νέρθεν εὐτρεπῆ ποιοῦ, γύναι, 'continue to win over the powers of the Underworld' (497) which follows, if τὰ νέρθεν has the meaning 'those (personified) forces below'.[118]

---

[116] On this stasimon as an *enkomion* (i.e. as a song of praise addressed to a mortal), see Parry 1965: 363.

[117] On the reception of the *paian* in tragedy, see Rutherford 1995 (124–5 on the second stasimon of *Heracles*).

[118] See Bond 1981 ad loc.: '497 is usually supposed to mean "continue with the preparations for the underworld". But D. S. Robertson, *CR* 52 (1938), 50, takes it to mean "continue to win over those who are below". This makes a much more effective reference to Megara's appeal to Heracles (490–496), and emphasizes Amphitryon's appeal to Zeus as parallel to it.'

Apart from the parallelism between Heracles and Apollo, a parallel is also drawn between the Chorus and the Delian Maidens, respectively, as the performers of the *paians* in honour of Heracles and of Apollo (687–700).[119] Although the references to Heracles' god-like status are counterbalanced by references to his piety (e.g. his establishment of an altar to Ζεὺς Σωτήρ after his victory over the Minyans, 48–50; his dedication of the trophy won in the Amazonomachy to a temple (alluded to at 416–18); his intention to honour the gods of his home on his return, 599–609), it is true that his liminal state between humanity and divinity puts him into an unstable position, which is constantly threatened by transgression.[120] His return from Hades, which marks his overcoming of mortality, serves as the best indication of this transgression.[121] In the madness scene, Heracles also shows signs of it, when he wishes to destroy the Cyclopian walls of Mycenae (944); his delusion of divinity could be implied at 943–6, where the verb used, 'violently shatter as with a trident' (συντριαινῶσαι, 946), a Euripidean hapax, is otherwise found in connection with Poseidon.[122] It is the duality of the nature of Heracles' violence that can give him god-like power as well as reduce him to wildness. It is the function of this duality that makes Heracles' power prove beneficent as well as cruel, and thus reveal its potential for both good and bad; it is also the duality of Heracles' power, the fusion of two contradictory

---

[119] The reference of the tragic Chorus to the performance of the Delian Maidens is discussed by Henrichs 1996a as an example of what he calls 'choral projection'. According to Henrichs, choral projection occurs 'when the Choruses locate their own dancing in the past or the future, in contrast to the here and now of their immediate performance, or when Choruses project their collective identity onto groups of dancers distant from the concrete space of the orchestra and dancing in the allusive realm of the dramatic imagination' (49). Henrichs considers choral projection as an important corollary to what he calls 'choral self-referentiality', i.e. the Chorus' self-conscious references to their performances within the particular tragedy's dramatic and ritual context. On choral self-referentiality, see Henrichs 1995.

[120] It is interesting that the Chorus' glorification of Heracles in the second stasimon contains none of the traditional warnings, found in epinician poetry, about human limits; on this issue, see Parry 1965: 364 and 371.

[121] Cf. Burnett 1971: 179. [122] See de Jong 1991: 166.

forces and the subsequent confusion that marks Heracles' 'monstrosity'.

We may also consider the impact that Heracles' presence on stage, wearing the lion-skin, may potentially have had for the spectators. It may have been a constant reminder of Heracles as the slayer of the lion, and thus as the possessor of over-whelming power (symbolized by the lion), and, at the same time, of Heracles as almost one with the beast.[123] The Greek preoccupation with the definition of human nature and its relation to the divine and bestial spheres reveals an anxiety over the transgression of the borderlines of each realm.[124] In extant Greek tragedy in particular, the fragility of the 'human' status is well exemplified, in metaphorical terms, in the case of Orestes in *Iphigenia among the Taurians*, where the hero is for a moment presented in a god-like status (267–8) only to be described as a lion soon afterwards (297). Apart from mere metaphor, the crossing of the borders implied in the hierarchy god-human-beast is evident at the end of *Bacchae*, where we learn that Cadmus, who was born mortal, will be tranformed into a snake and will eventually reach the land of the blessed (1330–9).

Dionysiac metaphor and the mystic element

I turn now to the way in which the Dionysiac metaphor in the play also helps articulate Heracles' ambivalence.[125] In terms both of transgression and of equal potential for good and bad,

---

[123] The lion imagery may have different associations in different contexts. E.g. strength and companionship in Soph. *Phil.* 1436 (for Philoctetes and Neoptolemus); savagery and ferocity in Aesch. *Ag.* 1258 (for Clytemnestra) as well as in Eur. *Med.* 187; 1342; 1407 (for Medea). In the case of Heracles, the lion-skin indicates his supreme strength (he subdued the lion) but also his becoming almost one with the beast as he now wears its skin.

[124] For a discussion, see Meagher 1989, who in this respect calls the Heracles of the play 'metaphysically undefined' (95).

[125] See also Kirk 1977, in whose opinion Heracles is the most contradictory among Greek heroes; cf. Brelich 1958, esp. 365.

Heracles resembles Dionysus.[126] On the one hand Dionysus is the boundless god, who defies and transgresses any border and who takes whatever form he wishes (in *Bacchae* he is a god, a man, a bull); he himself crosses the borders that maintain hierarchy and human order, and he makes others cross them too. On the other hand, Dionysus also incorporates the polarity of benevolence and cruelty (as the *Bacchae* forcefully demonstrates).[127]

The abundance of Dionysiac imagery in the play may also be interpreted as a constantly strong allusion to the association of Heracles with Dionysus' familiar characteristics of transgression and of equal potentiality for beneficence or cruelty. This suggestion about the dynamics of the Dionysiac imagery in *Heracles* is intended to supplement other accounts of the function of the Dionysiac element in the play. Seaford,[128] for example, attributes the Dionysiac imagery to an influence of Aeschylus' *Lycurgeia*:

> In Aeschylus' *Lykourgeia* it seems that Dionysus in consort with Λύσσα punished the resistance of Lykourgos by making him kill his own son (and probably also his wife), and that this influenced this scene of the *Herakles*. Hence presumably the strong Dionysiac element in the *Herakles*: the Chorus recognize the presence of Λύσσα but describe her as in Bacchic frenzy, and the frenzy of Herakles is repeatedly called Bacchic, aimed specifically at destroying the household.

There may indeed be precise intertextual references here, but the frequent occurrence of Dionysiac imagery in other plays may suggest that it could also function independently of a particular set of allusions.[129]

---

[126] The bibliography on Dionysus and his associations in Greek tragedy is vast. For the purposes of my discussion, see esp. Otto 1965 [1933]; Gernet 1953; Vernant 1985; Henrichs 1979, 1982, 1984, 1993, 1996b; Bierl 1991; Seaford 1993, 1994; 1996; Friedrich 1996; Segal 1997 (revised edition of Segal 1982).

[127] In this respect I disagree with Alford 1992: 46–7, who makes a juxtaposition between Heracles and Dionysus as representatives of extreme clarity and confusion respectively. In Alford's view, Dionysus has a shifting identity, whereas Heracles does not.

[128] Seaford 1994: 353.   [129] For examples from tragedy, see Bierl 1991.

The Dionysiac element is introduced not only for the description of Heracles' madness, but also much earlier, for the depiction of what seems to be a festive celebration (673–86);[130] in this way, both the peaceful and the violent aspects of Dionysus are evoked in relation to Heracles. Henrichs[131] notes but overemphasizes the peaceful aspect of Dionysus in *Heracles*, and negates the inherently violent aspect of the god in the play; according to Henrichs, the Dionysus of this play has 'more in common with the predominantly benign Dionysos of Attic cult and comedy than with the ambiguous, polar Dionysos of *Bakkhai*', and he is 'drawn into the violent orbit' of Lyssa through his juxtaposition with this divinity. But surely it is rather the familiar Dionysiac ambiguity and polarity that the play seems to evoke, in order to hint at the association of Heracles with Dionysus.

To begin with the peaceful aspect, this is introduced in the second stasimon, where the Chorus assert, in the third stanza, their devotion to the Muses' gifts (673–86). The association between Heracles and Dionysus-Bromios is close, since the reference to the god immediately follows the very first mention of Heracles in this stasimon, where Heracles is the *laudandus*. The references to the joyful dances and songs in a stanza where Dionysus, the giver of wine, along with the Muses, sets the atmosphere of peaceful bliss, will be ironically reversed[132] in the words of Lyssa, where she describes her effect upon Heracles: τάχα σ' ἐγὼ μᾶλλον χορεύσω καὶ καταυλήσω φόβωι, 'I shall soon make you dance more wildly and I shall play upon you a pipe of terror' (871; cf. οὔπω καταπαύσομεν | Μούσας, αἵ μ' ἐχόρευσαν, 'I shall not yet repress the Muses who set me

---

[130] For the recurrence in Greek tragedy of a festive Dionysiac context before reversal and catastrophe, see Schlesier 1993: 104–7, where she discusses passages from *Choephori, Antigone, Trachiniae* and *Hippolytus*. For the association between the Dionysiac metaphor and the destruction of household, see Seaford 1993, esp. 132; Seaford 1994: 328–67. For the use of Dionysiac elements for pointing out the hero's reversal in *Heracles*, see Bierl 1991: 140–5. On the role of Dionysus in the play, see also Grassby 1969: 238–46.

[131] See Henrichs 1996a: 61–2.

[132] Cf. Henrichs 1996a: 61: 'At the climax of the play, choral dancing turns into pandemonium, and Heracles becomes the victim rather than the beneficiary of choral projection.'

50

dancing', 685–6; Λίβυν αὐλόν, 'Libyan pipe', 684). Her mention
of the perverted songs and dances is taken up by the Chorus
(875–9). Their next two references to the same perversion
clearly mention the substitution of wild frenzy for the peaceful
Dionysiac atmosphere (889–90 and 892–3).[133]

Dionysiac vocabulary often carries mystic overtones, and it
is worth looking at passages in the play where language of this
kind seems to deepen the sense of Heracles' ambivalence. The
bacchic imagery of the play culminates in the characterization
of Heracles by Amphitryon as a bacchic figure from Hades
("Αιδου βάκχος, 1119). Although the phrase is taken to be evo-
cative of the wild aspect of Dionysus and his cult, in which case
the term βάκχος would be equivalent to 'wild figure',[134] the
phrase, with its combination of Dionysus and Hades, may also
be reminiscent of (and consequently reversive of) another
peaceful aspect of Dionysus, that of the god (via his mystic
identity of "Ιακχος[135]) of the Eleusinian mysteries.[136] Such an
allusion may be corroborated by an earlier, explicit reference
to Heracles' initiation into these mysteries (613). The term
bacchos was of course used, along with the term *mystes*, to
refer to mystic initiates.[137]

The abnormal situation in which Heracles' family finds
itself trapped as a result of Lycus' evil, a situation which is

[133] For a discussion of the discourse of negative Dionysiac music in the play, see
Wilson 2000: 433–9.
[134] The phrase "Αιδου βάκχαι, 'Bacchants from Hades', is found in another Euripidean
context of wild violence: in Eur. *Hec.* 1077, Polymestor uses this phrase for the
women who tore his eyes out. See Bond 1981 on Eur. *HF* 1119.
[135] For the identification between Dionysus and Iacchus, cf. Soph. *Ant.* 1146–52;
TrGF IV F 959; Eur. *Ion* 1074; Eur. *Bacch.* 725–6; Ar. *Ran.* 316. See Graf 1974:
46–66: Gasparri et al. 1986: 414; Simon 1990; *contra* this identification see Clinton
1992: 64–71.
[136] Mylonas 1961, while discussing the possible role of Dionysus at Eleusis, concludes:
'Dionysus had no part in the Eleusinian Mysteries and all references to his
participation are later in date and are the result of his confused equation with
Iacchos' (309). Mylonas' view reflects his aim in his book of keeping the Eleusinian
Mysteries free from any religious syncretism. Clinton 1992: 123–5 (cf. 64–71)
expands on Dionysus' own cult at Eleusis, separate from the Eleusinian
Mysteries. On Dionysus' relation with the Eleusinian Mysteries, see Graf 1974:
40–78; Versnel 1990: 153–5. For a discussion of later iconography (from the fourth
century BC), see Metzger 1995.
[137] See Seaford 1996: 41 with examples.

elaborately illustrated by a dexterous exploitation of the dynamics of ritual, is restored to order with Heracles' return to Thebes. Heracles' words on arriving are: ὦ χαῖρε μέλαθρον πρόπυλά θ' ἑστίας ἐμῆς, | ὡς ἄσμενός σ' ἐσεῖδον ἐς φάος μολών, 'I greet my house and the doorway to my hearth. How happy I am to see you and to have returned to daylight!' (523–4). His expression ἐς φάος μολών, that is, 'having returned to light', recurs in Amphitryon's words to Heracles: ὦ φάος μολὼν πατρί (531), that is, 'having come *as* a light to your father'.[138] Similarly Electra greets her brother Orestes as 'dearest light': ὦ φίλτατον φῶς (Soph. *El.* 1224). In both cases, as Seaford[139] has argued, a hero who is supposedly dead returns and saves his kin, and this salvation is expressed in language which evokes mystic transition. In the case of Heracles, Seaford[140] holds, the mystic connotation implies that Heracles, apart from being an initiate himself (his initiation into the Eleusinian Mysteries is explicitly mentioned at 613), is also presented in the play as the bringer of mystic salvation for his family. This salvation corresponds to the many references to ἐλπίς, 'hope', in the first half of the play; the only hope that Heracles' family and the Theban elders of the Chorus have is Heracles himself. Ἐλπίς is a leitmotif in the play and its association in particular with Heracles recalls the hopes of initiates of Dionysus.[141]

Given the mystic context, the description of the garments of Heracles' family as funerary, which is understandable since the family is about to die at the hands of Lycus, may also have mystic associations, given that the clothes of initiands, who were imagined as dying, were also thought of as funerary.[142] However, the mystic salvation is subverted when Heracles kills

---

[138] On light and darkness in the play, see Assaël 1994.

[139] See Seaford 1994: 377–8. Seaford's discussion of mystic allusions in several Greek tragedies is stimulating, but the material calls for caution: for example, the frequent juxtapositions between light and darkness, hope and despair, life and death, may be said to be recurrent antitheses in Greek tragedy without necessarily carrying mystic allusions. However, *Heracles*, with its clear statement that the hero returns after a period in Hades, where he was fortunate to have seen the holy Mysteries (613), invites a reading of mystic overtones.

[140] See Seaford 1994: 378.   [141] See Bierl 1991: 140–4.

[142] See Seaford 1994: 378–9 with notes.

his family. Heracles' murder of his family in the madness scene is correspondingly taken by Seaford as the violent reversal of the mystic transition. Mystic terminology, as Seaford[143] remarks with reference to its use in Greek tragedy, evokes some of the intense emotions which many among the audience had experienced as participants in the Eleusinian Mysteries, and we might also argue that the portrayal of the murders as the reversal of a mystic transition is a further effective device for deepening Heracles' ambivalence.

With regard to the mystic allusions of the play as a whole, one may add to Seaford's remarks that the presentation of Heracles as silent, veiled and seated before Theseus, during a scene which marks the beginning of the *passage* of Heracles from despair to his integration into a new context, may be reminiscent of similar portrayals of Heracles in art, which refer to his association with the mysteries at Agrai; in fact, these mysteries were said to have been founded in order to purify Heracles from the killing of the Centaurs.[144] As Parker (1983: 373–4) remarks:

[A] rite that recalls that of murder purification seems to have formed part of initiation at Eleusis or Agrai. The sitting posture, veiled head, silence and passive submission of the candidate are all the same (. . .) it is generally agreed that the explanation lies in the common character of the two ceremonies as rites of passage. The candidate at Eleusis is inducted into the society of the initiated; homicide purification means the reacceptance of the killer into social and political life.

Theseus' promise of future purification to Heracles (1324) shifts the focus to Athens and to his integration into a new religious and social context. This integration, the realization of which lies outside the scope of the drama, constitutes in a way a positive transition and concludes the sequence of two 'initiations', the effectiveness of which had proved to be only temporary: firstly, Heracles' initiation into the Eleusinian Mysteries helped him to subdue Cerberus but was of no help when he returned to Thebes; secondly, the salvation of the

---

[143] See Seaford 1994: 373.   [144] See Parker 1983: 284–5.

members of his family from death at the hands of Lycus, which was described, as we saw, in terms of an initiation, resulted in their death at the hands of Heracles himself.[145]

Ritual and integration

The foregoing discussion has largely focused on the way in which a polarity between good and bad is given concrete character in a clear juxtaposition between Heracles and Lycus, but is ultimately undermined and subverted to reveal the ambivalence at the heart of Heracles' violence/valour. I have also shown how this process is accentuated by a dexterous exploitation, on the part of the playwright, of the dynamics of a ritual crisis, which culminates in the failure of his purificatory ritual. It remains to consider how this ritual crisis is confronted.

Foley,[146] who attributes the ritual crisis in the play to the failure of the community of Thebes to integrate the hero, argues that the resolution of this crisis is to be seen in the acceptance of Heracles' *arete* and in the consequent integration of the hero into a new community, that of Athens. My approach to the ritual crisis in *Heracles* has been from a different perspective, which has associated the themes of pollution and purification with the nature of his violence and *arete*. The reception of Heracles by Athens and the introduction of a cult in his honour (1332–3) (where sacrifices have a significant role and thus function as a 'reparation' of his interrupted sacrifice) follow the recognition of the dual nature of his valour and are determined by the establishment of the beneficent aspect of this valour in the future for both the hero and his new community (1334–5). In the case of Heracles himself, this integration is aptly demonstrated in his long conversation with his weapons (the means both of his heroic deeds and of his outrageous slaughter of his family; the symbols, in other

---

[145] For a discussion of these changes/reversals in a Dionysiac context, see Bierl 1991: 88; 140–4.

[146] Foley 1985: 162–7.

words, of the duality of his *arete*), where he debates whether to
keep or reject them:

(...) ὦ λυγραὶ φιλημάτων
τέρψεις, λυγραὶ δὲ τῶνδ᾽ ὅπλων κοινωνίαι.
ἀμηχανῶ γὰρ πότερ᾽ ἔχω τάδ᾽ ἢ μεθῶ,
ἃ πλευρὰ τἀμὰ προσπίτνοντ᾽ ἐρεῖ τάδε.
Ἡμῖν τέκν᾽ εἷλες καὶ δάμαρθ᾽· ἡμᾶς ἔχεις
παιδοκτόνους σούς. εἶτ᾽ ἐγὼ τάδ᾽ ὠλέναις
οἴσω; τί φάσκων; ἀλλὰ γυμνωθεὶς ὅπλων
ξὺν οἷς τὰ κάλλιστ᾽ ἐξέπραξ᾽ ἐν Ἑλλάδι
ἐχθροῖς ἐμαυτὸν ὑποβαλὼν αἰσχρῶς θάνω;
οὐ λειπτέον τάδ᾽, ἀθλίως δὲ σωστέον. (1376–85)

How painfully sweet it is to kiss them and how painful it is too to think of the
companionship of my weapons. I do not know whether to keep them or to let
them go. They will say as they brush against my side: 'It was with our help
you murdered your wife and children. In wearing us you wear the killers of
your sons.' Am I to carry them about? What am I to say? Yet strip me of the
very weapons with which I did the most glorious exploits in Greece and shall
I not then die in submission at my enemies' hands? I cannot leave them
behind, I must keep them, painful though it is.

As this passage shows, the role of Heracles' weapons in the
future will be defensive, while the characterization of his reten-
tion of them as painful (ἀθλίως, 1385) is a reminder of the grief
which remains as the price of what seems to be a fragile
integration, just as the restoration offered by Theseus and
Athens cannot entirely mitigate this price.

On the other hand, ambivalence is also inscribed in the play
in reference to the future (and extra-dramatic) status of
Heracles. Here I disagree with Dunn,[147] who entirely under-
estimates the significance of Theseus' offers to Heracles, taking
them as vague and even illusory promises with no historical
significance for the Athenian audience. In fact, popular religion, and in particular the establishment of a hero-cult, is often

[147] Dunn 1996 and 1997. Cf. Dunn 2000. For a similarly sceptical approach to the
question of Euripidean aitiology, see Scullion 2000, who, using *Iphigenia among
the Taurians* as an example, argues that aitiologies in Euripides are more fictitious
and less based on the spectators' contemporary reality (but contrast Tzanetou
2000, in the same volume, whose perceptive reading of the ritual in the same play
seems to point in the opposite direction).

considered by critics as a meaningful closural device in many Euripidean plays,[148] while Dunn seems to try to conform to his general thesis (especially in Dunn 1996) about Euripides' disregard for 'closure' in most of his plays. What I would claim, by contrast, is that ambivalence or 'openness' are not absent altogether but may be seen in another sense. Since Heracles will receive a hero-cult, he will have the standard attribute of any recipient of hero-cult, that is, he will have the power to be both beneficent and maleficent. Finally, *contra* Foley, who sees 'restoration' or 'resolution' of the sacrificial crisis of the play, it should rather be argued that ritual[149] does not solve a problem, that is, in our case, the problem of Heracles' moral ambivalence, but helps to accommodate the problem and deal with it in another context. It is the function of ritual in general to redefine problematic issues and hold them in equilibrium, not to eliminate them completely.

Conclusion

An examination of the play based on ritual and its related themes shows that Euripides presents us throughout with neither an idealized nor a hubristic Heracles. Accordingly, Heracles' disaster is not to be seen in terms of an undeserved or a deserved punishment; the central problem is rather the inherent ambivalence of Heracles and the way in which this ambivalence can be dealt with. The tragedy problematizes the nature of Heracles' heroism and the ways in which this heroism can be accommodated in a civilized world after the performance of his labours.

In the course of this chapter, irrationality has often been mentioned in connection in particular with Heracles' violence

---

[148] Cf. Mikalson 1991.

[149] A comparable example of the fact that ritual does not offer a definite solution is the function of certain ancient Mysteries which promised salvation and the overcoming of death. As Burkert 1987: 12–29 notes, participation in these Mysteries, where no dogmatic faith was involved, reflected personal needs, and had a 'therapeutic' effect on participants; in this respect the psychological factor was stronger than the actual belief in overcoming death.

or the interplay between normality and excess, which often reduced the hero to wildness. At the same time, however, the madness inflicted upon Heracles, which results in his murder of wife and children, is presented as divinely caused. In the next chapter I turn to an examination of the role of madness and of the divine in this tragedy.

CHAPTER 2

MADNESS AND THE GODS

Introduction

The central event of *Heracles* is the hero's murder of his wife and children in a fit of madness directly caused by Lyssa but ultimately induced by Hera's will. Divine involvement and human agency are thus brought together and are problematized by the dramatic device of madness. In this chapter I shift the focus to an examination of the interrelated themes of madness and the role of the divine in the play, setting them against the wider background of other presentations of madness and divine causation in Greek tragedy and especially in Euripides.

The typology of Heracles' madness

Madness[1] is a broad, multi-faceted subject, as anyone trying to define it soon discovers.[2] Each period or culture in human history from antiquity to nowadays has its own systems of recognizing and describing madness, its nature, types, causes, symptoms, development and cures. To look back at ancient cases of madness with the help of what is known about madness in the modern world may often enrich our understanding of these cases; for example, we may conclude that an ancient description of madness approximates to what nowadays and in

---

[1] On madness in Greek tragedy in general, see O' Brien-Moore 1924: 74–155; Waldmann 1962: 24–32; Mattes 1970: 74–92; Vasquez 1972; Gregory 1974; Ciani 1974; Simon 1978: 89–154; Feder 1980: 35–97; Segal 1981: 35–8; Aélion 1983, vol. I, 215–63; Padel 1981; 1992; 1995; Schlesier 1985b; Goldhill 1986: 168–98; Szlezák 1986; Bruni and Piccitto 1991: 7–34; Gill 1996.

[2] For a discussion of ancient and modern concepts of madness and the problems of definition, see more recently Hershkowitz 1998: 1–16.

current terminology would be identified as 'X'- category of madness. It has often been noticed, for instance, that Orestes' madness as portrayed in *Orestes* is close to what would be described nowadays as delirium.[3] Attempts to categorize the different types of madness and to describe them in scientific terms were not of course absent from antiquity, and discussion of madness along with other diseases features in ancient medical literature, which finds echoes in the vocabulary used by the tragedians.[4] But we should be wary of jumping to conclusions about their approach to the phenomenon of madness.

As a general rule, medical works substituted natural causes for divine causation in any type of bodily or mental disorder. Greek tragedy, on the contrary, is a literary genre that dramatizes myths; it may indeed be enriched by the vocabulary of ancient medicine, it may even at times seem, especially in the case of Euripides, to present its audience with almost clinical cases of madness, yet it retains the notion of divine causation of madness as established in literary tradition from Homer[5] onwards. So although there is much to learn from medical concepts of madness, whether derived from antiquity or from the present day, identifying a specific type of madness and categorizing it as such will not take us very far. Madness in Greek tragedy is a complex phenomenon and although, as will be argued below, the convention of recurrent dramaturgical elements suggests the existence of a 'typology' for the description of madness, yet the dramatists were selective in their use of such elements.[6] In other words, the playwrights were not

---

[3] See e.g. Mattes 1970: 193; Theodorou 1993: 146. Cf. Smith 1967. On Orestes' madness in this play, see esp. Vasquez 1972: *passim*; Ciani 1974: *passim*; Gregory 1974: 55–98; Hartigan 1987: 129–35; Diggle 1999: 287–9.

[4] On the importance of the ancient medical models for the representation of madness in Greek tragedy, see e.g. Giles 1916; Miller 1944; Collinge 1962; Smith 1967; Musitelli 1968; Long 1968: 56–7; Vasquez 1972: 411–75; Dumortier ²1975; Ferrini 1978; von Staden 1992. On the relation between Euripidean tragedy and ancient medicine, see more recently Craik 2001.

[5] On the (limited) role of madness in Homer, see Hershkowitz 1998: 125–60.

[6] It should also be noted that there is always a category difference between phenomena as represented in drama and as defined or known in life off stage.

interested in presenting case-histories but in dramatizing madness for certain artistic purposes.

In *Heracles* Euripides uses several different perspectives which are complementary and together contribute to a reconstruction of Heracles' mad actions for the audience.[7] The first perspective is given in the words of Lyssa,[8] madness personified, who describes her ongoing attack on Heracles in future tenses (861–4: εἶμι, 'I shall go', δραμοῦμαι, 'I shall run', καταρρήξω, 'I shall shatter', ἐπεμβαλῶ, 'I shall bring down'). These are then followed by a series of present tenses (867–70: τινάσσει, 'he is shaking', ἑλίσσει, 'he is rolling', οὐ σωφρονίζει, [his breathing] is uncontrolled, μυκᾶται, 'he bellows'), which describe the effect that she already has upon her victim, and which are followed in turn by words with future reference (ἐπιρροιβδεῖν, ὁμαρτεῖν, 'to follow in full cry', 860; χορεύσω, καταυλήσω, 871; 'I shall make dance and I shall play a pipe upon', δυσόμεσθ᾽, 'I shall enter', 874), foretelling the continuation of her influence upon Heracles.[9] The second perspective is given immediately afterwards by Amphitryon, himself a witness of the scene, in his dialogue with the Chorus. The comments made by the Chorus (875–85) and the Chorus' lyric exchange with Amphitryon provide the audience with concurrent information on what happens inside the palace (875–909). The simultaneity between the off-stage action and its description, as well as the emotional involvement of both Amphitryon and the Chorus, do not allow a clear idea of what is happening. A clearer perspective will be given by the Messenger, who gives a relatively detailed description of the events after their completion (922–1015). Finally, after

[7] Cf. the use of multiple perspectives in Sophocles' *Ajax* for the reconstruction of what happened during Ajax's madness; on this, see Segal 1995b. On Ajax's madness in Sophocles, see esp. Starobinski 1974: 11–71; Winnington-Ingram 1980: 11–56; Segal 1981: 126–35; Goldhill 1986: 180–98; Davis 1986; Padel 1995: 66–72; Gasti 1998.
[8] On Lyssa as the personification of rage, see in general Kossatz-Deissmann 1992; on the etymology from λύκος, 'wolf', see Lincoln 1975. For the appearances of Lyssa in Greek tragedy, see Aélion 1983, vol. II, 202–5; on Lyssa in *Heracles*, see esp. Duchemin 1967; on the scene between Iris and Lyssa in the play, see Lee 1982.
[9] On the switch from Lyssa, the exterior agent, to Heracles in Lyssa's words, see Franzino 1995.

Heracles' recovery references are still made to his madness by Amphitryon, while with the coming of Theseus and his exchanges with Heracles the emphasis now shifts to the implications of his madness for the future. In that part it is Heracles' own perspective which is of interest, in the sense that, as the victim of madness who knows nothing of the Iris and Lyssa scene, he interprets and re-evaluates the meaning of what has happened to him.

Heracles' madness may be said to be traditional in its typology.[10] Its divine/external causation is established beyond doubt in the scene which brings Iris and Lyssa before the eyes of the audience. It is also implied in the way in which the Chorus elaborate on the unspeakable character of Heracles' murders in a short ode where they mention similar mythic *exempla*.[11] They begin with what hitherto[12] was the worst crime anyone had heard of, the killing of their husbands by the daughters of Danaus, and go on to say that the present events are worse. In this stanza (1016–20) they do not bring in the madness idea, but only the degree of awfulness of what has just happened. It is noticeable that they mention Heracles in the dative, not as subject of the verb; what he has done has 'happened' to him:

τάδε δ' ὑπερέβαλεν παρέδραμεν τὰ τότε
κακὰ τάλαιν̣ διογενεῖ κόρωι. (1019–20)

But these terrible events that have come to the unhappy son of Zeus have surpassed, outrun those old crimes.

In the comparison with Procne's infanticide in the second stanza (1021–4) the degree of horror is measured in terms of the number of children killed (Procne killed one child while Heracles killed three children), and the implied difference is that what Heracles did he did in his 'fated madness': λυσσάδι μοίραι (1024).

---

[10] On conventional symptoms in tragic presentations of madness, see esp. Vasquez 1972; Ciani 1974; Padel 1995.
[11] On this ode, see Angiò 1989. For the use of mythological parallels, cf. Aesch. *Cho.* 585–638; Soph. *Ant.* 944–87; Soph. *Phil.* 676–9.
[12] Note the mention of τότε twice (1017, 1019).

Those old crimes constitute mythological precedents for Heracles' murders; they express the Chorus' shock and their tentative attempts to place what has happened in some sort of context. But there are also themes implicit in their choice of analogies that help the audience to think further about the implications of what Heracles has done. The crimes committed by the Danaids and Procne were voluntary killings, whereas Heracles' murders were carried out in madness. It may be argued that examples which are closer to Heracles' murders, but not mentioned by the Chorus, would be those of Lycurgus or Agave, both of whom kill their sons in madness. Thus, although Heracles is the agent of his children's death, his murders are said to be the result of necessity (1022–4).[13]

Such a combination of human agency and external necessity is found in a similar example in *Medea*, where the Chorus use the expression αὐτόχειρι μοίραι, 'with a fate brought about by your own hand' (1281), to refer to Medea's infanticide, and where they also try to find a mythological precedent for this murder (1279–84). The reference to Ino's killing of her children seems to be a variation of the myth to suit the parallelism with Medea; in other sources, it is Athamas, Ino's husband, who is maddened and kills one of their sons, followed by Ino's leap into the sea with their other son.[14] The fact that Ino is said to have been maddened by the gods, however, also distances Medea from Ino. It is true, of course, that an infanticide is such a notorious crime that it can be called 'madness', in the way that any type of extreme or abnormal behaviour could be taken to manifest madness. But the suggestion is that Ino has been maddened by the gods, in the way in which Agave or Heracles was, whereas Medea's infanticide, however extreme, is presented as the result of careful deliberation and wish for revenge. No matter how abnormal her behaviour is, starting from the very way that she is described by the Nurse (esp. 24–36, 89–95), she is not maddened by a god.[15]

---

[13] See Bond 1981 on Eur. *HF* 1024.

[14] See Page 1938 on Eur. *Med.* 1284; on Ino see Gantz 1993: 176–80.

[15] Cf. Padel 1995, who, discussing infanticide in Greek tragedy, notes: 'The worst, strangest thing about Medea is that she is *not* mad' (208). But the extreme character

This difference between Ino and Medea serves to stress that Medea's crime is even more terrible than Ino's, since it was not committed under divinely inflicted madness. Conversely, in the case of Heracles, the implication of the comparison with the Danaids and Procne made by the Chorus, who have witnessed the Iris–Lyssa scene, is that Heracles' murders are even more terrible *because* they were involuntary.

Heracles' mad fit is also typical in that its course is well defined. It consists in a single episode with a clear beginning (930–4, cf. 867) and a clear end (1005–8). It also combines a number of conventional physical and mental symptoms. This is how Lyssa describes the first symptoms of Heracles' madness:

ἢν ἰδού· καὶ δὴ τινάσσει κρᾶτα βαλβίδων ἄπο
καὶ διαστρόφους ἑλίσσει σῖγα γοργωποὺς κόρας,
ἀμπνοὰς δ᾽ οὐ σωφρονίζει, ταῦρος ὣς ἐς ἐμβολὴν,
δεινὰ μυκᾶται δέ. (867–70)

Look at him! He is already shaking his head at the start of his race, rolling his distorted flashing eyes without speaking. His breathing is uncontrolled like a bull ready to attack and he bellows terribly.

The tossing of the head is a sign of madness, as can be seen also for example in *Bacchae* (862–5). Sudden abnormality in the eyes is a symptom which is a very common feature in descriptions of mad people.[16] This is understandable in view of the familiar connection between sight and knowledge. Already in *The Sack of Troy* (fr. 1.8 Davies) Ajax's madness was diagnosed from the abnormality of his eyes. The rolling eyes, or the Gorgon-like eyes, appear as symptoms on several occasions. At 883 Lyssa herself is described in similar terms to Heracles in a way which shows the fusion of the two; she is said

of her crime could be interpreted in a way that represented Medea as acting under the influence of madness. This is clear from artistic representations of her which have a Rage-type demonic figure driving her chariot. See Sourvinou-Inwood 1997: 272–4, discussing two such representations: 'The Λύσσα-figure creates the notion that Medea was the victim of forces beyond her control' (274) and 'she [sc. Medea] is thus shown as being at the mercy of an undefeatable power, in that respect no less a victim than Heracles under the sway of Λύσσα' (294).

[16] It is used as a symptom in both cases of madness and other kinds of affliction; e.g. Eur. *Or.* 219–20, 224, 253, 259; Eur. *Med.* 92, 187–8, 1174–5, 1183; 1197. See Vasquez 1972: 203–13.

by the Chorus to be Νυκτὸς Γοργὼν ἑκατογκεφάλοις ὄφεων ἰαχήμασι Λύσσα μαρμαρωπός, 'her eyes flashing, Lyssa, a Gorgon of Night (surrounded by) a hundred hissing snakes'. The eyes of the gods who madden a hero are often abnormal; e.g. Athena when she maddens Ajax is described with the epithet γοργῶπις, 'fierce-eyed' (*Aj.* 450). In *Choephori* Orestes sees blood dripping from the eyes of the Erinyes, who are also Gorgons (1048, 1058). In the Messenger's speech one of the first signs of madness recalled is the change in Heracles' eyes: ὁ δ᾽ οὐκέθ᾽ αὑτὸς ἦν, | ἀλλ᾽ ἐν στροφαῖσιν ὀμμάτων ἐφθαρμένος | ῥίζας τ᾽ ἐν ὄσσοις αἱματῶπας ἐκβαλών, '(suddenly) he was no longer himself. His face contorted, he rolled his eyes so that their bloodshot roots protruded' (931–3). Heracles is also described as ἀγριωπὸν ὄμμα Γοργόνος στρέφων, 'rolling his eyes with a Gorgon's savage glare' (990). The rolling of the eyes appears also e.g. in *Prometheus Bound* (for the madness of Io: 673, 882), in *Ajax* (69–70, 447–8), *Trachiniae* (794–5, with reference primarily to Heracles' physical pain), or in *Bacchae* (for Agave: 1122–3, 1166–7; cf. 1087).

Rolling of the eyes together with silence and foam at the mouth appear in Hippocrates (*Morb. sacr.* 7) as symptoms of epilepsy. Apart from *HF* 934, foam at the mouth appears also for example in *Iphigenia among the Taurians* (308, 310–11), in *Orestes* (219–20) or in *Bacchae* (1122). Outside the context of madness it can also be used as a symptom of disorder; thus in *Medea* Glauce's suffering is manifested in a number of symptoms, including foaming at the mouth (1173–4) and rolling of the eyes (1175) as if in an epileptic fit. The conventional use of the symptom of foaming in contexts of disorder also leads to metaphorical uses of the term; for example, the Aeschylean Cassandra is like a wild horse which foams (*Ag.* 1066–7), while in *Trachiniae* it is not Heracles himself but the poisoned robe which foams blood (702).[17] As for silence, the Aeschylean Cassandra remains silent before her ouburst (*Ag.* 1050–2), and Philoctetes too is silent before the outburst of his pain (*Phil.* 730–1). Silence and tossing of the head, followed by

[17] Cf. Vasquez 1972: 216.

foam and loud cries, also appear together, apart from *HF* 867–70, in *IT* 282–308, in a passage which in this regard strongly resembles our passage from *Heracles* (*IT*: ἔστη κάρα τε διετίναξ᾽ ἄνω κάτω, 'he stood and tossed his head up and down', 282; κἀνεστέναξεν ... βοᾷ, 'and he moaned aloud ... and he cried out', 283–4; στάζων ἀφρῶι γένειον, 'dripping foam down his chin', 308). The simile of the bull[18] along with the mention of fiery eyes appears in Euripides' *Syleus* (fr. 689). As for the look and the animal-like cries,[19] in *Frogs* (560–8) a female innkeeper says that Heracles gave her a fierce look, kept roaring (ἔβλεψεν εἴς με δριμὺ κἀμυκᾶτό γε, 562), and set about drawing his sword looking like a madman (καὶ τὸ ξίφος γ᾽ ἐσπᾶτο μαίνεσθαι δοκῶν, 564).

Irregular, mostly heavy, breathing, mentioned by Lyssa at 869, is also a symptom of disorder.[20] At 1092–3, although Heracles is sane upon waking up, his breathing has not yet become regular (πνοὰς θερμὰς πνέω | μετάρσια, 'my breath comes hot and unsteady'). Orestes also awakes from a fit still panting (*Or.* 277). Conversely, regaining normal breathing is a sign of Ajax's recovery (*Aj.* 274).

Another physical symptom of madness is extreme agitation as manifested in wild movement.[21] Heracles was dashing about the palace, as the Messenger mentions at 953 (ὁ δ᾽ εἶρπ᾽ ἄνω τε καὶ κάτω κατὰ στέγας). In *Orestes* (268–72) Orestes rushes up and down wildly shooting arrows at the Furies he sees. Ajax is described as going in and out of his tent (*Aj.* 287, 290, 301). Cassandra runs in a state of frenzy in *Trojan Women* (307).

---

[18] In Greek tragedy Ajax too is compared to a bull, although in a different context (Soph. *Aj.* 322). Apollonius Rhodius compares his Heracles with a bull stampeded by a gadfly in a context where Heracles' grief over the disappearance of Hylas exhibits symptoms of insane frenzy (*Argon.* 1. 1261–5).

[19] The metaphor (cf. also Soph. *OT* 1265: δεινὰ βρυχηθείς, 'roaring terribly'; Soph. *Trach.* 805: βρυχώμενον, 'roaring') conveys the connotation of wildness or alterity. The same holds for animal-like glances (e.g. Eur. *Med.* 92).

[20] See Vasquez 1972: 218, who describes it as an almost medical symptom.

[21] On the wild restlessness and motion associated with madness, see Vasquez 1972: 188–96 and 224.

In the imagery of madness[22] in *Heracles*, too, there are familiar elements. For example, hunting imagery is used by Lyssa when she calls on the Fates from Hell to follow as the hounds follow the huntsman (ὡς κυνηγέτηι κύνας, 860). The imagery is used here for the divine persecution of a mad victim; for example, Io is hunted down by Argos in *Prometheus Bound* (572). But it can also be used to refer to the aggression of the madman when he becomes the huntsman. Thus Heracles will also turn into a huntsman who hunts down his children, as Amphitryon notes (896) and as becomes evident in the madness scene. Conversely in *Bacchae* Pentheus turns from the role of the hunter to that of the hunted (e.g. 954–8, 1020–3). Another image used in *Heracles* to evoke aberration is that of horses or chariots driven outside their course. In *Choephori* Orestes uses this image to refer to his imminent madness (1021–4). In *Orestes* too the verb τροχηλατεῖ, 'drives about' (36), refers to Orestes' madness. In *Heracles* this type of imagery is used to refer to Lyssa's agency (863, 880–1) against Heracles, while in the madness scene it describes Heracles himself as agent of the infanticide (947–8, 1001).

The use of images of whipping, stinging or goading is also common in descriptions of madness. In *Prometheus Bound* for example, Io is presented as tormented by *oistros*. In *Ajax* the actual whipping of animals is the result of the hero's delusion (239–42, cf. 108–10). In *Bacchae*, the Chorus call on the hounds of Frenzy to goad the bacchants to madness (ἀνοιστρήσατε, 'goad to madness', 979). In *Heracles* the Chorus say that Lyssa uses her κέντρον, 'goad' (882), while in the madness scene Heracles imagines that he is on a chariot lashing out with an imaginary whip (947–9).

Bacchic elements and the use of music and dance are also recurrent features in contexts of madness.[23] For example, Cassandra in *Trojan Women* is presented in bacchic terms.[24]

---

[22] On the imagery of madness in Greek tragedy, see Vasquez 1972: 12–37. On imagery in Euripides in general, see Barlow 1971.

[23] For the link between tragic madness and Dionysiac religion, see esp. Seaford 1994: *passim*.

[24] See Papadopoulou 2000a.

So in *Heracles* the presentation of madness is pervaded by terms associated with Dionysus. As for the use of music and dance in contexts in which their joyful tone is negated, as in *Heracles* (e.g. 871, 879, 889–90 etc.), a comparable example is in the binding song of the Erinyes in *Eumenides* (328–33).

As for psychological traits, fear occurs often in the victims of madness.[25] For example, in *Prometheus Bound* the madness of Io is described as a terrified flight from the gadfly (e.g. κραδία δὲ φόβωι φρένα λακτίζει, 'my heart in terror knocks at my ribs', 881 etc.) and the mad Orestes is in constant terror of the Furies (e.g. *Cho.* 1050; *Or.* 270 etc.). In *Heracles* Lyssa foretells that she will soon 'play the pipe of terror' upon Heracles (καταυλήσω φόβωι, 871). But the madman can also cause terror himself when his madness leads to violence against others. This is what happens in *Heracles* when the hero attacks his children, who flee in terror (οἱ δὲ ταρβοῦντες φόβωι, 971).

On other occasions, and this is the case where, as with Heracles, the victim of madness becomes in turn an aggressor, madness causes not fear but a state of wild joy. In *Bacchae* for example, Agave in her delusion rejoices in her ill-fated hunt (1144), and exults in bringing her prey to Thebes (1198). Ajax is also presented as rejoicing at what he thinks he has achieved with his killings; as Tecmessa tells us, Ajax laughed loudly at all the violence he had inflicted upon his enemies (303).[26] The ominous character of maniacal laughter goes back to *Odyssey* 20.345–9, and the insatiable laughter that Athena causes there in the suitors, whose manipulation by the goddess approximates to possession.[27] A deluded Heracles too, as the Messenger reports, was laughing (γέλωτι παραπεπληγμένωι, 'with a maniacal laugh', 935) at the beginning of his strange activity, which made the by-standers wonder in turn whether

[25] See Vasquez 1972: 36.
[26] The sinister laughter of the deluded Ajax later became proverbial: Αἰάντειος γέλως (Zen. 1, 43). On Ajax's laughter, see in particular Grossmann 1968. On laughter and its usually sinister connotations in Greek tragedy, see Dillon 1991. See also Arnould 1990.
[27] On this, see esp. Colakis 1986.

they should laugh at Heracles' joke or tremble at what was a manifestation of madness (950–2).

Another feature found in *Heracles* which recurs in other contexts of madness or other types of physical or mental anguish is sleep that brings temporary release or total cure.[28] For example, sleep provides Orestes with some relief from the torments of his fits (*Or.* 166–86). In *Heracles* madness is a single episode and not, as in the case of the Euripidean Orestes, a series of recurrent fits. Accordingly, it has a clear end, which is marked in the play by the sleep into which Heracles falls following Athena's intervention (1004–6). Heracles may be sleeping a sleep that is terrible since it follows his murders (1034), but at least it brings rest and release from the mad seizure (1042–4).[29]

Sleep is a conventional element to mark the end of anguish. A feature that recurs after the end of madness is amnesia.[30] In *Orestes*, for example, the hero is confused as to what happened both upon wakening from his sleep (215–16) and following a fit of madness later on (277–9). In *Orestes* the hero is amnesiac, yet he is not totally unaware of his general state when madness attacks him, since his fits are a recurrent and not a single episode. In *Heracles* the hero is totally confused upon waking up. His dialogue with Amphitryon provides him with information on what has happened. This kind of dialogue will later be used by Euripides in his *Bacchae*, where Cadmus gradually brings Agave to a realization of what she has done during her madness. In contrast to Heracles, who is informed of the events by Amphitryon, Agave is here helped by Cadmus to recall for herself what happened.[31]

Apart from the physical symptoms of madness or the imagery used to describe it, hallucinations play an important role in

[28] See Vasquez 1972: 300–12.

[29] On Heracles' sleep after labour with regard to the double meaning of πόνος as 'labour' and 'calamity', see Willink 1988; On sleep scenes generally, see Dieterich 1891.

[30] On amnesia and confusion after madness, see Vasquez 1972: 251–5.

[31] See Devereux 1970.

presentations of madness.[32] The distorted vision of the victims makes them see imaginary objects or misperceive objects that exist. For example, in the final scene of *Choephori* Orestes sees the Erinyes whom the Chorus do not see.[33] In the madness scene in *Heracles*, the Messenger reports a variety of delusions in Heracles. At the beginning he can still recognize Amphitryon and declares his decision to kill Eurystheus; he then imagines that he is going to Mycenae and whips the horses of an imaginary chariot. He prepares a banquet, wrestles with an imaginary adversary and then says he has arrived at Mycenae. Up to this point Heracles seems to be engaged in a world which is the product of his own imagination. But his activities, such as banqueting and wrestling, as well as his promised revenge, are in accord with his normal activity. There is nothing there which is out of place compared with Heracles' character in sanity; it is madness that twists the otherwise normal nature of Heracles' actions here and thus makes them strange and inappropriate.

As the Messenger continues, it becomes evident that Heracles not only sees imaginary things but also now misidentifies the people around him; he sees them but mistakes their identity. So he does not recognize Amphitryon but mistakes him for Eurystheus' father in the same way as he mistakes his own children for Eurystheus' children. His recovery will take place gradually and will be expressed in terms of regaining his sight; thus at first he cannot recognize the dead bodies around him as those of his own children (1097) and he is confused as to where he is (1101–5). He is not entirely sane yet, or else he would understand what he sees, as Amphitryon points out (1117). Amphitryon points to the bodies, and Heracles then sees and understands correctly (1131–2). Heracles' misperception of reality during his madness is found also in *Ajax* (51–8 etc.), where Ajax thinks that he is attacking his enemies whereas in fact he is attacking the cattle. Orestes in *Iphigenia among the Taurians* (285–300) is comparable in misperceiving the cattle for the

---

[32] On various types of hallucination during madness, see Vasquez 1972: 241–51.
[33] Cf. Brown 1983; Garvie 1986: 317–18; Whallon 1995.

Furies and thinking that he is attacking his opponents whereas in reality he is only attacking the cattle. In *Bacchae* hallucinations have an even greater role, as in that play it is both Pentheus and Agave who hallucinate. Agave's hallucination is closer to that of Heracles, for in both cases we are presented with a wild scene of deluded infanticide. Agave fails to recognize her son and sees him as a beast of prey (1107–8), a delusion which lasts even after she has returned to Thebes.

To conclude: in general, as I have argued, the presentation of madness in *Heracles* follows conventional tragic patterns. The external causation, the clear beginning and end of the mad fit, and the use of standard symptoms, all show this, but the conventional character of Heracles' madness is limited to these formal features. The peculiarity of his madness, and this is the insight given by Euripides, lies specifically in the way in which the madness scene problematizes the image of the sane Heracles as well. The mad Heracles repeats patterns of behaviour known from his heroic past; the imposition of madness upon him does not launch him on an activity which is altogether alien to him; the use of violence is an essential part of Heracles' personality when he is sane, and in his madness he uses the same violence, only against the wrong victims. One may compare, by contrast, the way in which Euripides will later present Agave in his *Bacchae*; apart from their similarity in the sense that they both kill their children, the use of violence and the way, in general, in which Agave's mad behaviour is described have nothing to do with her normal behaviour, indeed are the reversal of it. So, there is something inherent in Heracles whether he is sane or mad, and in particular, it is the very position of Heracles after the completion of the labours that Euripides invites his audience to think about.

Tradition and models of causation

Although the dramatization of myths about Heracles in Greek tragedy was not rare, we have no information about tragic treatments of Heracles' madness before Euripides. Nor have we any way of knowing the reaction of the original audience of *Heracles* to the presentation of the divinely induced madness. A third century AD Oxyrhynchus papyrus[34] which contains a list of μελέται, rhetorical exercises, says that for showing Heracles going mad in a play at the Dionysia Euripides was prosecuted for impiety (κρίνεται ἀσεβείας). This recalls the statement in Satyrus' *Life of Euripides* that Cleon prosecuted Euripides for impiety, but neither of these can be taken as reliable evidence.[35]

Whatever the reaction of the audience to the portrayal of a mad Heracles, the scene in which Iris and Lyssa appear suddenly in mid-action must have been startling and unexpected.[36] Euripides often brings on gods at the beginning or at the end of his dramas. *Bacchae* is a special example in that here Dionysus appears as a god but also remains on the stage in human disguise and interacts with the other characters.[37] We may also think of the appearance of Athena in Sophocles' *Aias Lokros* (fr. 10c) or that of Apollo and Artemis in Sophocles' *Niobe* (fr. 441a).[38] But the appearance of Iris and Lyssa is striking because it is wholly unexpected.[39] Even more so because it contrasts sharply with the previous ode, a celebratory song of triumph, in which the Chorus praise Heracles' achievements and the divine concern for justice.

The double divine epiphany with its announcement of Heracles' madness was certainly meant to be startling. But what were the changes that Euripides chose to make to the

---

[34] *P Oxy.* 2400, vol. 24, pp. 107–9, ll. 10–14.

[35] On this, see Arrighetti 1964: 125–6. If the two are related, then the date of the play would be before Cleon's death in 422 BC. However, the fact that the papyrus contains rhetorical exercises makes it dangerous to press a historical meaning on the passage. See also Calder 1960: 128.

[36] Cf. Lee 1982: 44.

[37] In *Rhesus*, probably not by Euripides himself, the use of Athena in mid-action and of her disguise as Aphrodite is odd. The Euripidean authorship of *Rhesus* has been defended by e.g. Ritchie 1964, but the play is considered by most critics as spurious (e.g. Ebener 1966; Hall forthcoming).

[38] For the frequency of divine appearances in the three dramatists, see Lefkowitz 1989: 70 and notes. On modalities of divine appearances in Greek tragedy, see Sourvinou-Inwood 2003: 459–500.

[39] Euripides often surprises his audience in his tragedies, and *Heracles* as a whole may be said to be a prime example. See especially Arnott 1973 and 1978.

tradition about Heracles' madness? The question is important, for a poet's innovations or conscious selections from tradition reflect his re-interpretation of myth. So, in this section I focus on some aspects of the relation between tradition and the Euripidean treatment with regard to the myth of Heracles' madness,[40] and on their implications for an understanding of the play's concerns and aims.

In the catalogue of the heroines seen by Odysseus in *Odyssey* 11, Megara is referred to as wife of Heracles along with his mother Alcmena (269–70), but there is no mention there of Heracles' madness. As we learn from Proclus' *Chrestomathia*, in the *Cypria* Nestor told Menelaus about τὴν Ἡρακλέους μανίαν,[41] 'Heracles' madness', along with the stories of Oedipus and Theseus. It is likely that the purpose of telling these stories was to console Menelaus for the loss of Helen by saying that Paris' 'mad' action under Aphrodite's influence would be punished. In this case, the common denominator underlying these stories would be madness[42] and its consequences. However, if Heracles' *mania* refers to an action comparable to that of Paris, then this *mania* could be not the madness during which Heracles killed his family but that during which, as a consequence of his passion for Iole, he killed Iphitus. Yet, the lack of any other evidence makes it impossible to give a conclusive answer as to what exactly the *mania* of Heracles referred to in its context.[43]

Stesichorus[44] handled the theme of Heracles' madness, as we learn from Pausanias. In his description of Thebes (9.11.2) Pausanias mentions a memorial to Heracles' children by Megara and implies that Stesichorus and Panyassis[45] both referred to his madness but did not include either the attempted murder of Amphitryon or Athena's hurling of a

---

[40] On the madness of Heracles before and after Euripides with regard to Euripides' innovations, see esp. Cropp 1975: 1–17; a summary based on Cropp is given by Bond 1981: xxvi–xxx. See also Billerbeck 1999: 1–10 for a concise account up to Seneca's *Hercules Furens*.

[41] Bernabé *PEG*, p. 40, 28.   [42] See Jouan 1966: 378–83.

[43] Cropp 1975: 3.   [44] *PMGF* 230, p. 220 Davies.

[45] Bernabé, *PEG*, fr. 1.

stone to put an end to his frenzy. Panyassis wrote a *Heraclea*, an epic on Heracles' heroic career, but the fragments which have come down to us have nothing to say about the exact place of madness in his life. If Pausanias is correct in implying that Panyassis' version resembled Stesichorus', there was no mention here, either, of the attempted murder of Amphitryon or of Athena's role. Given that Panyassis mentions Heracles' murder of Iphitus and sack of Oechalia, it is likely that the Euripidean introduction of Theseus in the last part of *Heracles* and the turn towards an Athenian context were absent from Panyassis' account.

Pherecydes[46] treated Heracles' career at length in his prose work *Histories*. We do not know much about his treatment of the madness; he mentions five children (whereas Euripides gives three) and says that Heracles threw his children into a fire (by contrast with *Heracles*, where Heracles attacks them with weapons). The burning motif used here recalls similar attempts to achieve immortalization by means of fire; for example, in the Homeric *Hymn to Demeter* (231–64) Demeter, who has become the nurse of the child Demophoön, tries to make him deathless by hiding him in the fire every night, until she is detected by the child's mother and her attempts are thus thwarted. The burning motif in the case of Heracles also recalls his own death on the pyre on Mt Oeta, which was the prelude to his deification. If Pherecydes made Heracles' throwing of his children into a fire an act of madness (as opposed to an attempt by a sane Heracles to immortalize them),[47] then death by fire was one alternative pre-Euripidean version of their death. Death by fire also appears after *Heracles*. A fourth-century (350–325) south-Italian crater[48] portrays a dramatic scene in which a helmeted Heracles holds a child over a fire, while Megara flees through a door and Mania, Alcmene and Iolaus are looking on from above. Also, Apollodorus (*Bibl.* 2.4.12) mentions that Heracles, in

---

[46] *FGrH* 3 F 14 (= schol. Pind. *Isth.* 4, 104g Dr.).   [47] On this, see Cropp 1975: 14–15.
[48] It is known as the Kelch-Crater by Assteas of Paestum (Archaeological Museum of Madrid 11094).

his madness caused by Hera, killed his children as well as two children of Iphicles by throwing them into a fire. The fire-slaying is also mentioned by Tzetzes (*Chil.* II, 36.232).

Pindar[49] mentions that Heracles' eight children by Megara have a tomb at Thebes and receive heroic honours (holocaust and heroic games) in connection with cult (a feast and decorated altars) given to the deified Heracles. Pindar describes the sons as 'dying bronze equipped' (χαλκοαρᾶν ὀκτὼ θανόντων), which means that they were not killed when they were children but fighting as warriors. Absolving Heracles of infanticide is a plausible Pindaric version when we think of the hero's importance in Pindaric poetry as well as Pindar's well-known tendency to dismiss versions of which he disapproved.[50] Also, a Pindaric scholium on χαλκοαρᾶν refers to the accounts given by two historians (Lysimachus and Socrates), that Heracles' children were not in fact killed by their father but by Lycus or some strangers (Lysimachus) or by Augeas (Socrates). However, it has also been suggested[51] that the difficulty can be removed if χαλκοαρᾶν is explained in its cultic context, that is, if Heracles' children are understood as heroes now imagined as warriors who protect Thebes along with their father.

These sources, of course, constitute only a partial picture of what was available to Euripides when he composed his play, and we are left guessing whether the episode of the madness was included in such accounts or what was its exact position in the course of Heracles' career.

Then there is the question of how far Euripides' placing of Heracles' madness after the completion of his labours was original. No certain answer can be given because of the obscurity of the pre-Euripidean accounts which have come down to us. We only know that the sequence madness–labours was given by three later writers, two historians, Nicolaus of Damascus[52] and

[49] Pind. *Isthm.* 4.67–70.
[50] Cf. Pindar's rejection of the old traditional story about Pelops in *Olympian* I, for which see, e.g., Howie 1983.
[51] See Krummen 1990: 59–75. [52] Nic. Dam. in his *Historiae* (*FGrH* 90 F 13).

Diodorus,[53] and one mythographer, Apollodorus.[54] Pherecydes is often mentioned in Apollodorus and could be the mythographer's direct or indirect source as to Heracles' career; as for the madness, we saw for example how Apollodorus mentions the fire-slaying which was given by Pherecydes. If Apollodorus was also following the same chronology of the labours, then Pherecydes too placed Heracles' madness before the labours.[55] Pausanias' reference to Stesichorus and Pherecydes gives no clue to the sequence they used. Also, the predominance of the 'madness–labours' sequence after the Euripidean play despite its popularity in later times[56] may suggest that Euripides deviated from the traditional order of Heracles' madness and labours. But even if the Euripidean order was not in fact an innovation but the product of selection from extant tradition, the question remains the same: what was the dramatic aim of presenting Heracles' madness after and not before the labours?

To begin with, the motivation behind the performance of the labours is different. In Diodorus (4.10.6), by contrast, where they come earlier, the labours are portrayed as a serious threat to Heracles' stability. Heracles was commanded by Eurystheus to perform the labours; he at first refused, but Zeus insisted. He then went to Delphi, where he was told that the labours would eventually lead to his immortalization.[57]

---

[53] Diod. Sic. 4.10.6.   [54] Apollod. *Bibl.* 2.4.12.

[55] See Cropp 1975: 10 and 15. On Pherecydes as source for Apollodorus, see van der Valk 1958: 117–31 and 143–57.

[56] On the popularity of the play in the Hellenistic period, see Sifakis 1967: 80 and 84; Xanthakis-Karamanos 1980: 30. The use of the 'labours–madness' sequence elsewhere may derive directly or indirectly from Euripides (Asclepiades of Tragilos in his *Tragoidoumena* (*FGrH* 12 F 27 = Schol. Hom. *Od.* 11.269 TV), Seneca's *Hercules Furens*; Hyg. *Fab.* 32; schol. Lycoph. *Alex.* 38; Eust. *Od.* 11.268). In the case of the vase-painting by Assteas mentioned above, apart from all other thematic differences, the presence of Iolaus, Heracles' traditional colleague in the labours, rather suggests the Euripidean sequence 'labours–madness'.

[57] For deification as a reward for the labours, cf. Hes. *Theog.* 950–5 (with West (1966) on 947–55). References to Heracles' deification are found also in Hes. *Cat.* frs. 25.26–33 and 229.6–13, and in *Od.* 11.602–4, but in all cases the passages were athetized in antiquity. Heracles' deification appears later (see West 1966: 417), and according to Pausanias (1.15.3, 32.4) he was first worshipped as a god at Marathon. See also Stinton 1987.

Heracles then fell into extreme distress and was maddened by Hera. In Apollodorus (*Bibl.* 2.4.12) we read that Heracles was maddened by Hera, killed his children, and was then told by the oracle at Delphi to perform the labours. Here they are presented as an act of expiation, the penalty that Heracles had to pay in order to atone for his crimes. However, neither the association of the labours with a threat to Heracles' state of mind, nor the view that they were an atonement, can have any place in the Euripidean play, where they precede the madness and the motivation behind them is different.

Amphitryon mentions more than one motive in the prologue (17–21). Two of these have implications in particular for the way in which the gods are perceived in the play. Firstly, he suggests that Heracles may have undertaken the labours at the instigation of Hera, 'subdued by her goads' (κέντροις δαμασθείς, 21). The labours can thus be Hera's way to make Heracles' life troublesome. Hera's enmity towards Heracles was a well-known datum of myth, while the word κέντροις used here, and repeated when Lyssa attacks Heracles (882), may recall another famous victim of Hera, that is, Io and her plight in *Prometheus Bound.* Another reason, according to Amphitryon, is an impersonal force, that is, τὸ χρεών (21). Whether this force is subordinate to or independent of the gods is left unspecified. Iris echoes the idea of necessity when she says at the beginning of her speech that before the completion of the labours Heracles could not be harmed, for τὸ χρή νιν ἐξέσωιζεν οὐδ᾽ εἴα πατὴρ | Ζεύς νιν κακῶς δρᾶν οὔτ᾽ ἔμ᾽ οὔθ᾽ ῞Ηραν ποτέ, 'destiny kept him safe and his father Zeus would not let me or Hera hurt him' (828–9). Here Zeus is in control of τὸ χρή or at least makes sure that it is not violated. We might recall Pindar's *Olympian* 3, where it is said that Heracles was compelled to perform the labour of hunting the hind of Artemis εὖτέ νιν ἀγγελίαις Εὐρυσθέος ἔντυ ᾽ἀνάγκα πατρόθεν, 'when through Eurystheus' orders his father's compulsion moved him' (28). Iris' words also imply the importance of Heracles' labours as deeds which had to be performed. Amphitryon too stresses their significance when he says that the purpose of Heracles' labours is ἐξημερῶσαι γαῖαν, 'to free the earth of violence' (20).[58]

So far then we have seen that Heracles' labours in the Euripidean play were taken to be either a toil imposed by Hera's hatred, or part of a larger divine plan, which needed Heracles to be safe until, but no longer after, the completion of his deeds. If the labours are regarded as part of such a divine plan, the importance of Heracles is restricted to the performance of the labours, while after their completion he may be as vulnerable to the gods as anyone else. If Hera wishes to destroy him, even Zeus cannot protect him. It is not unheard of that sometimes gods do not interfere in other gods' business, or at least give way to one another so that each party is content.[59] For the moment, let us bear in mind Hera's role but also the presence of wider divine workings at play. I say more on this at the end of this chapter.

Amphitryon's words at 17–21 give one more important motive for the labours: Heracles undertook them in service to Eurystheus out of familial piety, that is, in order to occupy Argos, from where Amphitryon had fled. This helps to create a sense of free will as opposed to the imposition of the labours. This juxtaposition between free will and compulsion is explicitly noted in a comic context; in Epicharmus' *Heracles with Pholus* (fr. 66 K–A), a play in which Heracles prefers Pholus' hospitality to his labours, he says 'But of necessity I do all these; I believe no one of his own free will suffers labours or disaster.'[60] In the Euripidean context the mention of this motive, not

---

[58] One may here recall the [Hesiodic] epic *Shield*, where it is said that Zeus's plan in fathering Heracles was ὥς ῥα θεοῖσιν | ἀνδράσι τ' ἀλφηστῆισιν ἀρῆς ἀλκτῆρα φυτεῦσαι, 'to beget one to defend gods and bread-eating men against destruction' (28–9).

[59] This may be said to outline a general principle, although in many cases it seems to be an *ad hoc* invention by the poet to explain away some god's questionable role. Euripidean gods, in particular, often find themselves in deep trouble at the end of the plays, and are liable to claim that they have been acting under orders, or subject to some higher authority. For examples, cf. the words of Artemis in Eur. *Hipp.* 1328–30 and of Hera in Hom. *Il.* 4.50–63. With regard, in particular, to Heracles, cf. *Il.* 18.118–19, where Achilles says that Zeus's love for Heracles could not protect him from Hera's anger.

[60] But in later times, when deification was taken as the prize for the labours, these labours were supposed to have been undertaken not so much because they were

known from elsewhere, is particularly important, because it presents an affectionate and, to put it more generally, an all too human side of Heracles. The brief outline of this aspect of Heracles is a significant hint, given already in the prologue, at the presentation of Heracles as a family man upon arriving at Thebes and meeting his family.[61] When Heracles hears about the great danger in which his family have found themselves during his absence, his concern is immediately to defend them against Lycus, and he emphasizes the priority of his family over everything else when he bids farewell to his labours:

τῶι γάρ μ᾽ ἀμύνειν μᾶλλον ἢ δάμαρτι χρὴ
καὶ παισὶ καὶ γέροντι; χαιρόντων πόνοι·
μάτην γὰρ αὐτοὺς τῶνδε μᾶλλον ἤνυσα.
καὶ δεῖ μ᾽ ὑπὲρ τῶνδ᾽, εἴπερ οἵδ᾽ ὑπὲρ πατρός,
θνήισκειν ἀμύνοντ᾽· ἢ τί φήσομεν καλὸν
ὕδραι μὲν ἐλθεῖν ἐς μάχην λέοντί τε
Εὐρυσθέως πομπαῖσι, τῶν δ᾽ ἐμῶν τέκνων
οὐκ ἐκπονήσω θάνατον; οὐκ ἄρ᾽ Ἡρακλῆς
ὁ καλλίνικος ὡς πάροιθε λέξομαι. (574–82)

For whom should I protect if not my wife and children and father? Goodbye to my labours! They are useless in comparison to these. If they, the children, were prepared to die for their father, I must die in defending them. Otherwise what shall we say is so glorious about doing battle with a hydra and a lion on Eurystheus' orders, if I do not exert myself over the death of my children? I shall never then be called as I was once, 'gloriously conquering' Heracles.

In Euripides' *Auge* Heracles is also presented as the family man and there too (fr. 272) he says that he loves his children and that he prefers them to his labours. A more humanized figure emerges in both cases, where a tension is implied between Heracles the violent hero of the labours and a more civilized human being. In this passage from *Heracles*, his farewell to his labours means, of course, not that he dismisses them

---

imposed or because their goal was an altruistic service to mankind, but because of the hero's eagerness to achieve immortality; cf. e.g. Hercules in Seneca's *Hercules Furens*.

[61] Grummond 1983 examines Heracles' entrances in *Heracles* and *Alcestis* with regard to the hero's ability to relate to the other characters, but he is completely unjustified in arguing that in *Heracles* the hero is unable to bridge the gap between himself and his family's world because of their different kinds of reality.

as insignificant, but that they are less important to him than the defence of his family which is now at hand. He will still be the καλλίνικος Heracles in trying to avert the murder of his family; and in fact this defence will be as appropriate a labour as the labours of his heroic career. But the continuation of the heroic past in the present situation will prove disastrous; it will be the καλλίνικος Heracles who will murder his family, and the verb ἐκπονήσω, used here in the meaning 'exert oneself over', also hints at the meaning 'complete the labour of killing my children';[62] at 1279 Heracles will refer to his infanticide as the last labour he has endured (τὸν λοίσθιον δὲ τόνδ' ἔτλην τάλας πόνον).

The image of Heracles as the family man has already been developed earlier in the play. In her first speech in the Prologue Megara reports her children's anxious waiting for their father to come (72–9); every time they heard the door make a sound, Megara tells us, they stood up ὡς πρὸς πατρῷον προσπεσούμενοι γόνυ, 'as if to fling themselves in supplication at their father's knees' (79). In the madness scene, however, one of the children is described by the Messenger as γόνασι προσπεσὼν πατρός, 'having fallen at his father's knees' (986), in a vain attempt to stop his father from murdering him. When Megara brings her children to be led to their death she utters a speech in which she juxtaposes their past happiness to their present plight. Part of her speech is devoted to a happy scene where Heracles used to play with his children and in the game allocate to them the different kingdoms they were to inherit upon coming of age (462–75). Here the heroic past is mingled with a joyful domestic scene but again in a sinister manner; the club and the arrows mentioned here in a peaceful context will be the weapons that Heracles will use to kill his children. It is the family man whom we see when his children clutch his clothes and he takes them by the hand and draws them to safety like a ship drawing its little boats (627–36). The second episode, which began with the family in despair, ends with this scene and Heracles' reflections on the love of the whole human race for its children (632–6). Its peacefulness

---

[62] On the ambiguity of the verb ἐκπονήσω at 581, see Bremer 1972.

will again be reversed in the madness scene, where Heracles' strength will be used to murder his family.

The examples mentioned above show the dexterous way in which Euripides both juxtaposes and intertwines the images of Heracles in sanity and in madness.[63] The madness that strikes Heracles uses the hero's modes of activity, familiar from his labours, and reverses them. The violence that he uses is the same violence he would use in another context of fighting against enemies while sane. He is still the mighty and victorious hero of the labours, but the problem now is that his violence is directed against the wrong victims because he is mad. The co-existence of the heroic past and the domestic present in one and the same person becomes deeply problematic, while at the same time the relevance of the violent past to the civilized present is questioned.

To conclude: the dramatization of madness in the play effectively problematizes the place that Heracles, the famous performer of heroic deeds, may have in human society. Whereas in versions of the story which give the 'madness–labours' sequence the labours are one step before Heracles' deification, in Euripides there is no such thing, and the dramatist presents the gradual humanization of Heracles, away from the hero who is depicted as close to divinity in the first part of the play, to the person who dismisses Zeus and chooses Amphitryon as his only father.[64] Madness becomes the catalyst that forces Heracles to choose humanity over divinity, but the play's end, with Theseus' promises of future cult for Heracles, eventually gives a secure place for the hero after the completion of his labours. It seems, indeed, that the value of Heracles' place in human society can only be securely affirmed after his death with the establishment of his cult.[65] Finally,

---

[63] See the previous chapter for a detailed examination of Euripides' sophisticated interrelation of the two images of Heracles in the play.

[64] The eventual solution of the problem of the double paternity is central to Gregory's 1974 reading of the play, which follows her thesis that Euripides was unique in making dilemmas a factor in madness. For discussions of other aspects of the theme of fatherhood in the play, see e.g. Ferguson 1969; Mikalson 1986; Padilla 1994; Mirto 1997: 15–38; Kraus 1998: 144–9.

[65] Cf. Padilla 1992: 12.

along with Heracles' move towards humanity, and along with the question of the exact relevance of his heroic past within a civic context, the play also treats the question of human *arete* (excellence) and the ways in which this notion is re-defined after Heracles becomes mad.[66]

So far, in discussing the presentation of Heracles' madness we have found that Euripides stresses the role of forces outside rational human control and at the same time turns the spotlight inwards to Heracles' own character. He is thus working along traditional lines in dramatizing a divine causation for Heracles' madness, and is innovative in using madness as a device which problematizes Heracles' character and status within a civilized context. The importance of the different models of causation is shown by means of the startling scene between Iris and Lyssa, as well as by the fact that Hera is held by all characters to be ultimately responsible. But interpreters both ancient and modern have wanted to account for the madness of Heracles in less literal terms, using physiological or psychological models, and particularly in modern times views of Euripides' 'rationalism' or his symbolic treatment of Olympian deities have influenced the way the causation of Heracles' madness is understood.[67]

Several Greek physicians, for example, described Heracles' madness as epilepsy, the so-called ἱερὰ νόσος, 'sacred disease', which was in turn also known as Ἡρακλεία νόσος.[68] In the Pseudo-Aristotelian *Problemata*[69] Heracles' affliction is also said to be epileptic, and the author lists the hero among those eminent people who are melancholics and vulnerable to afflictions caused by black bile. Modern scholars have also described Heracles' madness as a case of an epileptic fit, as if

---

[66] The Athenian context and the play's treatment of the notion of human *arete* are discussed in the next chapter.

[67] For a general overview of the history of Euripidean interpretation, see Michelini 1987: ch. 1. On the culturally determined notions of Euripidean theology, see more recently Sourvinou-Inwood 2003, esp. 291–300.

[68] For a list of the relevant sources, see Robert 1921: 629 n. 3.

[69] Arist. [*Pr.*] 30.1, p. 953a (Ruelle); for a discussion of this particular *Problem* and the question of melancholy in general, see Pigeaud 1988. On melancholy in ancient theories of medicine in particular, see also Flashar 1966.

Euripides' purpose was to dramatize a case-history of epilepsy.[70] Others have rightly stressed that epilepsy may seem to provide a model for the symptoms of Heracles' madness, without however implying that Euripides intended to portray Heracles as an epileptic or that other models should be excluded.[71] After all, Greek dramatists, as was pointed out at the beginning of this chapter, were free to choose material from many different sources for their own portrayals of madness.

The view that Heracles' madness originated from psychological causes was also put forward in antiquity. For example Diodorus (4.10.6) thought that it was depression upon learning that he must undertake the labours that made him go mad. Some modern scholars have taken a similar line: Kamerbeek[72] held that Heracles' madness in the play was the hero's psychological reaction to the strains of his burdensome life during his labours. More recently, Barlow[73] ends her introduction to the play by pointing out that Heracles' madness recalls modern categories of mental diseases, such as manic depression,[74] no matter that such terms are modern and no matter that the play explicitly makes gods the cause. I would agree in principle that finding several links between an ancient play and modern concerns is often helpful for making the play more relevant for a modern audience; but care should be taken so that modern readings do not misinterpret the ancient play. Thus, in the case of *Heracles*, the building of an entire scene between Iris and Lyssa, and consequently the clear announcement for the

[70] See esp. Blaiklock 1945 and 1952: 122–40. According to Blaiklock, Euripides portrayed a human Heracles overcoming a mental affliction. For Heracles' madness as an epileptic seizure, see also e.g. Pohlenz ²1954: 298–9; Devereux 1970: 35 n. 6 and 38 n. 23.

[71] See esp. Temkin ²1971; cf. Mattes 1970; Jakob 1998: 85. An interesting exception is Pigeaud 1981: 416–17 and 1987: 38, who suggests that the description of Heracles' madness in Eur. *HF* 953–67 (especially his imaginary fighting) is very close to the description of the Hippocratic *Internal Affections* 48 (= VII L 285–6), in which case the Euripidean portrayal could have influenced the medical description.

[72] Kamerbeek 1966.

[73] Barlow 1996: 15–16 and n. 52.

[74] The association of Heracles' madness with manic depression is not new; Dodds 1929: 100–1, adopting Verrall's views about the negation of anthropomorphic religion by Euripides, argued that Euripides presents in his Heracles the case of a manic depressive.

audience of divine causation, should caution against interpretations which choose to ignore the obvious.[75]

It may seem surprising that the obvious, that is, the explicitly dramatized divine causation of Heracles' madness, has been ignored in many approaches to Euripides' play.[76] To begin with the most influential study, according to Wilamowitz[77] Heracles' madness and downfall were the result of his own megalomania. The Heracles that Wilamowitz identified in the Euripidean play was the all-mighty Dorian hero, who falls victim to his own strength, and who does not even have to be maddened suddenly because he is already mad upon his arrival at Thebes. Wilamowitz's main interpretation of the play is nowadays hardly acceptable; Heracles has rightly emerged as a panhellenic hero as opposed to a strictly defined Dorian hero, and it has also been stressed that Heracles in the Euripidean play is not a mad megalomaniac hero when he arrives home; his violence may seem at times excessive, yet he is not presented as inherently mad.

Ancient criticism of Euripides, especially in comedy,[78] as impious or even an atheist, has had a wide influence on modern approaches to Euripides' dramaturgy.[79] The critique of the myth and of the gods in his plays has often been considered clear evidence for Euripides' own 'radical' and iconoclastic beliefs. Thus in modern times, the view, especially associated with Nietzsche,[80] that myth was destroyed by Euripides, was influential, as was also the idea that Euripides attacked the gods and the whole system of anthropomorphic religion.[81] The

[75] The most extreme case where a critic completely disregards the importance of the Iris–Lyssa scene is the rationalist approach by Verrall 1905, according to whom the scene was nothing more than a dream of the Chorus (168).
[76] For useful overviews of scholarly approaches to the theology of *Heracles*, see esp. Grassby 1969: 45–82 and 168–82; Cropp 1975: 24–40.
[77] Wilamowitz ²1895.
[78] See more recently Sourvinou-Inwood 2003: 294–7.
[79] On the relation between ancient criticisms and modern approaches to Euripides, see Grassby 1969: 4–82.
[80] On this, see esp. Henrichs 1986.
[81] For the development of this view, see esp. Schlesier 1986; Lefkowitz 1987. The bibliography on the Euripidean treatment of the gods is vast. For a defence of the poet against the wide-spread accusations of impiety and atheism, see in particular Lefkowitz 1989.

widespread belief in Euripides as the enlightened enemy of traditional religion lies behind several works which were published after Wilamowitz's book on *Heracles*, and which also chose to ignore the divine causation of Heracles' madness. For Verrall and Greenwood for example, Euripides invited his audience to disbelieve and to rationalize the stories that he dramatized with all their divine and mythical elements.[82] In the case of *Heracles* this approach meant among other things the negation of the role of the gods, of Heracles' divine paternity and of his heroic labours.

Another approach which refuses to accept Hera as the divine agent that causes Heracles' madness is that which interprets Hera (and her agents) symbolically as an abstract, impersonal force in the universe. For some scholars, Hera symbolizes the hostile, irrational and unknown forces which bring suffering to humans.[83] Accordingly, it is τύχη, 'chance', and not the anthropomorphic gods, which governs the universe and human affairs.[84] The word τύχη in various forms indeed appears quite frequently in *Heracles*,[85] suggesting the existence of a capricious world which would in turn make human life all the more fragile. Although the emphasis on τύχη does not *per se* conflict with ancient religious beliefs, the denial of significance to the anthropomorphic gods in the play would be a clear attack on the religious framework of the drama. However, as Busch and Grassby have argued, taking into consideration the role of τύχη in Euripidean drama in general, τύχη in *Heracles* cannot be said to be independent of or above the gods.[86]

---

[82] Verrall 1905; Greenwood 1953.

[83] E.g. Kitto ³1961: 244–7; Arrowsmith 1954: *passim* and 1956: 55; Chalk 1962: 16; Vellacott 1975: 241; Erbse 1984: 180.

[84] E.g. Hendrickson 1919: 29; Parmentier and Grégoire 1923: 9; Kroeker 1938; Drexler 1943/9: 329–30.

[85] On the notion of τύχη in Euripides, see Busch 1937, who concludes that it varies to the extent that its exact meaning must be decided in its context each time. Cf. Giannopoulou 2000 for the role of τύχη in *Ion*. See also Bond 1981 on Eur. *HF* 1393. For a discussion of τύχη along with other abstract forces in *Heracles*, see Grassby 1969: 261–78.

[86] Busch 1937: 41, 45–6, 55; Grassby 1969: 278. A similar conclusion is reached for the role of τύχη in *Ion* in Giannopoulou 2000: 271; cf. Matthiessen 2004: 86–8.

Heracles contains what has often been regarded as the most compelling evidence not simply of Euripides' polemic against traditional religion, but, even more, of his virtual erasure of the traditional gods. For this reason, the theology of *Heracles* must be of primary importance for every discussion of the religious universe of Euripidean plays. The tendency to ignore the role of the gods in the play can be seen as part of a more general trend from antiquity onwards, which considered Euripides as the enemy of traditional religion. This view has repeatedly been challenged,[87] but what comes out most strongly from the continuous study of Euripidean tragedies is a sense that their religious dimension is a complex and multi-dimensional issue.[88] In the case of *Heracles*, religious problematization has a significant role, and issues such as divine presence and divine motivation, as well as human response, contribute to the understanding of the play.

Poetic lies and Heracles' notion of divinity

The passage which has given rise to a great variety[89] of approaches to the theology of *Heracles* is part of the dialogue between Theseus and Heracles, where Heracles seems to introduce a new notion of divinity, different from the anthropomorphic divinities portrayed in the play. Here is what he says:

Ηρ.   οἴμοι· πάρεργα < > τάδ' ἔστ' ἐμῶν κακῶν·
      ἐγὼ δὲ τοὺς θεοὺς οὔτε λέκτρ' ἃ μὴ θέμις
      στέργειν νομίζω δεσμά τ' ἐξάπτειν χεροῖν
      οὔτ' ἠξίωσα πώποτ' οὔτε πείσομαι
      οὐδ' ἄλλον ἄλλου δεσπότην πεφυκέναι.
      δεῖται γὰρ ὁ θεός, εἴπερ ἔστ' ὀρθῶς θεός,
      οὐδενός. ἀοιδῶν οἵδε δύστηνοι λόγοι. (1340–6)

---

[87] Cf. e.g. Schmid and Staehlin 1929–48, 1.3: 701–26; Grube 1941: 41–62; Schlesier 1986; Lefkowitz 1989 and 1987; Nikolakakis 1993; Matthiessen 2004: 54–96.

[88] Cf. e.g. Yunis 1988; Mikalson 1991; Seaford 1994; Sourvinou-Inwood 2003.

[89] For bibliography on the various interpretations of this passage, see esp. Halleran 1986 and Lawrence 1998.

Alas! All this is incidental < > to my troubles. I do not believe that the
gods acquiesce in illegitimate love and have never thought them capable
of chaining each other up. I shall not believe that nor that one god is
tyrant over another. A god if he is truly god needs nothing. These are the
miserable tales of poets.

At first glance, this passage indeed seems to undermine the
whole system of anthropomorphic gods as they are known
from tradition, since such gods certainly engaged in the kind
of activities denounced by Heracles. Heracles' words also seem
to undermine the very presuppositions of the plot of Euripides'
play, in which he himself is the product of Zeus's intercourse
with Alcmena. In his dialogue with Theseus Heracles affirms
his divine parentage, although he chooses his human one. His
decision to consider Amphitryon his father in place of Zeus is
Heracles' way of showing gratitude to the caring Amphitryon
as opposed to Zeus's lack of concern, yet Zeus's fatherhood
remains a fact: Ζεὺς δ᾽, ὅστις ὁ Ζεύς, πολέμιόν μ᾽ ἐγείνατο |
῭Ηραι (σὺ μέντοι μηδὲν ἀχθεσθῇις, γέρον· | πατέρα γὰρ ἀντὶ
Ζηνὸς ἡγοῦμαι σ᾽ ἐγώ), 'Zeus, whoever Zeus is, engendered me
to be a source of enmity for Hera. (Do not take offence,
Amphitryon. I consider you as my father, not Zeus)'
(1263–5). The belief in Zeus's fatherhood is after all also
stressed by the fact that Heracles, Amphitryon and Theseus
never doubt that Heracles' madness was caused by Hera's
jealousy of her husband's illegitimate son.[90]

Furthermore, the notion of a perfect divinity that has no
needs, as outlined by Heracles, certainly conflicts with Hera
and her agents in the drama.[91] So, is there a contradiction

[90] Amphitryon's criticism of the union between Zeus and Alcmena at 344–5 is not
negation of this union but expression of Amphitryon's complaint that sharing his
bed with the great god proved to be in vain, since Zeus did not intervene to save
Heracles' family. Only Lycus disbelieves Heracles' divine parentage (148–9). Iris'
phrase ὅν φασιν εἶναι Ζηνὸς᾽ Ἀλκμήνης τ᾽ἄπο, 'who men say is Alcmene's son by
Zeus' (826), shows contempt for Heracles rather than doubt for his divine origin.
The Chorus' phrase Διὸς ὁ παῖς, 'it is Zeus' son' (696), was a climax in view of their
earlier scepticism (353–4); the prompt return of Heracles, which is interpreted by
the Chorus as a sign of Zeus's intervention, is regarded as unquestionable proof of
Heracles' divine parentage.
[91] Lee 1980: 45, argues that Heracles' notion of divinity at 1345–6 can still apply to the
anthropomorphic gods of the play, if one paraphrases δεῖται οὐδενός as 'the gods

between this passage and the divine and mythical universe of the entire play as this is dramatized? Does Euripides perhaps deny the traditional gods and invite his audience to demythologize the dramatic action? Also, what about the mention of 'poetic lies'? To be sure, there are self-referential passages in Euripidean tragedy which imply that the audience are asked to think about the function of poetry.[92] But one has to wonder about the implications that the reference to poetic lies in our passage may have for the understanding of the play as a whole. In other words, if poets are indeed guilty of conveying to their audiences false accounts of the gods, is Euripides here subverting his own play?

One way of approaching this passage would be to deny that it relates to the understanding of the whole drama.[93] On this view, Heracles' words echo, and are only meant to be the reply to, the arguments earlier used by Theseus in his attempt to dissuade Heracles from committing suicide:

Θη. παραινέσαιμ' ἄν μᾶλλον ἤ πάσχειν κακῶς.
     οὐδεὶς δὲ θνητῶν ταῖς τύχαις ἀκήρατος,
     οὐ θεῶν, ἀοιδῶν εἴπερ οὐ ψευδεῖς λόγοι.
     οὐ λέκτρ' ἐν ἀλλήλοισιν, ὧν οὐδεὶς νόμος,
     συνῆψαν; οὐ δεσμοῖσι διὰ τυραννίδα
     πατέρας ἐκηλίδωσαν; ἀλλ' οἰκοῦσ' ὅμως
     Ὄλυμπον ἠνέσχοντό θ' ἡμαρτηκότες.
     καίτοι τί φήσεις, εἰ σὺ μὲν θνητὸς γεγὼς
     φέρεις ὑπέρφευ τὰς τύχας, θεοὶ δὲ μή; (1313–21)

> I would advise you rather than to give in to your suffering. No man can be untouched by fate, no god either, unless the poets lie. Have they not committed adultery among themselves in defiance of law? Have they not, for the sake of power, dishonoured their fathers by casting them into chains? None the less they live on Olympus and have borne their crimes. So what is

get what they want'. But this paraphrase is surely a wrong interpretation of the passage. At all events, the notion of a perfect god is incompatible with the gods presented in the play.

[92] E.g. in a much quoted passage from the *Trojan Women* (1242–5), Hecuba, in her attempt to create some reason and order in the midst of utter despair, mentions the future 'survival' of Troy as a subject of song for future generations. Cf. also, in our play, the Chorus' description of Procne's infanticide as 'a sacrifice to the Muses' (1021–2). For discussions of the self-referential character of Heracles' mention of poetic lies, see e.g. Pucci 1980: 175–87; Michelini 1987: 275–6.

[93] See e.g. Bond 1981 on Eur. *HF* 1341–6.

your defence then, if you, a mere mortal, complain excessively about fate when the gods do not?

Here Theseus' λέκτρ' ἐν ἀλλήλοισιν, ὧν οὐδεὶς νόμος, 'adultery among themselves in defiance of the law' is echoed in Heracles' λέκτρ' ἃ μὴ θέμις, 'illegitimate love'; his δεσμοῖσι διὰ τυραννίδα, 'chains for the sake of power', is echoed in Heracles' δεσμά τ' ἐξάπτειν χεροῖν, 'chaining up', and δεσπότην, 'tyrant'; and finally, his ἀοιδῶν εἴπερ οὐ ψευδεῖς λόγοι, 'unless the poets lie', is echoed in Heracles' ἀοιδῶν οἵδε δύστηνοι λόγοι, 'these are the miserable tales of poets'. So, Heracles' words are meant to correspond directly to specific points made by Theseus.

It is true that Heracles' phrase λέκτρ' ἃ μὴ θέμις may at first be taken as implying also Zeus's union with Alcmena.[94] After all, Hera and her jealousy are important in the context of both Theseus' and Heracles' words about illicit divine unions. This becomes evident when one thinks that the dialogue between Theseus and Heracles is informed by the emphasis on Hera's jealousy as the cause of Heracles' downfall, and also that Theseus' divine *exempla,* which form the core of his argumentation, follow Heracles' words about his destruction by Hera (1303–10). But if Heracles' words are taken as the direct reply to Theseus' arguments, then his phrase λέκτρ' ἃ μὴ θέμις means adultery among the gods alone. Thus, his words do not imply Zeus and Alcmena, in which case Heracles is not in fact denying the circumstances of his divine parentage.[95]

Another solution would be to take the passage as an extra-dramatic intrusion by Euripides, who takes the opportunity to voice, via Heracles, his own religious or philosophical beliefs.[96] One may compare Hecuba's invocation of Zeus in *Trojan Women* (884–8). In that passage Hecuba prays to Zeus in a manner which seems to mingle religious feeling and philosophical speculation.

---

[94] Cf. earlier references to this union: τὸν Διὸς σύλλεκτρον, 'who shared his wife with Zeus' (1), τἀλλότρια λέκτρα, 'someone else's wife' (345), γυναικὸς οὕνεκα λέκτρων, 'for a woman's bed' (1308–10).

[95] Cf. Grube 1941: 58; Gregory 1977: 273 and Gregory 1991: 153 n. 51; Bond 1981 ad loc.

[96] See Brown 1978. Bond 1981: 400, allows for the possibility that the passage 'may well represent Euripides' own considered view'.

The peculiar character of her prayer is evident also in Menelaus' reaction to what he considers a novelty: τί δ'ἔστιν; εὐχὰς ὡς ἐκαίνισας θεῶν, 'what is this? How strange and novel these prayers of yours to the gods!' (889). Although traditional elements are not of course absent from Hecuba's prayer,[97] it sounds peculiar with all its allusions to philosophical theories current in Euripides' time. The association of Euripides with philosophy recurs in the *Lives* of the dramatist, Aristophanes parodied this association in his comedies, and Euripides was taken seriously as a philosopher in antiquity, from Aristotle to Cicero, as becomes evident from the numerous quotations from his dramas in philosophical works. He was also known in antiquity as 'the philosopher from the stage'.[98] The ancients certainly thought that dramatists spoke through the mouth of their characters, as Aristophanes' parodies show, especially in the *Frogs*. Also, ancient scholiasts criticized Euripides for this kind of intrusion,[99] while Lucian, on the contrary, notices it rather approvingly, since he himself does the same in his own works; in his dialogue *Zeus Rants*, he has a character say that, although there is no truth when Euripides shows that gods destroy villains and save the pious, nevertheless the dramatist can be heard speaking the truth when he says what he thinks, without being limited by the requirements of the plots; what Euripides puts forward in these cases is the type of innovative theology which appears in the passage from *Heracles* and *Trojan Women:*

[Damis]: ἐπεὶ καθ'ἑαυτὸν ὁπόταν ὁ Εὐριπίδης, μηδὲν ἐπειγούσης τῆς χρείας τῶν δραμάτων, τὰ δοκοῦντά οἱ λέγηι, ἀκούσηι αὐτοῦ τότε παρρησιαζομένου,

---

97 Lefkowitz 1989 tries to prove the traditional character of Hecuba's prayer over its philosophical overtones; but its peculiarity should not be underestimated: Menelaus' surprised reaction makes this clear, and one may recall that Aristophanes satirized this type of innovative religion (e.g. *Ran.* 889–92).
98 Cf. ὁ ἐπὶ τῆς σκηνῆς φιλόσοφος, Clem. Al. *Strom.* 5.11.70; σκηνικὸς φιλόσοφος, Ath. IV p. 158 E; XIII p. 561 A; Sext. Emp. *Math.* I 288.
99 Cf. schol. Eur. *Hipp.* 953: περὶ ἑαυτοῦ γὰρ αἰνίξασθαι βούλεται ὁ Εὐριπίδης. τοιοῦτος δέ ἐστιν ἀεί, τὰ ἡρωϊκὰ πρόσωπα εἰσάγων φιλοσοφοῦντα, 'for Euripides wishes to hint at his own art. He is always like this, introducing characters who speak like philosophers'; schol. Eur. *Alc.* 962: ὁ ποιητὴς διὰ τοῦ προσώπου τοῦ χοροῦ βούλεται δεῖξαι ὅσον μετέσχε παιδεύσεως, 'through the persona of the Chorus the poet wishes to show how learned he is'.

ὁρᾶις τὸν ὑψοῦ τόνδ' ἄπειρον αἰθέρα
καὶ γῆν πέριξ ἔχονθ' ὑγραῖς ἐν ἀγκάλαις;
τοῦτον νόμιζε Ζῆνα, τόνδ' ἡγοῦ θεόν.

[from a lost play; the verses are translated by Cicero, *Nat.D.* II 25, 65]

for when Euripides, using his own devices, says what he has in mind without being under any constraint imposed by the requirements of his dramas, you will hear him speaking freely then:

'Do you see on high this boundless air
that embraces earth in moist arms?
Hold this to be Zeus, and consider it god.'

καὶ πάλιν,

Ζεύς, ὅστις ὁ Ζεύς, οὐ γὰρ οἶδα, πλὴν λόγωι
κλύων. [from the lost *Melanippe the Wise*. Cf. Plut. *Mor.* 756 c]

καὶ τὰ τοιαῦτα. (Lucian, *Zeus Rants* 41)

And again:
'Zeus, whoever Zeus is, for I do not know him, except by hearsay,' and so on.

The philosophical overtones of Heracles' notion of divinity are evident from the similarities with ideas expressed elsewhere. In particular, Heracles' criticism of the immorality of the anthropomorphic gods and his notion of a self-sufficient divinity recall Xenophanes (A 32 DK): ἀποφαίνεται δὲ καὶ περὶ θεῶν ὡς οὐδεμίας ἡγεμονίας ἐν αὐτοῖς οὔσης· οὐ γὰρ ὅσιον δεσπόζεσθαί τινα τῶν θεῶν· ἐπιδεῖσθαί τε μηδενὸς αὐτῶν μηδένα μηδ' ὅλως, 'he declares with reference also to the gods that there is no sovereignty among them; for it is not sanctioned for any god to be mastered. And none of them is in need of anything not in the least.' The same idea is possibly found in Antiphon the sophist (B 10 DK): οὐδενὸς δεῖται οὐδὲ προσδέχεται οὐδενός τι, ἀλλ' ἄπειρος καὶ ἀδέητος, if the subject of the phrase is ὁ θεός: 'he does not need anything nor receives anything but he is infinite and self-sufficient'.[100] The notion of a self-sufficient divinity occurs also in Xenophon's *Memorabilia* (1.6.10), as part of Socrates' reply to Antiphon's view, which

[100] On the possible relation of the Euripidean passage with Xenophanes and Antiphon, see Bond 1981: 400. Cf. Conacher 1998: 17–19.

implied that happiness consists in luxury; according to
Socrates, to have no wants is divine (τὸ μὲν μηδενὸς δεῖσθαι
θεῖον εἶναι), and to have as few as possible is what comes next
to the divine. In general, the tone of the passage in *Heracles*
seems to be influenced by philosophical discussions current in
Euripides' time, which may have suggested to the audience that
the notion of divinity as envisaged by Heracles is a rationalized
one which moves away from the traditional system of anthropomorphic gods.[101]

As for the reception of the passage, it is known from
Plutarch that philosophers praised it because already in it
they found elements used later in their theories. In chapters
38–45 of *Stoic Self-Contradictions* (*Mor.* 1052 e40), Plutarch
tries to show that Chrysippus' view that Zeus or the universe
alone of the gods is indestructible and self-sufficient contra-
dicts other statements made by this philosopher. In chapter
40 in particular, Plutarch quotes *HF* 1345–6 as applauded by
the Stoics because it is in agreement with the philosophical
view that the conception of the gods includes happiness,
blessedness and independence (τὸ εὔδαιμον καὶ μακάριον καὶ
αὐτοτελές).

The interpretation of the Euripidean passage by philosophers
after Euripides' time as an early reflection of philosophical doc-
trines is certainly no proof that the passage should be taken as
inherently philosophical at the time it was written. As happens
with the later reception of every writer of antiquity, so in the case
of Euripides later writers used excerpts from his dramas, often
out of context, depending on their own interests. Clement of
Alexandria for example quoted *HF* 1345–6 in a discussion of
sacrifices in antiquity,[102] taking the phrase 'the god, if he is truly a
god, needs nothing', as meaning that the true god does not need
sacrifices and other offerings. According to Clement then, this is a
laudable piece of wisdom by Euripides, which is in accord, as he
goes on to say, with similar beliefs in Plato and St Paul.

---

[101] For fifth-century rationalism in discussion of divinity and the relation to the
passage from *Heracles*, see Lawrence 1998: 132.
[102] Clem. Al. *Strom.* 5.11.75.

But it is worth examining whether there is in fact a dramatic relevance in what may at first seem to be a sudden and irrelevant authorial intrusion. In the passage from the *Trojan Women* for example, Hecuba's peculiar prayer to Zeus may indeed recall philosophical trends for an informed audience, but it can also be explained in context, that is, as a cry of despair to a god who seems to have abandoned the Trojans completely.[103] In *Heracles* also, even if Heracles' words evoke for the audience philosophical ideas which were current in their time, it would be strange if Euripides had his character speak these lines in a way that undermined and invalidated the divine universe as he dramatized it. For these reasons, there is a stronger argument to be made against the 'authorial intrusion' model; even if the innovative character of Heracles' notion of divinity is acknowledged, one should attempt to explain it in the context of the drama.

It is essential for an appreciation of the famous passage to examine how Heracles' view of the gods expressed there is related to his attitude to the gods after his madness. He has no knowledge, of course, of the Iris–Lyssa scene. Amphitryon first informs him of a disaster sent by Hera, before he describes the murders he committed during madness (1127–9). When Theseus arrives and hears from Amphitryon what Heracles did in a mad fit, he immediately considers Hera the cause: "Ἥρας ὅδ᾿ ἀγών, 'this is Hera's contest' (1189). The calamity that has fallen upon Heracles is enormous, as everyone agrees. When Heracles asks Theseus if he knows anyone unhappier, Theseus answers that Heracles' unhappiness reaches the sky (1240).[104] It is this extreme unhappiness that makes Heracles' life unbearable and leads to his determination to die (1241). There follows a lacuna at

---

[103] Meridor 1984 compares the *Trojan Women* and *Heracles* and finds them similar in that in both plays, which also lack a divine epilogue, humans come to realize that they have nothing to hope for from the gods. On the pessimism expressed as to the question how one is to live in a world abandoned by the gods, see Schmidt 1987 with reference to *Heracles*.

[104] The phrase ἅπτηι οὐρανοῦ, 'to touch the sky', is proverbial; see Bond 1981 on Eur. *HF* 1240. However, it may have some sort of relation to the ancient belief that Heracles touched the sky when he was admitted to Olympus.

1241 f., and from what follows, it becomes evident that in his extreme suffering and anger he says things that challenge the gods:

Θη.   δοκεῖς ἀπειλῶν σῶν μέλειν τι δαίμοσιν;
Ηρ.   αὔθαδες ὁ θεός, πρὸς δὲ τοὺς θεοὺς ἐγώ.
Θη.   ἴσχε στόμ᾽, ὡς μὴ μέγα λέγων μεῖζον πάθηις.
Ηρ.   γέμω κακῶν δὴ κοὐκέτ᾽ ἔσθ᾽ ὅπηι τεθῆι.
Θη.   δράσεις δὲ δὴ τί; ποῖ φέρηι θυμούμενος;
Ηρ.   θανών, ὅθενπερ ἦλθον, εἶμι γῆς ὕπο (1242–7)

THESEUS: Do you think the gods care at all for your threats?
HERACLES: As the gods are stubborn towards me, so am I towards them.
THESEUS: Hold your tongue. You may suffer even more for your presumption.
HERACLES: I am full of suffering as it is and there is no room for more.
THESEUS: What are you going to do then? Where does your anger drive you?
HERACLES: To death. I shall return beneath the earth from which I came.

Like Hyllus at the end of *Trachiniae* (1264–74), Heracles here revolts against the injustice of the gods. His strong reaction may actually recall the epic Heracles, who fought against the gods.[105] The great difference of course is that in the Euripidean context Heracles is not the θεομάχος, 'one who fights the gods', known from tradition; his reaction against the gods is his complaint at having been treated unjustly by them. But Heracles considers himself as on almost equal terms with the gods, in the sense that he will also be αὐθάδης, 'stubborn', to the gods as the gods have been to him. His reaction is indeed strongly defiant, and is followed by Theseus' advice to him to hold his tongue lest he suffer even more. A comparison of Heracles with Oedipus in *Oedipus the King* and *Oedipus at Colonus* is helpful here.[106] Both Heracles and Oedipus committed horrible crimes ultimately induced by gods. Oedipus knows that Apollo is responsible

[105] Cf. Galinsky 1972: 63.
[106] Euripides' *Heracles* was probably composed between the two Oedipus plays. For comparisons between Heracles and Oedipus in Sophocles' *Oedipus the King*, see Bartosiewiczová 1987–8: 10; Yunis 1988: 170–1; Padilla 1992: 9–10; Lawrence 1998: 145–6. Braden 1993: 246–7 compares the Euripidean Heracles with Oedipus in both Sophoclean plays in terms of the hero's survival in each play.

(*OT* 1329–30) but does not rebel against the gods in the way that Heracles does. Instead, as becomes obvious in *Oedipus at Colonus,* he seems to recognize a pattern behind his experience. On the contrary, Heracles refuses to come to terms with the fact that the gods have acted against him.

In the speech in which he explains to Theseus why his life is unbearable (1255–1310), Heracles refers to Zeus as follows: Ζεὺς δ', ὅστις <ὁ> Ζεύς, πολέμιόν μ' ἐγείνατο | "Ηραι, 'Zeus, whoever Zeus is, engendered me to be a source of enmity for Hera' (1263–4). The form of the phrase 'whoever Zeus is' is a traditional formula in prayers and hymns, which shows the human recognition of the inscrutability of the divine.[107] In *Agamemnon* for example the phrase is used in a hymn to Zeus (160). In Euripides the phrase appears several times but it should not be considered a cliché.[108] Each time it occurs, the contextualization of the Euripidean use is essential for defining the meaning or the connotation of the phrase. We have seen for example that Hecuba uses a similar formula in her prayer in *Trojan Women* (885), but in a way which may be interpreted as both traditional and radical. In *Bacchae* 894, the Chorus' speculation on 'whatever it is that is divine' (ὅτι ποτ' ἄρα τὸ δαιμόνιον) seems to be a pious expression of the unknowability of the divine. But when Pentheus earlier in the play uses the formula to refer to Διόνυσον, ὅστις ἔστι, 'Dionysus, whoever he is' (220), he does so in a contemptuous manner. By contrast, when the Messenger asks Pentheus to accept τὸν δαίμον' οὖν τόνδ', ὅστι ἔστ', 'this god, whoever he is' (769), because he is powerful and gives blessings to people, the use of the phrase is quite traditional and conventional. In *Orestes* 418 Orestes' statement δουλεύομεν θεοῖς, ὅτι ποτ' εἰσὶν οἱ θεοί, 'we are slaves to the gods, whatever the gods are', is rather subversive of the formula and may have negative connotations, given that it is spoken in a context where Apollo is portrayed unfavourably.

Heracles' reference to Zeus as 'Zeus, whoever Zeus is' in *HF* 1263 is startling because it uses a traditional formula of prayers

---

[107] On the use of the phrase, see Bond 1981 on Eur. *HF* 1263.
[108] West 1987 on Eur. *Or.* 418 considers it a Euripidean cliché.

outside prayer, and, more importantly, in a context that describes both Zeus and Hera unfavourably. As Heracles puts it, Zeus begat him to be an enemy to Hera from the moment of his birth. The implication of Heracles' phrase 'whoever Zeus is' is 'what kind of a god would allow what happened to Heracles?'. Heracles' phrase also implies that Zeus has suddenly become strange to him, that is, Heracles no longer has any understanding of Zeus. The gods have proven themselves different from what Heracles used to think about them before his calamity. It is his calamity and his unfair treatment by the gods which causes an unbridgeable breach in his view of the gods and suddenly makes the gods unintelligible to him. The implications of this breach will lead to his famous lines expressing his sophisticated notion of divinity.

Before this famous passage, however, there is another instance which constitutes an important stage in the development of Heracles' attitude towards the gods. At the end of his speech which explains to Theseus that his life is intolerable, his anger and frustration over his unjust treatment by the gods are developed further:

τί δῆτά με ζῆν δεῖ; τί κέρδος ἕξομεν
βίον γ' ἀχρεῖον ἀνόσιον κεκτημένοι;
χορευέτω δὴ Ζηνὸς ἡ κλεινὴ δάμαρ
+κρόουσ' Ὀλυμπίου Ζηνὸς ἀρβύληι πόδα + .
ἔπραξε γὰρ βούλησιν ἣν ἐβούλετο
ἄνδρ' Ἑλλάδος τὸν πρῶτον αὐτοῖσιν βάθροις
ἄνω κάτω στρέψασα. τοιαύτηι θεῶι
τίς ἂν προσεύχοιθ'; ἢ γυναικὸς οὕνεκα
λέκτρων φθονοῦσα Ζηνὶ τοὺς εὐεργέτας
Ἑλλάδος ἀπώλεσ' οὐδὲν ὄντας αἰτίους. (1301–10)

Why then should I live? What advantage would I gain, now that my life is both useless and accursed? Let Zeus' celebrated wife dance + pounding with her sandal ... of Olympian Zeus +. She achieved what she wished and overturned, foundation and all, the foremost man in Greece. Who could pray to such a goddess? Out of jealousy for a woman loved by Zeus she destroyed the saviour of Greece who was guiltless.

Heracles here complains that Hera destroyed him, the fore-most man of Greece, out of jealousy. Heracles' reaction, though understandable in view of his suffering, is again rebellious. He refuses to be called the victim of Hera and attacks Hera instead. This is unequivocal denunciation of Hera, but it does have some sort of precedent in Amphitryon's criticism of Zeus:

ὦ Ζεῦ, μάτην ἄρ' ὁμόγαμόν σ' ἐκτησάμην,
μάτην δὲ παιδὸς κοινεῶν' ἐκλήιζομεν·
σὺ δ' ἦσθ' ἄρ' ἥσσον ἢ' δόκεις εἶναι φίλος.
ἀρετῆι σε νικῶ θνητὸς ὢν θεὸν μέγαν·
παῖδας γὰρ οὐ προύδωκα τοὺς ' Ηρακλέους.
σὺ δ' ἐς μὲν εὐνὰς κρύφιος ἠπίστω μολεῖν,
τἀλλότρια λέκτρα δόντος οὐδενὸς λαβών,
σώιζειν δὲ τοὺς σοὺς οὐκ ἐπίστασαι φίλους.
ἀμαθής τις εἶ θεὸς ἢ δίκαιος οὐκ ἔφυς. (339–47)

It was all for nothing then, Zeus, that you shared my marriage, all for nothing that we said you shared my son! You turned out after all to be less of a friend than you seemed. I am only a man but I surpass you, a great god, in my principles, for I did not betray the sons of Heracles. You knew how to come secretly into my bed and take someone else's wife without being invited. Yet you do not know how to save those you love. You are either an ignorant sort of god or else your nature is plain unjust.

According to Amphitryon, Zeus was either stupid or unjust, because he did not intervene to help Heracles' family, while on the contrary he himself, Heracles' mortal father, showed concern for his son's family and was thus proven to be superior to Zeus in excellence. Underlying Amphitryon's criticism of Zeus here is his belief that a god must in general reciprocate and show concern, be sensitive and just. Amphitryon criticizes Zeus in despair, because he realizes that all his prayers were in vain. In a similar manner, at the end of *Trojan Women*, Hecuba's despair and scepticism about the gods (cf. 469, 1240) culminates when she interrupts a prayer which she has hardly started, wondering why she should call upon the gods, since they did not listen when they were appealed to before (ἰὼ θεοί· καὶ τί τοὺς θεοὺς καλῶ; | καὶ πρὶν γὰρ οὐκ ἤκουσαν ἀνακαλούμενοι , 1280–1).

But Heracles' ironical question 'who would pray to such a goddess?' (1307–8) goes one step further. It does not just convey the complaint that a god does not have the qualities that humans associate with divinity (Amphitryon's view) or the despair at finding oneself in a world which is devoid of caring gods (Hecuba's view). Heracles here implies that humans should stop worshipping gods who do not meet the standards that humans set for them. This view is radical in the sense that divinity *per se* is no longer the criterion for human worship; it is now reciprocity from the gods that becomes the prerequisite.[109] The rebellious attitude that Heracles adopts here is the development of his earlier threats and anger against the gods. There (1243) he asserted his determination not to remain the victim of divine injustice, but to strike back and attack the gods in the same way as they attacked him; in this passage now comes his first line of attack when he argues that this type of god should no longer be honoured by humans. By doing this he also gives power to humans over the gods, in the sense that the role of the divine will be conditioned by human standards.

Gods of course will still be gods, but gods also need human recognition and worship. For example, Dionysus in *Bacchae* is a god, but he also wants to establish his worship in places where his divinity is not recognized by humans. In *Hippolytus* Aphrodite is an established divinity, but she takes offence when a mortal refuses to honour her, for, as she says, gods in general enjoy being honoured by humans (7–8). The status of the gods and their wish to be honoured are used to a comic effect in Lucian's *Zeus Rants*, where the central issue is a discussion between two philosophers about the existence or not of the gods. The amusing thing is that this discussion takes place within a divine framework, that is, the gods attend the discussion. So, the gods as portrayed by Lucian exist irrespective of what humans believe about their existence,[110] yet they are worried that if the outcome of the debate is that they do not exist, they will no longer be worshipped by humans.

The next development in Heracles' view of the gods will be in the famous lines 1341–6, which correspond directly to the

---

[109] Cf. Lawrence 1998: 143–4.
[110] Cf. the situation presented in Aristophanes' *Birds*.

arguments used by Theseus in his attempt to dissuade his friend from putting an end to his life. The core of Theseus' argumentation (1313–21) was that if gods indeed commit terrible crimes, yet live with the consequences of their actions, then this should apply even more to humans.[111] The divine *exempla* used by Theseus represent the type of *a fortiori* argumentation which Euripides uses elsewhere and Aristotle later recommends it (*Rh.* 1397b). In the agon between Hecuba and Helen in *Trojan Women*, Helen argues that she was compelled by Aphrodite to follow Paris to Troy and that it would be impossible for her to resist Aphrodite's power, for even Zeus could not resist it (948–50). Helen's use of an *a fortiori* argument here is presented as an attempt to justify her action in the past. This type of argument is used also in *Hippolytus*, this time in order to justify immoral action in the future with regard to Phaedra's passion for Hippolytus. According to the Nurse, the power of Cypris is indeed irresistible (442–50). The Nurse then uses mythological examples in a passage which has similarities with Theseus' argumentation in *Heracles* 1313–21. As she tells Phaedra:

[Τρ.] ὅσοι μὲν οὖν γραφάς τε τῶν παλαιτέρων
  ἔχουσιν αὐτοί τ᾽ εἰσὶν ἐν μούσαις ἀεί
  ἴσασι μὲν Ζεὺς ὥς ποτ᾽ ἠράσθη γάμων
  Σεμέλης, ἴσασι δ᾽ ὡς ἀνήρπασέν ποτε
  ἡ καλλιφεγγὴς Κέφαλον ἐς θεοὺς Ἕως
  ἔρωτος οὕνεκ᾽· ἀλλ᾽ ὅμως ἐν οὐρανῶι
  ναίουσι κοὺ φεύγουσιν ἐκποδὼν θεούς,
  στέργουσι δ᾽, οἶμαι, ξυμφορᾶι νικώμενοι.
  σὺ δ᾽ οὐκ ἀνέξηι; χρῆν σ᾽ ἐπὶ ῥητοῖς ἄρα

---

[111] Theseus' saying that no god is ταῖς τύχαις ἀκήρατος, 'untouched by fate' (1314) may be taken either as 'no god is untouched by misfortunes', or 'no god is untouched by fate', depending on whether one takes τύχαι to mean misfortunes or some impersonal force. In the latter case, Theseus implies that there is a hierarchy of powers and that τύχαι are independent forces which actually control the gods. Busch 1937: 41, 45–6, 55, dismisses the passage as a sophistic attempt by Theseus to encourage Heracles. See also Grassby 1969: 272, who discusses the uses of the term within the drama, and suggests accepting the meaning 'misfortunes'. Also, although gods are presented as victims in Theseus' words, it is true that the word ἡμαρτηκότες (1319) seems to leave open the possibility that the gods' acts were voluntary and not the result of compulsion, as for example in the case of Iris and Lyssa in *Heracles*; on this, see Yunis 1988: 157.

πατέρα φυτεύειν ἢ 'πὶ δεσπόταις θεοῖς
ἄλλοισιν, εἰ μὴ τούσδε γε στέρξεις νόμους. (*Hipp.* 451–61)

Now those who know the writings of the ancients and themselves are
constantly engaged in poetry know how Zeus once desired a union with
Semele, and they know how beautiful shining Eos once snatched
Cephalus up into the company of the gods, because of desire; but still
they dwell in heaven and do not flee out of the way of the gods, but they
put up, I think, with being conquered by misfortune. And will *you* not
bear it? Then your father ought to have begotten you on set conditions
or under the rule of other gods, if you will not put up with these laws.[112]

The Nurse says that the tales about the gods' amours are
known to those who are familiar with the γραφαί ('written
texts' or 'paintings')[113] of the ancients and those who are themselves engaged in poetry. Theseus also referred to the source of
the mythical stories when he said that 'No god is untouched by
tychai, and no man either, unless the stories of the poets are
false' (ἀοιδῶν εἴπερ οὐ ψευδεῖς λόγοι, *HF* 1315). In both examples used by the Nurse in *Hippolytus,* a divinity (Zeus, Eos)
desires a mortal (Semele, Cephalus), and the core of her argument is that if gods yield to passion and put up with (στέργουσι)
having to live in a state they cannot resist, then Phaedra, who is a
mere mortal, should all the more do so. Similarly Theseus argues
that the gods commit crimes yet are not troubled by them (ἀλλ᾽
οἰκοῦσ᾽ ὅμως | Ὄλυμπον ἠνέσχοντό θ᾽ ἡμαρτηκότες, 'none the
less they live on Olympus and have borne their crimes', *HF*
1318–19). And if the gods do not complain, then Heracles, who
is a mortal, should not either (καίτοι τί φήσεις, εἰ σὺ μὲν θνητὸς
γεγὼς | φέρεις ὑπέρφευ τὰς τύχας, θεοὶ δὲ μή; 'so what is your
defence then, if you, a mere mortal, complain excessively about
fate when the gods do not?', *HF* 1320–1).

In *Trojan Women* and *Hippolytus,* no one questions the truth
of the divine *exempla.* No one doubts that Zeus was a slave to
Aphrodite as Helen says, or that Zeus and Eos were the victims
of passion. But Heracles' response to Theseus' mythological
examples is different. He says that he does not believe that gods

---

[112] Translation by Halleran (1995).
[113] On the meaning of γραφάς at 451, see Halleran 1995 on Eur. *Hipp.* 451–2.

perform the misdeeds that Theseus described. These, he explains, are the miserable tales of the poets.[114] Does Heracles then deny that the Olympian gods behave badly? Is it the case that traditional gods are perfect and poets lie? It is worth noting that Theseus' expression ἀοιδῶν εἴπερ οὐ ψευδεῖς λόγοι, 'unless the poets lie' (1315), which anticipates Heracles' ἀοιδῶν οἵδε δύστηνοι λόγοι, 'these are the miserable tales of poets' (1346), is in itself a strange qualification added by Theseus to his arguments. At this point, in order to make sense of Heracles' statement, we need to set it in a wider context, examining the association of poetry with lies, and particularly Euripides' critique of myths.

Poetry was traditionally associated with lies and deception, but 'lying' could be either denounced by those who equated poetry with truth-telling, or approved of by those who recognized the status of poetry as fictional invention. The relation between factual and fictitious reality in poetry and the tension between two opposing approaches to the idea of fiction, which may be summarized as 'fiction = fabrication, hence reprehensible' vs 'fiction = creative invention, hence part of a poet's job', are complex issues which have an important role not only in ancient works of criticism but also in literary works.[115] One need only recall the famous passage from Hesiod's *Theogony* where the Muses claim to know how to speak false things as though they were true, as well as to utter true things (ἴδμεν ψεύδεα πολλὰ λέγειν ἐτύμοισιν ὁμοῖα, | ἴδμεν δ᾽, εὖτ᾽ ἐθέλωμεν, ἀληθέα γηρύσασθαι, 27–8). This phrase is usually associated with the way in which Odysseus is described after his false tale to

---

[114] On the misleading character of stories in general, cf. what is said by Megara and then by Amphitryon, on telling stories to Heracles' children in order to reassure them: ἐγὼ δὲ διαφέρω | λόγοισι μυθεύουσα, 'I put them off with stories, telling them mere tales' (76–7); παρευκήλει λόγοις, | κλέπτουσα μύθοις ἀθλίους κλοπὰς ὅμως, 'soothe them with your talk as you beguile them with stories, pitifully misleading though they may be' (99–100). The use of such passages may be said to imply the deceptive character of story-telling in general. It may also prepare for the emphasis that will later be given to the relation between Heracles' life and the implications of his *mythos*.

[115] For discussions of these issues in antiquity in general, see Gill and Wiseman 1993; Pratt 1993. For a discussion of ancient scholiasts' attitudes to similar issues in Greek tragedy in particular, see Papadopoulou 1998 and 1999a.

Penelope in *Odyssey* 19: ἴσκε ψεύδεα πολλὰ λέγων ἐτύμοισιν
ὁμοῖα, 'he moulded many lies to resemble truth' (203), and it
should be noted that if a character can create false stories, so the
poet, by implication, can create fictions.[116]

Pindar is the poet usually associated with a tendency to
attack the lies that myths tell about the gods, and to dissociate
himself from other poets who convey these lies in their works.
His first *Olympian ode* is a famous example of his approach. In
it he rejects the traditional story about Pelops' ivory shoulder
following the feast of the gods, implying that the story is false
(Pind. *Ol.* 1. 28–9). But, by going on to argue that the power of
poetry to deceive is due to Charis (30), a quality (here personified) which he uses elsewhere to refer to his own poetry, he
implies that all poetry, including his own, is deceptive and
persuasive, that is, it makes what is unbelievable sound believ-
able.[117] It is also important that Pindar introduces his own
account not by means of a reference to truth vs falsehood but
in terms of appropriateness or *decorum*: ἔστι δ᾽ ἀνδρὶ φάμεν
ἐοικὸς ἀμφὶ δαιμόνων καλά· μείων γὰρ αἰτία, 'it is proper for a
man to speak well of the gods, for the charge is less' (35).
Saying good things about the gods to incur less blame is
certainly not the same as truth-telling. Similarly, Pindar says
later on that he stands apart from speaking ill about the gods
because the lot of slanderers is impoverishment (53). What is
again emphasized here is propriety, not truth.

Also, in his *Olympian* 9, Pindar begins to tell the story of
Heracles' fight against the gods (Poseidon, Apollo, Hades)
only to interrupt it suddenly with the following remarks:

ἀπό μοι λόγον
τοῦτον, στόμα, ῥῖψον·
ἐπεὶ τό γε λοιδορῆσαι θεοὺς
ἐχθρὰ σοφία, καὶ τὸ καυχᾶσθαι παρὰ καιρὸν
μανίαισιν ὑποκρέκει.

---

[116] But the extent to which the notion of fictional invention as opposed to truth-telling
may be recognized in Hesiod and Homer remains debatable. A striking example
comes from two different approaches in the same collection of essays. See Bowie
1993, esp. 8–23, and Gill 1993a, esp. 70–1.
[117] See Gerber 1982: 59–60 and Pratt 1993: 124.

μὴ νῦν λαλάγει τὰ τοιαῦτ᾽ · ἔα πόλεμον μάχαν τε πᾶσαν
χωρὶς ἀθανάτων.(35–41)

Cast this story away from me, my mouth! for rebuking the gods is a hateful
craft and boasting inappropriately strikes a note of madness. Do not babble
such things! Keep war and all fights far from the immortals.

Here again there is no mention of truth vs lies, but Pindar
asserts that poetry should give appropriate accounts of the
gods; and gods should not be portrayed unfavourably. In
Pindar's poetry, in general, different standards apply to his
mythical narrative and the praise of the victor. He may criticize
his predecessors' versions of myths, but he never claims that he
is the one to provide the truth;[118] his claim is that his version is
appropriate. On the contrary, Pindar makes claim to truth
when he wants to assert the validity of the praise that he sings;
for this reason also, when he speaks about the victory events he
makes sure that he provides some sort of testimony.[119]

Xenophanes[120] is another interesting case; critics have repeatedly noticed the similarity to the extent that the Euripidean
passage is often called 'Xenophanean'. Xenophanes' critique
of Homer and Hesiod for their attribution to the gods of blame-
worthy acts is strange when one considers that his notion of
divinity was not necessarily anthropomorphic. In view of the
fragmentary state of Xenophanes' works, it is impossible to
determine whether his views of divinity developed during the
course of his life. But from what we have of his work it seems
that his purpose is not to invalidate the traditional anthropomorphic religion.[121] His criticism of the poets' portrayals of the

[118] His attitude towards Homer is interesting in this respect. In *Nem.* 7.20–30, Pindar
says that Homer has enhanced Odysseus' fame beyond the hero's worth, and,
referring to the Judgment of Achilles' arms which led to Ajax's death, comments
on the power of fiction and persuasion. Homer and Odysseus are here brought
very close together, but Pindar's main intention is to criticize Odysseus, not
Homer. On this issue, see Pratt 1993: 127–8. Cf. Pindar's praise of Homer with
regard to the treatment of Ajax in *Isthm.* 4.41–3.
[119] See Pratt 1993: 122–3. On Pindar's attitude to truth and lies in poetry, see
Komornicka 1972 and 1981; Pratt 1993: 115–29; on the development of the notion
of truth in archaic Greek thought in general, see Detienne 1996.
[120] On Xenophanes, see Babut 1974; Pratt 1993: 136–40.
[121] See Eisenstadt 1974 for the view that Xenophanes' views were not meant to over-
throw the traditional religious system.

anthropomorphic gods is based, like that of Pindar, on ethical grounds. Thus in his first elegy (B I DK)[122] about behaviour at a symposium, he says that one should not narrate in this context the tales about the Titans, the Giants and the Centaurs, which are the inventions (πλάσματα) of previous generations. However, Xenophanes here clearly places emphasis not on the falsehood of these tales, but on their lack of appropriateness. In other words, Xenophanes does not reject stories because they are false, but because they are not ethical. The underlying criterion is that poetry should serve a social, and in particular, moral function.

Taking into account that appropriateness and moral function with regard to poetry are given most weight even by Pindar and Xenophanes, who have often been taken as more radical in their attack on the falsehoods in myth and poetry, let us examine what happens when similar issues are raised in Euripidean drama. Euripides often has characters criticize the truth of mythical accounts in his dramas, but does this criticism amount to outright demolition?[123]

In the agon between Hecuba and Helen in *Trojan Women*, Helen refers to the Judgment of Paris (924–31). She says that Paris was the arbiter of a beauty contest between Hera, Athena and Aphrodite, and she mentions what each goddess promised him if he would judge in her favour. Athena promised him that he should destroy Greece, Hera that he should rule over Asia and the boundaries of Europe, and Cypris (Aphrodite) that he should take Helen as a gift. In her reply (969–82), Hecuba says that she will defend the three goddesses against Helen's unjust words. Like Heracles, she puts forward her own explanation of the goddesses' motives. It is not entirely clear from Hecuba's answer whether she doubts that the Judgment actually took place.[124] What she clearly doubts is that the goddesses could be so inconsiderate as to sell Argos and Athens to the Trojans over a beauty contest, which, in itself, would be unimportant

---

[122] On this elegy, see Bowra 1938; Defradas 1962; Pratt 1993: 138–9.
[123] Cf. the discussions by Stinton 1976; Jakob 1998: 50–5.
[124] See Barlow 1986 on Eur. *Tro.* 975. The Judgment of Paris was alluded to by Poseidon in the prologue (23–34), while it was also prophesied by Cassandra in

for deities. Thus, according to Hecuba, either the Judgment never took place, or the goddesses did not promise Paris what Helen said they did. As for Hecuba's questioning of the god-desses' actions and motives, which reflects her own 'idealized' view of the divine, it is here similar to Heracles' view of the gods as not engaging in questionable activities. But the play shows its audience that gods behave in various ways often not pleasing to mortals. Thus, if in the prologue the audience witness Athena as the guardian of human propriety, and hear that the future destruction of the Greeks is a punishment for outrage, they also hear about a capricious Athena, who is fickle in her attitudes towards humans (cf. 67–8), and whose destruction of the Trojans was merely the result of her failure in a beauty contest.

Another example comes from *Iphigenia among the Taurians*. Here Iphigenia accuses Artemis of duplicity, in that she requires ritual purity on the one hand and takes pleasure in human sacrifices on the other. But then she attempts to absolve the goddess by using myth as well as rationalizations:

τὰ τῆς θεοῦ δὲ μέμφομαι σοφίσματα,
ἥτις βροτῶν μὲν ἤν τις ἄψηται φόνου
ἢ καὶ λοχείας ἢ νεκροῦ θίγηι χεροῖν
βωμῶν ἀπείργει, μυσαρὸν ὡς ἡγουμένη,
αὐτὴ δὲ θυσίαις ἥδεται βροτοκτόνοις.
οὐκ ἔσθ' ὅπως ἔτεκεν ἂν ἡ Διὸς δάμαρ
Λητὼ τοσαύτην ἀμαθίαν. ἐγὼ μὲν οὖν
τὰ Ταντάλου θεοῖσιν ἑστιάματα
ἄπιστα κρίνω, παιδὸς ἡσθῆναι βορᾶι,
τοὺς δ' ἐνθάδ', αὐτοὺς ὄντας ἀνθρωποκτόνους,
ἐς τὴν θεὸν τὸ φαῦλον ἀναφέρειν δοκῶ·
οὐδένα γὰρ οἶμαι δαιμόνων εἶναι κακόν. (380–91)

As for the goddess's wisdom, I deplore it. When any of us mortals has contact with bloodshed, or even touches childbirth or a corpse with their hands, she bans them from her altars, judging them polluted – while she herself relishes human sacrifices. In no way could Zeus's consort Leto have given birth to such uncouthness! I for my part do not believe the story of

---

Alexandros, the first play of the Trojan trilogy. On the Judgment of Paris and its treatment by Euripides, see Stinton 1965. On Euripides' *Alexandros* and the Trojan trilogy as a whole, see Scodel 1980b with bibliography.

Tantalus' feast for the gods – that they relished a meal of his son! The people here, I think, being murderous themselves, ascribe their weakness to the goddess. I do not believe that any deity is bad.[125]

Iphigenia's attitude to myth is entirely based upon a belief in divine virtue as such; a divinity, in other words, cannot be charged with ἀμαθία, a word which conveys both intellectual (e.g. *HF* 347) and moral associations (e.g. *Ion* 916). But then her move to another myth is problematic; from the negation of divine pleasure in human killings (the case of Artemis) her thought moves to the alleged divine pleasure in human eating (the case of Tantalus' cannibalistic meal offered to the gods). Although she gives a rationalizing explanation of the impure ritual of human sacrifice, by arguing that it is not Artemis' wish but the projection of the human (the Taurians') murderous instinct onto the goddess, the mythical example of cannibalism remains unexplained (cf. Pind.*Ol.* 1. 37–51, discussed above).[126] The audience are left in doubt whether Iphigenia's thoughts are anything more than mere speculations. So, Iphigenia's 'idealized' notion of divinity may seem sophisticated and appealing, but its validity is far from certain.[127]

In the second choral ode of Euripides' *Electra* (699–746), the Chorus tell 'a story which endures among our greying tales' (κληδὼν | ἐν πολιαῖσι μένει φήμαις, 700–1), about Thyestes and his brother Atreus, who were in dispute over the kingdom. The gods sent Pan to Atreus carrying a golden lamb as evidence that the gods recognized his claim to the kingdom. But Thyestes, who had seduced Atreus' wife Aerope, stole the lamb with her help and announced to the assembly that he had the golden lamb which gave him claim to the throne. Zeus then

---

[125] Translation by Cropp (2000).

[126] The use of the word ἄπιστα (388) may of course imply that the myth is considered a fiction made up by human beings.

[127] Iphigenia's view of the goddess must be informed by her own experience at Aulis: Artemis had asked for the sacrifice of Iphigenia, but for Iphigenia the goddess is credited only with her salvation. In the play in general, Artemis may be said to function also as a dramatic device that problematizes the otherwise clearly drawn distinction between the categories Greek and barbarian.

intervened by reversing the course of the sun.[128] At this point, the Chorus end their ode with the following remarks:

λέγεται <τάδε>, τὰν δὲ πί-
στιν σμικρὰν παρ᾽ ἔμοιγ᾽ ἔχει,
στρέψαι θερμὰν ἀέλιον
χρυσωπὸν ἕδραν ἀλλάξαν-
τα δυστυχίαι βροτείωι
θνατᾶς ἕνεκεν δίκας.
φοβεροὶ δὲ βροτοῖσι μῦθοι
κέρδος πρὸς θεῶν θεραπείαν.
ὧν οὐ μνασθεῖσα πόσιν
κτείνεις, κλεινῶν συγγενέτειρ᾽ ἀδελφῶν. (737–46)

These things are said, but meagre is the credit they hold with me – that the golden sun did turn and change its torrid station, to the detriment of men, for a mortal cause's sake. But fearful tales are profitable to men in furthering the service of the gods. Unmindful of such tales you have killed your husband, sister of glorious brothers.[129]

Here the Chorus express their scepticism concerning the story of Zeus's intervention and his alteration of the sun's course. The problem is that they cannot believe that Zeus, only for a mortal's sake, caused so much misery to all humans through his interference with the climate (741–2). It has been argued that the Chorus only disapprove of the divine motivation, yet allow for the possibility that the story about Zeus's intervention may be true.[130] But the Chorus' scepticism about the story surely amounts to disbelief in the truth of Zeus's intervention altogether and is based on their denial of the god's motivation. The logic behind the passage is not 'the story may be true, but we disapprove of the god's motivation', but rather 'we cannot believe this motivation of a god, so we hardly believe in the truth of the story'.[131] What the Chorus disbelieve is not that the sun actually changed its course, but

---

[128] On the change of the course of the sun, see Denniston 1939 on Eur. *El.* 726–32 and Cropp 1988 on Eur. *El.* 727–36.

[129] Translation by Cropp (1988).

[130] This is the interpretation given by Stinton 1976: 79–81, and followed, e.g., by Jakob 1998: 52–3. See *contra* Cropp 1988: on Eur. *El.* 737–46.

[131] This is in fact similar to the phrase ἄπιστα κρίνω, 'consider unbelievable', in Eur. *IT* 388.

that the purpose of this phenomenon was for Zeus to intervene
and settle a dispute.

But the Chorus' scepticism about the story does not make
them reject it. What is important for them is not so much the
truth of a story as its function and purposes.[132] As they go on
to say, φοβεροὶ δὲ βροτοῖσι μῦθοι | κέρδος πρὸς θεῶν θεραπείαν
(743–4), that is, fearful stories such as the one they have just
narrated may not be wholly true in content, but they serve a
valuable purpose; they encourage mortals to worship gods.
Thus in the story about Atreus and Thyestes, the narration
of Zeus's intervention may present the god's motivation as
questionable, but it serves a higher purpose because it makes
humans believe that crimes are not left unpunished by the
gods. And the Chorus conclude that Clytemnestra did not
draw the moral from such stories of divine intervention, but
was unmindful of them, or else she would have been deterred
from killing Agamemnon (745–6).

When in *Iphigenia at Aulis* the Chorus refer to Helen, they
envisage how the Trojan women, fearing for their future misfortunes, will blame her:

διὰ σέ, τὰν κύκνου δολιχαύχενος γόνον,
εἰ δὴ φάτις ἔτυμος ὡς
+ἔτυχε Λήδα+ ὄρνιθι πταμένωι,
Διὸς ὅτ᾽ἀλλάχθη δέμας, εἴτ᾽
ἐν δέλτοις Πιερίσιν
μῦθοι τάδ᾽ἐς ἀνθρώπους
ἤνεγκαν παρὰ καιρὸν ἄλλως. (794–800)

Because of you, the offspring of the long-necked swan, if indeed it be a true
report that + Leda bore you + to a winged bird, when Zeus transformed
himself, or whether, in Pierian tablets [poetic texts], fables have carried
these tales to people, inappropriately.

According to the story, Zeus took the form of a swan in
order to approach Leda, Helen's mother. But here Helen's

---

[132] The important issue is not truth but moral function. This attitude of the Chorus
here is reflected in several critical approaches to poetry and story-telling in antiquity. Plato, for example, argued that although certain ancient stories were false,
they were important for propagating values (on Plato's attitude to fiction in
general, see Gill 1993a; Pratt 1993: 146–56).

divine origin is brought into question, and truth is juxtaposed
to poetic accounts of myths. The miraculous birth of Helen
may well have sounded patently incredible and thus fabricated.
Ancient Greek poetry was full of similar features, and critics
often drew a line between true and obviously fabulous elements in myths. Already at the end of the sixth century
Xenophanes uses the term πλάσματα in his first elegy (B 1.22
DK) for the tales of the Giants, Titans and Centaurs in a way
which indicates that he objects to these stories.[133] Also, ancient
scholia, especially on Homer, abound in comments on miraculous stories included in poetry. In the Hellenistic typology of
narratives, which uses as its criterion the degree of truthfulness
in an account, one category was μῦθος or μυθικόν, where
genealogy belonged, according to Asclepiades of Myrlea (Sext.
Emp. *Adv. Gramm.* 253).[134] From the examples given by Sextus
(264) it is obvious that Asclepiades means the miraculous births
and also the metamorphoses in mythology, which are incredible
at first sight and are thus readily taken as untrue.[135]

So, our example from *Iphigenia at Aulis,* which refers in
particular to genealogy, is an early example, found within
poetry itself, of the kind of criticism of the truth of a mythic
account which was to develop into theoretical systematization
in the Hellenistic period. To use another example of criticism
of myth in Greek tragedy, one may recall the story about
Dionysus' miraculous birth from the thigh of Zeus in
Bacchae, which is rejected by Pentheus as false (242–7) and
accepted by Teiresias as true (286–97). No matter that the
myth seems incredible and no matter that what Teiresias does
is to rationalize it in seemingly absurd terms, we must remember that Pentheus himself attributes the myth to the
Stranger.[136] So it is reasonable to say that for the audience,
who are the only ones to know that the Stranger is Dionysus in
human disguise, the myth must carry weight, and it is indeed
possible that they recognize allusions to mystic elements in

[133] His objection is based on moral grounds; cf. pp. 102–3 above.
[134] See now Blank 1998.
[135] For this category of narrative, see in general Meijering 1987: 78–84.
[136] On Teiresias and the Stranger in the play, see Papadopoulou 2001b.

Teiresias' account.[137] Thus one needs to consider carefully both the context and the dramatic purpose while examining instances where myth is criticized.[138]

In the passage from *Iphigenia at Aulis*, it is important that it is the Trojan women who are presented as speaking through the Chorus; in other words, the Chorus imagine and create the Trojan perspective. It is the Trojan women who question Helen's miraculous origin. Why then their concern with Helen's origin at this point? The easy solution would be to disregard the issue and say that it is just one example, out of many, where Euripides finds an opportunity to juxtapose myth and 'reality'.[139] But here Euripides (and his Chorus) dexterously has Helen's origin questioned by Trojan women. They are in despair and blame their misfortunes on Helen. The question then is, how could a person of divine origin, indeed the daughter of Zeus, cause the destruction of Troy and bring so many misfortunes on the people? The passage resembles Andromache's outburst against Helen in *Trojan Women*, at the climactic point when she has to hand her son over to Talthybius to be taken away to his death:

ὦ Τυνδάρειον ἔρνος, οὔποτ' εἶ Διός,
πολλῶν δὲ πατέρων φημί σ' ἐκπεφυκέναι,
' Ἀλάστορος μὲν πρῶτον, εἶτα δὲ Φθόνου
Φόνου τε Θανάτου θ' ὅσα τε γῆ τρέφει κακά.
οὐ γάρ ποτ' αὐχῶ Ζῆνά[140] γ' ἐκφῦσαί σ' ἐγώ,

---

[137] See for examples the connotations of the word *aither* at 293 as interpreted by Seaford 1996 on Eur. *Bacch.* 286–97.

[138] This instance is different from the other examples discussed in that Dionysus is already a character in the play. In Eur. *HF* 140–54, Lycus' rejection of Heracles' divine paternity and his rationalization of Heracles' exploits, which deprives them of any heroic status, may also be said to be in a way a criticism of the myth of Heracles. Heracles is of course a character of the play but he is presented as a legendary figure, renowned throughout for his achievements. Lycus may use sophistic arguments of the type that was popular in the fifth century, but the myth of Heracles remains valid both inside and outside the play.

[139] On this use of the myth by Euripides, see Eisner 1979. There is certainly an interplay between myth and reality in Euripidean drama (*Helen* is a prime example), but it is wrong to presuppose, as Eisner does, that Euripides' concern is to attack myth.

[140] If there is here an allusion to the etymological affinity between Ζεύς, 'Zeus' and ζῆν, 'to live', then the use of the word κήρ, 'doom', 'ruin' for Helen in the next line might further imply that Helen cannot be the daughter of Zeus, for she brings death instead of life. On this point, see Lee 1976 on Eur. *Tro.* 770.

πολλοῖσι κῆρα βαρβάροις" Ελλησί τε.
ὄλοιο· καλλίστων γὰρ ὀμμάτων ἄπο
αἰσχρῶς τὰ κλεινὰ πεδί᾽ ἀπώλεσας Φρυγῶν. (766–73) [141]

You scion of Tyndareus' house, you were never born from Zeus, but I declare you are the child of many fathers, of the Avenging Curse, of Envy, of Murder and Death and all the plagues the Earth breeds! Zeus never begot you, I am certain, you who are a pestilence to countless Greeks and barbarians alike. May you die! With your lovely eyes you have brought ugly death to the famed plains of Troy.[142]

At the point where Andromache's grief culminates, it is understandable for her to attack Helen, who is held responsible. Helen is called the child of Tyndareus and not of Zeus. She is the child of whatever plague the earth breeds. Andromache confidently asserts (cf. αὐχῶ, 770) that Helen is not the child of Zeus, because if she had been, she would not have brought so many calamities on Trojans and Greeks alike.

The question of Helen's divine origin is raised also in *Helen*. This time, the issue is raised by Helen herself. In the prologue of the play she has this to say:

ἡμῖν δὲ γῆ μὲν πατρὶς οὐκ ἀνώνυμος
Σπάρτη, πατὴρ δὲ Τυνδάρεως· ἔστιν δὲ δὴ
λόγος τις ὡς Ζεὺς μητέρ᾽ ἔπτατ᾽ εἰς ἐμὴν
Λήδαν κύκνου μορφώματ᾽ ὄρνιθος λαβών,
ὃς δόλιον εὐνὴν ἐξέπραξ᾽ ὑπ᾽ αἰετοῦ
δίωγμα φεύγων, εἰ σαφὴς οὗτος λόγος· (16–21)

As for myself, my fatherland is no obscure place. It is Sparta, and my father is Tyndareos, though there is of course a story that Zeus transformed himself into a bird, a swan, and flew to my mother Leda. He pretended to be fleeing an eagle's pursuit and consummated his love through a trick – if this tale is true.[143]

Here Helen wonders, in terms closely echoed by the Chorus of *Iphigenia at Aulis,* if her miraculous birth from Zeus, who took the form of a swan to approach Leda, was a true story. The juxtaposition between what is true and what seems to be

[141] For the rhetoric of 766–9, cf. Patroclus' words to Achilles in *Il.* 16.33–5.
[142] Translation by Barlow (1986).
[143] Translations from *Helen* are by Morwood (1997).

true but is false, in other words the anthithesis between reality and appearance, which permeates the whole play,[144] is introduced a few lines below by Helen, when she refers to the *eidolon* that Hera gave to Paris in anger for the outcome of the Judgment:

δίδωσι δ'οὐκ ἔμ᾽ ἀλλ᾽ὁμοιώσασ᾽ἐμοὶ
εἴδωλον ἔμπνουν οὐρανοῦ ξυνθεῖσ᾽ἄπο,
Πριάμου τυράννου παιδί· καὶ δοκεῖ μ᾽ἔχειν,
κενὴν δόκησιν, οὐκ ἔχων. (33–6)

[Hera] gave to the son of King Priam not my real self but a breathing phantom which she had moulded in my likeness from heavenly ether; and he believes he possesses me – but it is a vain belief, for he does not.

The juxtaposition is made again when Helen mentions that Hermes, following Zeus's orders, transferred her to Egypt when the Trojan War started so that she could be safe. Everyone on both the Greek and the Trojan side believed the War was fought over Helen in Troy, whereas the real Helen was in the house of Proteus (36–53). Helen acknowledges that her transportation to Egypt was obvious proof of Zeus's concern (45–6). However, the situation as it is depicted at the beginning of the drama is no longer safe for Helen. She is now in despair (53; 56). Not only does she have a bad reputation in Greece and Troy, despite her innocence, but now that Proteus has died Helen is a suppliant at Proteus' tomb trying to escape his son's advances (56–67). The emphasis on Helen's present plight and on the urgency of the situation is clear not only in her words, but is also made obvious for the spectators from the very beginning as Helen is presented as a suppliant.

Once again, it would be simplistic to attribute this to Euripides' tendency to question myth at every opportunity; Helen's statement in this passage can be explained in terms of her despair. She is presented as the innocent victim who has suffered intensely. She is the one who took the blame for the Trojan War and she is now hated and vilified. Zeus showed his concern for his daughter by making sure she would never reach Troy, and he has also promised, as Hermes told her (56–9),

---

[144] On this, see Segal 1986b.

that her reputation will eventually be restored and that she will return to Menelaus in Sparta; but her sufferings contradict her divine origin, because, despite being the child of Zeus, she is deeply miserable.[145] And now that she is threatened and has taken refuge there is no sign that she has not been abandoned by Zeus. So, Helen's reference to her divine origin is not in fact criticism of the truth of it but rather an expression of her disappointment that Zeus does not intervene to help his own child. Similarly in the Parodos the Chorus' reference to Helen's miraculous birth from Zeus, which is presented as a fact, is made in a context which enumerates Helen's misfortunes (211–28).

In general, a god's intervention on a human being's behalf is considered by characters in the plays to be adequate proof of that person's divine descent. In *Heracles* for example, Heracles' prompt return to save his family is taken by the Chorus as proof of Zeus's intervention and makes them say confidently that Heracles is indeed Zeus's son (Διὸς ὁ παῖς, 'it is Zeus's son', 696). It is not of course the case that the Chorus ever doubted the divine paternity of Heracles. But the absence of Zeus when his son's family were in utter despair was constantly stressed. It made Lycus find reason to deny Heracles' origin (148–9), and it also caused Amphitryon's outburst against the god (339–47) who was called the divine father of Heracles in vain.[146] As for divine intervention which proves divine origin, one may recall Theseus' curse against his son in *Hippolytus*. Theseus invokes Poseidon, his divine father, mentions the three curses he once promised him, and asks him to

---

[145] Cf. the comments by Kannicht 1969, vol. II, on Helen's state in the prologue of the play; Stinton 1976: 74–9; Jakob 1998: 52. Cf. also Heracles' words to Odysseus in *Od.* 11.620–1: Ζηνὸς μὲν πάϊς ἦα Κρονίονος, αὐτὰρ ὀϊζὺν | εἶχον ἀπειρεσίην, 'my father was Zeus, the son of Cronus, yet I suffered measureless grief'.

[146] Cf. also Euripides' *Antiope* (fr. 48 Kambitsis (see now Diggle 1996)), where Amphion says that 'if Zeus is our father he will rescue us and punish our enemy'. When Hermes later appears, he refers to the union of Zeus and Antiope as a fact, which means that Amphion is indeed of divine origin. But Amphion is not questioning his divine origin, and a few lines below in fr. 48 (10–14) he seems to say that if Zeus does not intervene, the union between Antiope and Zeus was in vain. Therefore, there is no scepticism concerning the truth of the divine origin, but emphasis is given to the urgent need for Zeus's intervention. See Kambitsis 1972 on Eur. *Ant.* fr. 48, on l. 2.

use one in order to cause Hippolytus' death (887–90; 895–6). When later in the play the Messenger brings the news that Hippolytus is barely alive, and that it was the curses that Theseus addressed to Poseidon against his son that destroyed Hippolytus (1166–8), Theseus exclaims: ὦ θεοί, Πόσειδόν θ᾽ · ὡς ἄρ᾽ ἦσθ᾽ ἐμὸς πατὴρ | ὀρθῶς,[147] ἀκούσας τῶν ἐμῶν κατευγμάτων, 'O gods and Poseidon, how you truly are my father, since you have listened to my curses!' (1169–70). Theseus of course knew all along that Poseidon was his father, but, in a way, the god's answer to his prayers provided him with what he considered to be the strongest proof of his divine origin. Conversely, although Helen too knows that she is the child of a god, that is, Zeus, and although she recognizes that Zeus has shown his concern for her before, she is made to wonder about her divine origin because she now considers herself neglected by the god.

This section has focused on examples from Euripidean plays where the truth of myths is brought into question by dramatic characters. What I hope to have shown is that the purpose of this criticism is not to invalidate the myths in question. In other words, Euripides does not use his characters in order to undermine myth. Contextualization is what helps to define the meaning of the criticism each time, and any attempt to disregard the importance of the dramatic context runs the risk of misinterpreting the function of the relevant passages within each tragedy. The examination has shown that in each case,

---

[147] The use of ὀρθῶς here is interesting, for it also appears in *HF* 1345, to refer to Heracles' notion of a true divinity. Barrett 1964 on Eur. *Hipp.* 1169–70 takes the phrase to mean ' "you really are my father" (he had no guarantee of it before), not "you are a real father, a father worthy of the name" ', and compares Eur. *Alc.* 636 οὐκ ἦ σθ᾽ ἄρ᾽ ὀρθῶς τοῦδε σώματος πατήρ, 'which is not "you don't deserve the name of father" but "you aren't really my father at all" (he goes on to allege that he is a changeling)'. Barrett is certainly right, but the difference is subtle. Theseus is now certain that Poseidon is his true father, but the idea behind this is also that Poseidon acted in the way that Theseus expected a true father would act, that is, he helped his son. Also, in *Alcestis*, Admetus' assertion that Pheres was not his real father results from the fact that Pheres failed to meet the standards that Admetus associated with a proper father. Thus, the word ὀρθῶς, which means 'really', also has the connotation of the proper, as opposed to improper, application of the term which accompanies it (here 'father', in *Heracles* 'god'; more on the latter in the discussion of the passage from *Heracles* below, p. 115).

the scepticism expressed by a character was based on this character's notion of what a divinity is or how a divinity should act. It becomes obvious also that the human notion of divinity tends to be 'idealized', and that whenever gods are criticized, the criticism results from the gods' failure to meet the standards which the humans set for them.

In *Heracles*, the hero rejects Theseus' arguments because he does not want to accept Theseus' parallelism between the gods and himself. I have shown above how Heracles' reaction against the gods developed gradually. Heracles' response to Theseus' arguments is a clear indication that he refuses to find solace in the notion that gods too put up with imperfection. He wants to have nothing to do with imperfect gods and so Theseus' use of these gods as good examples causes Heracles' reaction. His decision whether to live or to die will have nothing to do with the gods to which Theseus refers. For this reason he calls Theseus' arguments πάρεργα, that is, of secondary importance or irrelevant.[148] In a way, then, given the context of Heracles' revolt against the gods, Theseus' *a fortiori* argumentation, though in itself strong and recommendable in other contexts, is doomed to fail when it is addressed to Heracles at this specific point. In his reply, Heracles denounces the divine character of the imperfect gods who have just been described by Theseus. If the gods put up with imperfection, Heracles will show himself superior to them. He will not accept imperfection and will refuse divine character to these gods.[149] It was discussed above how Hecuba in *Trojan Women* and Iphigenia in *Iphigenia among the Taurians*[150] also refused to believe that

[148] For the view that the word πάρεργα refers to Theseus' arguments (and not to Theseus' offers), see Halleran 1986: 175; Yunis 1988: 159.

[149] Cf. the line from Euripides' *Bellerophon* (fr. 292.7): εἰ θεοί τι δρῶσιν αἰσχρόν οὐκ εἰσὶν θεοί, 'if the gods behave shamefully, they are not gods'. On the play, see now Collard et al. 1995: 98–120.

[150] Jakob 1998: 55 persuasively suggests that, given the chronological proximity of the Euripidean *Trojan Women* (415 BC), *Iphigenia among the Taurians* (c. 415 BC) and *Heracles* (c. 415 BC), these three plays bring forward the need for a sophisticated, and morally advanced, notion of divinity. Such a notion of divinity would probably be appealing to the audience, and would all the more invite them to think about the gods as they were dramatically portrayed. But again it is a question of whether gods follow human standards or not.

gods are imperfect. Heracles moves one step ahead here because, realizing that gods have indeed proven to be imperfect, he not only criticizes them but refuses to call them gods. As has been shown by Yunis,[151] the use of the word ὀρθῶς at *HF* 1345 invokes the topic of ὀρθότης ὀνομάτων, 'correctness of names', which was of primary importance in fifth-century philosophy, and which refers to the relation between language and reality, and in particular to the ability of language to represent reality accurately. Thus Heracles makes a clear distinction between the right and wrong application of the term 'divinity'.

When Heracles says that he does not believe that gods engage in the kinds of activity described by Theseus, he does not of course deny that gods such as Zeus and Hera do behave badly. He does not deny for instance that Zeus overthrew his father or that he committed adultery. It is interesting that he uses the term δύστηνοι, 'wretched', to refer to the poetic accounts (that is, 'tales of wretchedness'), instead of a term to denote falsehood (that is, 'false tales').[152] Heracles' view is that it would be wrong to call the gods who perform these acts 'gods'; and poets are wrong to call them 'gods'. That is, the name 'god' is given correctly to those who do not commit the crimes mentioned by Theseus. Heracles does not say much about the notion of a perfect divinity; but one need not necessarily think here of a monotheistic notion, nor of a divinity which, in being self-sufficient, is somehow aloof from mankind like the gods that ancient philosophers discussed.[153]

It is interesting that Heracles says that his belief in the perfection of divinity is not a new idea; it has been his firm belief in the past (ἠξίωσα, 'thought capable of', 1343), it is in the present (νομίζω, 'believe', 1342) and will be the same in the future (οὔτε πείσομαι, 'I shall not believe', 1343).[154] Thus,

[151] See Yunis 1988: 161–6.
[152] See Yunis 1988: 163 and n. 45; cf. Jakob 1998: 54 n. 41. Cf. LSJ s.v. δύστηνος ((2 II) for the moral significance of the term after Homer.
[153] For the remoteness of the divinity envisaged by Heracles, cf. Desch 1986: 15; Lawrence 1998: 135–6. See *contra* Yunis 1988: 163–4 and n. 47.
[154] Despite the rhetorical overtones of the phrasing, Heracles here expresses a strong belief, which aims both at answering Theseus' earlier arguments and at revealing

Heracles does not suddenly turn into a philosopher in this passage. Divinity and perfection go together in Heracles' view and his present plight has become the catalyst for realizing that traditional gods can no longer be considered perfect; more specifically, they no longer deserve to be called proper gods. The gods who do not commit misdeeds are certainly one and the same with the god (a generic term) who needs nothing. But this notion of divinity is not separated from the traditional gods.[155] 'True gods', however, means the gods according to Heracles' idiosyncratic notion of divinity. Thus, his notion of divinity may seem sophisticated, because it is that of a perfect god, but it is neither out of character nor dramatically irrelevant.[156] The traditional gods exist but no longer meet the standards that Heracles believes that gods should meet.[157] His own experience, that is, his unfair treatment by these gods, has made him assert this belief even more. Although he does not deny the existence of the traditional gods, he rebels against them; in doing so he deludes himself into believing that he can banish the gods from the human universe by refusing to acknowledge their divinity.[158]

his own consistent attitude, past, present and future, towards the gods. Bond on Eur. *HF* 1342 f. quotes Eur. *Tro.* 467 for a similar play on tenses: πάσχω τε καὶ πέπονθα κἄτι πείσομαι, 'I suffer and have suffered and shall go on suffering'; here too the rhetorical effect helps to convey the continuity of Hecuba's suffering in past, present and future (cf. Barlow 1986: 180–1).

[155] Yunis 1988: 159 argues that Heracles expounds a new notion of divinity, which, according to Yunis, he has in mind throughout the whole passage, and which has nothing to do with the traditional gods.

[156] Critics who think otherwise conclude that Heracles' views of the gods in the play are necessarily incompatible; see e.g. Schlesier 1985a. For an attempt to understand the development of Heracles' views in the play, see Yunis 1988: 149–71.

[157] In Euripides' *Bellerophon*, the hero, like Heracles, is extremely angry with the gods, but in that case it is not that the gods act injustly towards humans, but that they do not show any concern about the situation on earth; thus, Bellerophon argues that there are no gods in heaven, but he probably goes to heaven himself in the course of the play to confront them. See Collard et al. 1995: 98–120.

[158] For Heracles as self-deluded, cf. Foley 1985: 165 and Mastronarde 1986: 208, who however, hold that Heracles denies the existence of the traditional gods. For the idea of Heracles' self-delusion, see more recently Matthiessen 2004: 61.

The incomprehensibility of the gods

In Euripides' plays, the way that gods act and the disastrous effects that their actions often have upon humans are manifestations of their power. The humans can criticize the gods for their behaviour but their criticisms are based on their demand that gods should behave in certain ways. Humans have certain notions of how a divinity should act, and when they are disappointed they criticize the gods for failing them. In *Hippolytus* for example, the Servant prays to Aphrodite to forgive Hippolytus, who spoke rashly about her, because, as he says, σοφωτέρους γὰρ χρὴ βροτῶν εἶναι θεούς, 'for gods should be wiser than humans' (120). The Servant presupposes that gods *qua* gods ought to be wiser, and hopes that Aphrodite in particular will prove the same, but his prayer is doomed to fail, as it follows the clearly stated plan of the goddess in the prologue to destroy Hippolytus. It is true that Aphrodite in the prologue describes a reciprocal relation between herself and mortals, that is, she treats well those who honour her and ruins those who disrespect her (5–6). Reciprocity between gods and humans is important because it reassures humans that gods will show concern for them as long as they are honoured by them. But Aphrodite's manifestation of power over Hippolytus, although justifiable according to divine standards, seems excessive according to human standards. The difference between divine and human standards becomes obvious also at the end of this play, where Artemis, in order to avenge the death of Hippolytus, announces her future revenge upon a favourite of Aphrodite, that is, upon another mortal (1420–2).

Similarly, in *Bacchae* Dionysus, when confronted by Cadmus' complaint that he should not have acted so excessively, justifies his actions by saying that he is a god and he suffered insult (1347). He also says that if they had been sensible before and accepted the god they would now be happy (1341–3). There is again an underlying sense of failed reciprocity; mortals fail to worship a divinity (as in the case of Hippolytus), and are punished. But the punishment also seems

excessive to the humans, and Cadmus asserts, in a formulation
that for many critics has raised questions which the plays seem
not to answer, that gods should not resemble humans in anger:
ὀργὰς πρέπει θεοὺς οὐχ ὁμοιοῦσθαι βροτοῖς (1348).[159]

The power of divinity in Euripidean tragedy may be inflicted
upon characters in what seems to be the harshest way. This
may be felt even more in the case of the Euripidean Heracles,
who is presented as the victim of Hera's jealousy. But the ways
of the gods remain ultimately unintelligible, and humans can
have only partial understanding of their gods. Accordingly,
humans speak about the gods, have certain notions of them,
hope that the gods will act in certain ways and criticize them
when they do not, yet they can never fully understand them.[160]

This becomes evident in the course of *Heracles*, where
humans think that they understand gods only to be proven
wrong. In the prologue, Amphitryon is confident that Zeus will
reciprocate and intervene to help his son's family; the implication is that Amphitryon thinks he knows and understands
Zeus too well. On the contrary, at the end of the first episode,

[159] Effe 1990 discusses *Bacchae*, *Hippolytus* and *Heracles* as examples which show the
contrast between the rationalistic optimism of the sophistic movement, which
eventually fails, and the irrational powers, exemplified by the traditional gods,
which eventually prevail.

[160] On these issues in Euripidean drama, see e.g. Schlesier 1985b; Kullmann 1987; cf.
Graf 1993, esp. 173. Contrary to this view, which holds that in Euripides characters
criticize the gods because they cannot understand that gods have their own
standards, irrespective of human ones, Jakob 1998: 54, argues that the important
role of reciprocity in Greek religion should not be ignored. However, although
reciprocity indeed plays a major role (cf. Gould 1985: 14–16; Yunis 1988: *passim*),
it should be stressed that the unknowability of the gods predominates over human
hope for reciprocity; in other words, humans can only hope, not demand, that gods
will reciprocate, while, at the same time, divine motivation often remains obscure.
To mention some examples: in *Il.* 22.168–72, there is a clear reciprocation between
gods and humans when it is said that Zeus's concern for Hector is based on
Hector's devotion to the god in sacrifice; but in *Il.* 24.525–30, Achilles, reflecting
on the nature of human misfortune, tells Priam how Zeus bestows blessings and
sorrows on mortals from his two separate urns, and there is always a likelihood
that one will get more bad fortune than good. Cf. Athena's failure to reciprocate
the prayers and offerings of the Trojan women in *Il.* 6.311. Solon too, whose work
emphasizes divine justice, says that sometimes good people are brought down,
whereas evil people enjoy good fortune (13, 63–70). One way of trying to get
further with this problem was of course to invoke the idea of inherited liability
for punishment. On the limitations of human knowledge in the presocratic philosophical tradition and in Sophocles' *Oedipus Tyrannus*, see Liapis (2003).

when he realizes that his hopes in Zeus are in vain, he goes on to reproach the god (339–47). Megara, on the other hand, emphasized from the very beginning of her speech the inscrutability of the gods: ὡς οὐδὲν ἀνθρώποισι τῶν θείων σαφές, 'how unclear are the ways of gods to men!' (62). The idea that gods and mortals have different standards is clearly stated by the Chorus in the second stasimon, when they say that, if gods had understanding and wisdom as humans conceive it (εἰ δὲ θεοῖς ἦν ξύνεσις | καὶ σοφία κατ᾽ ἄνδρας, 655–6), then gods would give good people a second life as an objective mark of their virtue. When the Chorus hear the cries of Lycus as he is being murdered by Heracles, they talk about justice and the gods. In the first stasimon, they had called the impending fate of Heracles' children ἄθεον ἄδικον, 'godless, unjust' (433–4). In the present reversal of that situation the Chorus now see the manifestation of theodicy; they exclaim against the mortal who questioned the power of the gods (757–9), they assert divine concern and justice (772–3) and conclude with what is in fact an implicit answer to Amphitryon's earlier accusation of Zeus. Now, the Chorus say, Zeus is vindicated, for he has made sure that his son returned from Hades to save his family; Heracles' divine parentage is now an unquestionable fact for the Chorus, who end with another affirmation of the gods' concern for justice (798–814). The optimism of the Chorus is however suddenly reversed, as their final remarks are followed by the appearance of Iris and Lyssa.[161]

So, up to this divine appearance, the play shows that there is a gap between gods and humans. Both the Chorus and Heracles' family hope at first that gods will reciprocate, but gradually come to think that they have been abandoned by the gods and consequently criticize them. The arrival of Heracles however proves them wrong and makes them reaffirm their belief in the gods' concern. And when Heracles is afflicted with divinely induced madness, they change their views of the gods once more. It is evident then from the play

---

[161] On the staging of this divine appearance, see Bond 1981: 280; Mastronarde 1990: 260–1, 268–9, 270.

that humans think that they can understand gods, but that gods remain obscure and ultimately unintelligible to them. The unknowability of the gods is an important fact which cannot be played down.

The motivation of the gods in particular is not a straightforward issue in the play. Although all characters attribute Heracles' calamity to the jealousy of Hera, the dialogue between Iris and Hera raises another issue. This scene has rightly been compared with that at the beginning of *Prometheus Bound*, that is, the dialogue between Kratos and Hephaestus (1–87).[162] In each case a god who does not appear in person (Zeus, Hera), sends agents (Kratos and Hephaestus, Iris and Lyssa) against a victim (Prometheus, Heracles). There Hephaestus was the sensitive foil to the ruthless Kratos in the same way as Lyssa is the sympathetic foil to the merciless Iris.[163] Hephaestus participates in the task of shackling Prometheus in fear of Zeus and expresses his sympathy for Prometheus, whereas Kratos exults over Prometheus. As Kratos says, Prometheus is to learn a lesson: δεῖ θεοῖς δοῦναι δίκην, | ὡς ἂν διδαχθῆι τὴν Διὸς τυραννίδα | στέργειν, φιλανθρώπου δὲ παύεσθαι τρόπου, 'he must be punished by the gods, so that he learns to put up with the sovereignty of Zeus and quit his championship of humans' (9–11). Similarly in *Heracles*, Lyssa expresses her sympathy for Heracles and urges Iris and Hera to refrain from inflicting great harm upon him, whereas Iris insists on the plan to destroy Heracles (822–57).

Iris is not simply the agent of Hera's will; apart from carrying out Hera's will, she expresses her own wish to harm Heracles: Ἥρα προσάψαι καινὸν αἷμ' αὐτῶι θέλει | παῖδας κατακτείναντι, συνθέλω δ' ἐγώ, 'Hera, with my co-operation,

---

[162] Some similarities between the two plays in general were noticed by Mullens 1939 and 1941. A detailed comparison of them is given by Jouan 1970. As Jouan concludes, the similarities are too important to be incidental, despite the chronological distance between the two plays. See also Aélion 1983, vol. II, 127–32 and 358–63.

[163] Webster 1967 also compares Talthybius in *Trojan Women*, who has to carry the orders of the Greek commanders but expresses his sympathy for the Trojans.

wants to involve him in kindred slaughter by making him kill his children' (831–2) and also: ὡς ἂν πορεύσας δι' Ἀχερούσιον πόρον | τὸν καλλίπαιδα στέφανον αὐθέντηι φόνωι | γνῶι μὲν τὸν Ἥρας οἷός ἐστ' αὐτῶι χόλος, | μάθηι δὲ τὸν ἐμόν· ἢ θεοὶ μὲν οὐδαμοῦ, | τὰ θνητὰ δ' ἔσται μεγάλα, μὴ δόντος δίκην, 'so that when by his own murderous hand he has made his crown of lovely children cross the river of Death, he may recognize the nature of Hera's anger, and learn mine. Otherwise the gods are worth nothing and men shall prevail, if Heracles does not pay the penalty' (838–42). There is then a sort of justice in the divine intervention and the words of Iris here invite the audience to think that human notions of justice, as presented in the play up to this point, are not the same as those of the gods.[164]

Also, the fact that not only Hera but Iris too is angry with Heracles may recall to the audience the tradition about Heracles' fights against the gods.[165] Heracles' outburst against the gods later on, when he says αὔθαδες ὁ θεός, πρὸς δὲ τοὺς θεοὺς ἐγώ, 'as the gods are stubborn towards me, so am I towards them' (1243), will recall his readiness to rebel against the gods; also, the very use of the term αὔθαδες, 'stubborn', applied to both Heracles and the gods who destroy him, recalls *Prometheus Bound*, where the word is often used both for Prometheus' self-assertiveness towards Zeus, and for Zeus's not very different attitude.[166]

So although after the madness the human characters emphasize the jealousy of Hera as the cause, the play also raises the question of the power of Heracles, which is considered a threat by some gods. The similarities with Prometheus also point in this direction; even the binding of Heracles in his sleep, and his subsequent presentation on stage in bonds when he wakes up, is reminiscent of the

---

[164] Cf. Lee 1982: 106.

[165] Cf. Padilla 1992: 112. Tradition presents Heracles not only as helping the gods in their fight against the Giants (as recalled in Eur. *HF* 177–80, 1190–4) but also as conflicting with or wounding various Olympians. See e.g. Gantz 1993: 445–56.

[166] For the use of the term in the Aeschylean play, see Griffith 1983, on Aesch. *PV* 64–5.

binding of Prometheus. Philostratus, describing a painting of
Heracles' madness which has many similarities with the
Euripidean play, concludes with the following remark: μέχρι
τούτων ἡ γραφή, ποιηταὶ δὲ προσπαροινοῦσι καὶ ξυνδοῦσι τὸν
Ἡρακλέα καὶ ταῦτα τὸν Προμηθέα φάσκοντες ὑπ'αὐτοῦ
λελῦσθαι, 'so far does the painting go; poets, however, treat
Heracles more violently and present him in bonds although
they claim that it was he who released Prometheus from his
chains'.[167]

The gods' exact motivation indeed remains obscure. Iris
says that while Heracles was performing his labours, τὸ χρή
νιν ἐξέσωιζεν, οὐδ' εἴα πατὴρ | Ζεύς νιν κακῶς δρᾶν οὔτ'ἔμ' οὔθ
Ἥραν ποτέ, 'destiny kept him safe and his father Zeus would
not let me or Hera hurt him' (828-9). This complicates the
divine universe which controls human affairs. τὸ χρή here
may denote Zeus's will, or it may signify a separate power
in the universe, which in this case acts in parallel with Zeus.[168]
The use of the term τὸ χρή here recalls the use of the term τὸ
χρεών, 'fate' (21), by Amphitryon, when he conjectures the
motivation behind Heracles' undertaking of the labours.

The motivation behind the gods' acts is not the only case
which is left obscure. The role of Zeus is also an issue which is
brought into question throughout the play. Amphitryon
hoped for Zeus's intervention only to criticize him when he
did not intervene, while Heracles' opportune return was interpreted as proof of divine intervention. After recovering from
his mad fit, Heracles even refuses to call Zeus father on the
basis of his obvious lack of concern for his son. Does Hera then
prevail, and does the play leave us with the sort of vindictive
gods we see at the beginning of *Hippolytus* or *Bacchae*?[169]
Paradoxically it is only Lyssa, the personification of madness

[167] Philostr. *Imag.* II 23.4 (378 K).
[168] See also Grassby 1969: 266; Bond 1981 on Eur. *HF* 828 f.
[169] These gods may be called vindictive, yet they may be said to reciprocate certain
traits of their victims' characters; on this view, see Wildberg 2000, who, in the case
of Heracles, holds that 'the protagonist is overwhelmed by the power of Hera in an
epiphany which reciprocates certain unsettling aspects of Heracles' (ultimately)
human nature and is in the end rescued by Theseus in a human quasi-epiphany,
reciprocating other aspects of Heracles' personality' (246 n. 31).

and therefore the bringer of disaster, who shows concern. But there is something more in *Heracles*, which may suggest that, although the play turns towards a more secular orientation, the divine workings may have another function. This is the introduction of Athena.[170]

If in *Ajax* Athena inflicts madness on the hero, in *Heracles*, on the contrary, she puts an end to madness. Athena's epiphany in *Heracles* is rather peculiar in the sense that it is short in duration, not visible to the audience and mute.[171] *Heracles* is dominated by divine presences as well as divine absences. The absence of Zeus is constantly emphasized from the beginning of the play; Hera is also absent, but, although she does not appear on stage herself, she is 'present' via Iris and Lyssa, who act on her behalf. The unexpected appearance of the two goddesses and their speeches have the effect of a second prologue in the play, and in fact Iris and Lyssa at this point play the directorial role that gods often have in a prologue. They are *didaskaloi*, or more correctly, *hypodidaskaloi*, since they follow the orders of Hera, who sets the action in motion via her two emissaries.[172] The epiphany of Iris and Lyssa however is not the only divine appearance which breaks in suddenly on human affairs. At 905 the Chorus cry out that a whirlwind is shaking the palace and that the roof is collapsing (θύελλα σείει δῶμα, συμπίπτει στέγη).[173] What the Chorus say at this point follows what Lyssa had said would happen after Heracles' murder of his children (864–5).

[170] For the representations of Athena in Greek tragedy in general, see Papadopoulou 2001c.
[171] See Bond 1981 on Eur. *HF* 886–909 and 906–9. The evidence points to cries from within, and while there are parallels for unseen supernatural events responded to from within, it would be harder to find a precedent for a god appearing in view of the audience and not saying anything.
[172] On the directorial role of a god as *didaskalos*, see Easterling 1993b: 80–6 (85 on *hypodidaskaloi*).
[173] What is said to be taking place in the palace here is similar to the palace miracle in *Bacchae* (585–603), for which see e.g. Fisher 1992; Jakob 2000. It is not known whether the fall of the roof and the collapse of the building were possible in Athenian staging or whether the audience had to imagine them; see Goldhill 1993: 6–8. For other examples from Greek tragedy, see Collard et al. 1995 on Eur. *Erec.* fr. 370 K 44–54.

But at 906–9 there is a further shock, and a voice is heard, that of Amphitryon,[174] identifying the presence of Athena: ἢ ἤ· τί δρᾷς, ὦ Διὸς παῖ, μελάθρωι; | τάραγμα[175] ταρτάρειον ὡς ἐπ᾽ Ἐγκελάδωι ποτέ, Παλλάς, | ἐς δόμους πέμπεις, 'Ah, ah! What are you doing, daughter of Zeus, in the palace? The ruin you bring to this house, Pallas, is from hell itself and like the one you brought upon Enceladus.'[176] It should be borne in mind that Amphitryon is at this point the only witness of the events of Heracles' madness, while neither the Chorus nor of course the audience have any direct access to them; this lack of access by the Chorus and the audience marks a strong contrast to their direct access to the stage appearance of Iris and Lyssa, which was in turn inaccessible to Amphitryon. So far there is a clear juxtaposition between two perspectives, an exterior (Lyssa, Chorus, audience) and an interior (Athena, Amphitryon).

Amphitryon's response to Athena's epiphany is further corroborated by the Messenger, another witness of Heracles' madness, who narrates the whole madness scene. His perspective seems to be shared not only by Amphitryon but also by a number of other servants who were present during the madness scene (950–1). After narrating Heracles' murder of his children and wife, the Messenger reports that Heracles was ready to attack the old man, that is, Amphitryon, when a phantom appeared, or at least so it

---

[174] It is not identified in the mss, but there is a strong case for taking it as Amphitryon; see Bond 1981 on Eur. *HF* 906–9.

[175] The word τάραγμα in its various forms is used in the play to express disequilibrium on many levels, from material as here, to psychophysical (836, 1091) to social (533, 605); on these uses, see Schamun 1997.

[176] Note in particular the surprise which the first sentence of Amphitryon causes, before any mention of Pallas Athena, and also the irony that it conveys (906): ἢ ἤ τί δρᾷς, ὦ Διὸς παῖ, μελάθρωι; The Chorus (and the audience) have no reason to doubt that Lyssa continues her disastrous work on Heracles, in which case they must be surprised since Lyssa was not the child of Zeus. In any case, since Amphitryon is unaware of Lyssa's plan, the phrase ὦ Διὸς παῖ must be temporarily taken to refer to Heracles himself as the agent of the collapse of the palace roof. If this is indeed the case, then Barlow 1996: 85, misses this irony by translating the word παῖ with 'daughter' and not e.g. 'child'. Bond 1981 (on 906–9) rightly rejects some critics' suggestions that the lines refer to Heracles and not at all to Athena, but does not note the irony conveyed by l. 906.

seemed, of Pallas Athena brandishing her spear; she hurled a stone at Heracles' breast which put an end to his rage and caused him to sleep (ἀλλ' ἦλθεν εἰκών, ὡς ὁρᾶν ἐφαίνετο | Παλλάς, κραδαίνουσ᾽ἔγχος ⁺ἐπὶ λόφω κέαρ⁺, | κἄρριψε πέτρον στέρνον εἰς 'Ηρακλέους, | ὅς νιν φόνου μαργῶντος ἔσχε κὰς ὕπνον | καθῆκε, 1002–6). Athena's phantom here, brandishing her spear, is also described in terms resembling her statue on the Acropolis.[177] Contrary to Amphitryon's view that Pallas Athena brings ruin to the palace, the Messenger's speech makes clear that in fact it was the intervention of Athena that prevented Heracles from killing his father.

Athena's sudden intervention, which prevents patricide, can be justified both by her association with patriarchal values and by her relationship with Heracles, which is evident both in literary tradition and in art.[178] There are two central aspects of this relationship, firstly the presence of Athena in many episodes in Heracles' life and especially in his labours, and secondly her role in Heracles' apotheosis.[179]

Athena's traditional patronage of Heracles was exercised under Zeus's will,[180] a fact which might hint at Zeus's indirect 'presence' here. In this regard, Athena, as Zeus's intermediary, would have a role parallel to that of both Iris and Lyssa, the intermediaries of Hera. Since her intervention modifies the action, Athena also has a directorial role; she does not set the action in motion beforehand, of course, but she still influences its development in a way that gives her the role of both director and actor. Whether hers alone or Zeus's, there seems to be a directorial authority and voice behind her silent

---

[177] See Bond 1981: on Eur. *HF* 1002. For the significance, cf. George 1994: 155.

[178] Cf. Soph. *Trach.* 1031, where Heracles in agony calls on Pallas, his divine protector. For a brief survey of the literary sources on the relation between Heracles and Athena, see *LIMC* v, 1, 143–4. On this relation in art, see e.g. Amburger 1949; *LIMC* ii, 1, 994–5 and v, 1, 144–54. For gods in the role of protectors, see Beckel 1961 (41–66 on Heracles and divine help).

[179] Other aspects found in art show Athena close to Heracles (often in the same chariot) in the Gigantomachy; on Olympus as Heracles' partner in assemblies of gods or attending Heracles' musical performances or his relaxation as symposiast.

[180] Cf. Hom. *Il.* 8.362–9, where Athena complains to Hera that Zeus does not remember how many times she has saved his son Heracles during his labours. Athena is thus presented as Zeus's intermediary in the role of Heracles' protectress.

presence. If the main function of epiphanic appearances on stage in Greek tragedy is indeed the manifestation of divine power in directing the dramatic action, in a way which recalls the poetic authority in shaping the plot,[181] then a comparison between the two epiphanies, the first of Iris and Lyssa, the second of Athena, seems to emphasize the effect of the former and almost to ignore that of the latter. Athena's epiphany is never mentioned thereafter, as if her appearance did not make any change at all, while her silence leaves her motivation obscure.

But should Athena's epiphany necessarily be taken as a sudden intervention which opposes or at least interrupts the plan set by Iris and Lyssa?[182] After all, when Athena intervenes, Lyssa's plan as foretold in her epiphany has already been fulfilled; to go one step further, the description of the madness scene not only verifies Lyssa's plan but also goes beyond it. Lyssa had foretold that the collapse of the palace would follow Heracles' murder of his children (864–5), but had said nothing about the murder of Megara or the attempted murder of Amphitryon, which are only reported by the Messenger. The implication is that Heracles' rage goes even beyond Lyssa's plan (Heracles in his madness in fact follows the familiar patterns of his heroic rage), to the extent that it causes Athena's sudden interference. The stone that Athena hurls at Heracles, the λίθος σωφρονιστήρ, which Pausanias (9.11.2) saw in the Herakleion at Thebes,[183] halts Heracles' rage (cf. οὐ σωφρονίζει, 'is uncontrolled', 869). Both Athena's sudden intervention and the stone that she uses suggest the urgency of the situation which the goddess comes to rectify and the difficulty of her task, which is further stressed by the comparison of her action here to that against Enceladus.[184]

---

[181] Easterling 1993b.
[182] Bond 1981 on Eur. *HF* 904 f., assumes different motivations between Lyssa and Athena.
[183] Bond 1981 on Eur. *HF* 1004.
[184] There is another instance where Athena hurls a stone: in *Iliad* 21.403–8 she throws a stone against Ares, who is often associated with the fury of the battle (but not only with this: in *Iliad* 15 it is his anger and wish for revenge which are described as madness, esp. 128, 138). The stoning of madmen appears in other contexts (e.g. Ar.

With the coming of Theseus and his support for Heracles the action moves towards an Athenian context. As Mikalson puts it, Euripides 'is dramatizing an aetiology of how Heracles came to be in Athens and why he is worshiped in the places he is'.[185] If Athena stopped Heracles from committing patricide,[186] Theseus prevents him from committing suicide. Thus, Athena's intervention could be viewed as a foreshadowing of the future role that Athens will play,[187] an idea which seems to be enhanced as soon as Theseus appears on stage. Theseus prefaces his promises to Heracles with an invitation to follow him to Athens. The phrase that Theseus uses for Athens is 'the city of Pallas Athena' (1323). Bond[188] comments: 'Tragedy is rich in synonyms for Athens'; his remark is correct but perhaps he fails to note the significance that the choice of this particular synonym may have. It is the city of Pallas Athena, the goddess whose narrated epiphany in the play contributed crucially to the development of the dramatic plot in halting Heracles' madness. In this respect, it is hard to detach Athena from the sequence of the dramatic events.

Conclusion

The presentation of Heracles' madness is traditional in that it dramatizes a divine causation for madness and it is also conventional in the description of the symptoms. The new

---

Vesp. 1491; Ar. *Av.* 524–6). For stones in relation to madness and its cures, see Mattes 1970: 53 and n. 1; Simon 1978: 152, 306 n. 53; for stones in relation to madness as pollution, see Padel 1995: 100–2; on stoning in general, see Rosivach 1987. Athena's intervention, which halts Heracles' rage, also signifies a change in the musical tune, that is, the end of the 'piping madness' (cf. 871: τάχα σ᾽ἐγὼ μᾶλλον χορεύσω καὶ καταυλήσω φόβωι, 'I shall soon make you dance more wildly and I shall play upon you a pipe of terror'; 894–5: δάιον τόδε | δάιον μέλος ἐπαυλεῖται, 'the tune being played on the pipe is truly murderous'), as she silences the wild sounds of madness; as Wilson 2000: 438 aptly points out, her throwing of the stone recalls her discarding of the aulos (Melanippides, *Marsyas* fr. 758. 1–2 *PMG*).

[185] Mikalson 1991: 223.
[186] Carrière 1972 interprets Athena's intervention allegorically, as a message of peace after Heracles' massacres, which are taken to symbolize the first years of the Peloponnesian War.
[187] Gregory 1991: 139–40.   [188] Bond 1981 ad loc.

aspect is that Heracles' insanity also problematizes the status of Heracles when sane. Madness does not impose upon Heracles an action which is entirely alien to his normal activity; he follows his familiar course of action throughout his mad fit, the only difference being that he is made to misperceive reality around him. The similarities between the behaviour of Heracles in both madness and sanity invite the audience to think about the unstable position of Heracles after the completion of his labours. His mad behaviour becomes a device that facilitates the gradual humanization of Heracles by making him choose humanity over divinity. The play's end, with Theseus' promises and the move towards an Athenian context, offers a place for Heracles in the establishment of his future cult.

Apart from the secular orientation of the play the function of the divine is an issue which is raised and runs parallel to it. The morality of the gods and their concern for humans are questioned, and humans have to come to terms with living in a world where gods destroy innocent victims. Humans measure the gods' behaviour according to their own standards and see that they are often superior to gods in excellence. The criticism of the gods, which results from human despair at finding the gods lacking, reaches a climax in this play where Heracles refuses to call them gods. But gods continue to exist, and human condemnation of them is ultimately irrelevant. Even more, the crucial point given emphasis is that humans fail to understand gods because they judge them by human standards. The divine universe has its own rules; gods can both destroy and show concern for humans as the scene between Iris and Lyssa, with the diametrically opposed views of the two goddesses, shows. The conclusions that human characters draw about the gods are not the last word that the play has to say. The intervention of Athena, with all the implications that this has for the role of Zeus, shows that the divine universe is not simply the one that Heracles has recognized, that is, full of imperfect gods. Gods may have been criticized severely by the suffering Heracles, but the religious context remains intact. It is important in this sense that the play ends with the announcement of a future cult for Heracles.

CHAPTER 3

ARETE AND THE IMAGE OF ATHENS

Introduction

The previous chapter focused on the interrelated themes of madness and divinity in the play. Madness becomes a dramatic device which problematizes the question of Heracles' valour, and which also moves the plot towards an Athenian context. When Heracles recovers from his mad fit, he resolves to commit suicide, but the intervention of Theseus, the representative of Athens, succeeds in dissuading him from killing himself. The crucial role of Theseus and of Athens invites a consideration of the political overtones of the play. At the same time, the change in the plot, with Heracles' decision to live, brings to the fore the issue of Heracles' *arete*, 'excellence', which is variously illuminated throughout the play. This chapter deals with the related issues of *arete* and the image of Athens, looking at what is distinctive about Heracles in relation to the rest of Euripides' surviving tragedies.

Amphitryon, Megara and Lycus

The motif of supplication is used in many tragedies.[1] Whereas the usual pattern is that suppliants find refuge in the territory of their potential rescuer, in *Heracles* the situation is different. In Heracles' absence, his father, wife and children,[2] threatened

---

[1] On supplication in general, see Gould 1973; on supplication in tragedy see also Lattimore 1964: 46–7; Kopperschmidt 1967; Burian 1972 and 1974; Aélion 1983, vol. II, 15–61; Rehm 1988; Mercier 1990.

[2] The presence of the children is meant to evoke pathos, especially since the play moves towards their murder by their own father. On children in Greek tragedy in general, see Sifakis 1979; in Euripides, see Masqueray 1906; de Romilly 1960, esp. 61–2; Menu 1992.

with death by the usurper tyrant Lycus, are sitting at the altar of Zeus the Saviour in a state of despair (44–54). Here the family confront an enemy instead of trying to secure help from a deliverer.[3] Supplication functions as a context for exposing the motivation of the people involved at a moment of impending crisis. In this sense, the main confrontation is that between suppliant (Heracles' family) and enemy (Lycus), while the usual confrontation, that between suppliant and deliverer, is postponed till Heracles' return. The situation is similar to that in *Andromache*, where the confrontation between the suppliant (Andromache) and the deliverer (Peleus) follows the long encounter between the suppliant and an enemy (Hermione and then Menelaus).[4] In *Heracles*, the significance of supplication as a ritual act seems in fact to be subordinated to the importance given to the secular confrontation between the suppliants and their enemy.[5] At the same time, the length of this scene, compared to the rest of the play, has often been considered unjustified and the content of it melodramatic or irrelevant.[6]

However, this part of the play is significantly relevant to Heracles and in particular it elucidates the theme of nobility and the course of action that nobility prescribes.[7] The confrontation between Amphitryon and Megara, and their different approaches to the dire situation they are in, anticipate Heracles' attitude and the decisions he has to make after he recovers from madness.[8] The kinds of action prescribed in

[3] The suppliants' attempt to persuade a potential deliverer to help usually takes the form of a confrontation between the two parties; this is the typical form in e.g. Aeschylus' *Suppliants*, in Sophocles' *Oedipus at Colonus*, and in Euripides' *Heraclidae* and *Suppliants*.

[4] See Maio 1977: 21–7. On the importance of supplication as a structural element in *Heracles*, see Karabela 2003.

[5] For the function of supplication in terms of its varying religious significance in Euripidean drama, see in general Jaekel 1972.

[6] This is an old view; cf. Ehrenberg 1946: 158; Norwood 1954: 46. On various approaches to the structure and unity of the play, see esp. the summary given in Barlow 1993: 193–4. Perhaps the most extreme view is that of Carrière 1952, who explained the seeming lack of unity in the play by arguing that Euripides must originally have written the part up to Heracles' arrival and deliverance of his family from Lycus as a separate drama.

[7] For a discussion of the theme of nobility in the play, see esp. Gregory 1991: 123–8.

[8] On these issues, see esp. Chalk 1962 and Adkins 1966: 209–19.

their different ways by Amphitryon and Megara, and the underlying motivation that the language suggests, are important because they relate closely to what Heracles, the 'best of men', stands for and because they foreshadow his preoccupations later on.

Since this scene brings out the importance of *arete* to Megara and Amphitryon, and its complete unimportance to Lycus, we need to ask what sort of *arete* this is. The dangerous situation of Megara and Amphitryon does not simply relate to anyone caught in frightful circumstances; it concerns the ways in which a noble person should act and more specifically how Heracles' family are expected to behave. In other words, Heracles' being *aristos* and the son of Zeus creates extreme difficulties and expectations for the family. The behaviour of Heracles' family is modelled on his exceptional status, and will be reflected, in turn, in his own decisions at the end of the play.

The range of words used to refer to Heracles' excellence centres upon the ideas of noble birth and bravery. The word *aristos* (150, 183) signifies particularly bravery or physical courage, while the word εὐγενής (50) refers primarily to Heracles' noble descent from Zeus.[9] The references to Heracles show that in fact he combines several qualities that make him outstanding. He is the son of Zeus, he is brave, he defends his people and offers service to the whole of mankind (220–6), he honours the gods (cf. 49), shows respect to his father (cf. 17–18), and is a good family man. *Arete*, excellence, is a term with a whole range of meanings, and each time the context is essential. For example, when Amphitryon exclaims that he surpasses Zeus in *arete* (342), the underlying implication here is specifically Amphitryon's willingness to help his son's family and not betray the relationship of *philia*.

Arete-related terms are used in the course of this scene not only to refer to specific persons but also in passages which have a gnomic character. The universal applicability of these sayings

---

[9] Being of divine origin and showing extreme bravery are interrelated. The two are clearly distinguished at 696–700, where the Chorus say that Heracles' bravery (<ἀρεταῖ>) has by far surpassed his divine descent (εὐγενίας).

further illuminates for the audience aspects of excellence and outlines the course of action which *arete* entails. At 105–6, Amphitryon ends his speech with a *gnome*: οὗτος δ᾽ ἀνὴρ ἄριστος ὅστις ἐλπίσιν | πέποιθεν αἰεί· τὸ δ᾽ ἀπορεῖν ἀνδρὸς κακοῦ, 'and the bravest man is one who has always put his trust in hope. To despair is the mark of a coward.' Here Amphitryon introduces a contrast between hopefulness and despair as the distinctive features of the best man and of the coward respectively.[10] Amphitryon's words serve as a reply to Megara's implicit identification of his tenacious clinging to hope and life as cowardice (90).[11] Amphitryon's optimism, which is contrasted throughout with Megara's resignation (88–106),[12] lies to a great extent in his trust in Zeus and in his confidence that the god will intervene in favour of his son, while in Megara's case her belief in the inscrutability of the gods (62) makes her see hope as futile.[13]

The placing of Megara's speech (275–311) immediately after the Chorus (very unusually) are given a long rhesis (252–74)[14] and unequivocally denounce Lycus, ending with the claim that the city is 'not of sound mind' (272) and 'sick with stasis' (173), suggests the complexity of the situation and makes the question of how one should behave in such circumstances all the more difficult. Since imminent death is inevitable, she suggests that the family should opt to die voluntarily rather than be murdered, that is, they should leave the altar where they have taken refuge and die willingly to preserve their good reputation.[15]

---

[10] On Amphitryon's use of the terms here, see Adkins 1966: 212 and Bond 1981: 90–1.

[11] Contrast Eur. *Heracl.* 533–4, where Heracles' daughter expresses her determination to die a glorious death rather than cling to life. On the idea that it is cowardice to prolong a life of shame and not choose an honourable death, cf. Soph. *Aj.* 473–4; Pl. *Ap.* 37c6.

[12] Hope in antiquity was sometimes regarded as good and sometimes as bad; see Bond 1981 on Eur. *HF* 105 f.

[13] For a reading of each relationship in the play, both with humans and with gods, in terms of the principle of reciprocation, see Becroft 1972.

[14] For choral reactions to threats, see Hose 1991: 360.

[15] Burnett 1971: 157–82 argues that leaving the altar means a violation of the ritual of supplication, and that Amphitryon and Megara are faithless suppliants. For a refutation of Burnett's thesis, see Bond 1981: xix.

Despite her affection for her children,[16] voluntary death is her preferred course of action, which is in turn discussed in terms of avoiding dishonour and the charge of cowardice (280–94). What could be a speech of hatred or despair is turned into a bold argument for behaving as *eugeneis*, 'noble' and 'courageous' people should.

Megara believes that the course of action she suggests follows Heracles' example (294: ἐμοί τε μίμημ' ἀνδρὸς οὐκ ἀπωστέον).[17] The heroic ethos that she wants to follow in accordance with Heracles' status disapproves of fighting against necessity, as this is a characteristic of the fool (σκαιόν, 283), and of being ridiculed by one's enemies (285–6), and recommends voluntary death instead of disgrace (289–93). Voluntary death is thus described as an act of courage (τόλμα μεθ' ἡμῶν θάνατον, 'brave death with us', 307), which is consistent with both Amphitryon's and Megara's noble birth and with their relation to Heracles and what he stands for.

The idea of behaving in a way consistent with one's noble descent appears in other contexts, again in relation to voluntary death. In *Heraclidae*, Heracles' daughter asserts her willingness to sacrifice herself by saying (507–14):

> ... ἐπεί τε καὶ γέλωτος ἄξια,
> στένειν μὲν ἱκέτας δαιμόνων καθημένους,
> πατρὸς δ' ἐκείνου φύντας οὓ πεφύκαμεν
> κακοὺς ὁρᾶσθαι· ποῦ τάδ' ἐν χρηστοῖς πρέπει;
> κάλλιον, οἶμαι, τῆσδ' - ὃ μὴ τύχοι ποτέ -
> πόλεως ἁλούσης χεῖρας εἰς ἐχθρῶν πεσεῖν
> κἄπειτ' ἄτιμα πατρὸς οὖσαν εὐγενοῦς
> παθοῦσαν "Αιδην μηδὲν ἧσσον εἰσιδεῖν.

for it deserves nothing but mockery if we sit and groan as suppliants of the gods and yet, though we are descended from that great man who is our father, show ourselves to be cowards. How can this be fitting in the eyes of men of nobility? Much finer, I suppose, if this city were to be captured

---

[16] The emphasis on Megara's love for her children (e.g. 70–9, 280–1, 451–89) intensifies the personal cost of her decision to subordinate her affection to her preoccupation with honour.

[17] On Megara as the surrogate for Heracles and on the relation between female and male roles, see Michelini 1987: 246–50. On Megara's discussion of nobility in terms of the male heroic code, cf. Evadne's words in Eur. *Supp.* 1059–63.

(God forbid!) and I were to fall into the hands of the enemy! Then when I, daughter of a noble father, have suffered dishonour, I shall go to my death all the same![18]

The determination to act nobly and do something worthy of one's kin is evident in *Orestes*, when Orestes urges Pylades as follows (1060–4):

ἀλλ' εἰ' ὅπως γενναῖα κἀγαμέμνονος
δράσαντε κατθανούμεθ' ἀξιώτατα.
κἀγὼ μὲν εὐγένειαν ἀποδείξω πόλει
παίσας πρὸς ἧπαρ φασγάνωι · σὲ δ' αὖ χρεὼν
ὅμοια πράσσειν τοῖς ἐμοῖς τολμήμασιν.

Now come on, let's make sure we do something noble and fully worthy of Agamemnon when we die! I'm going to prove my nobility to the city by stabbing to my liver with a sword; and you in turn must match my brave efforts.[19]

To return to *Heracles*, the choice of honourable death in the midst of utter despair is presented as the action that the family of Heracles, the outstanding hero, should follow. It is the way in which the father, wife and children of Heracles should behave in order to avoid disgrace and to live up to their reputation as members of Heracles' family. A similar choice of voluntary death will present itself as an option to Heracles himself when he has to come to terms with the aftermath of his mad fit.

---

[18] Translation by Kovacs 1995. For courage in association with self-sacrifice, cf. Eur. *Hec.* 347–8 (Polyxena): θανεῖν τε χρήιζουσ' · εἰ δὲ μὴ βουλήσομαι, | κακὴ φανοῦμαι καὶ φιλόψυχος γυνή, 'I desire to die: if I shall not be willing, I shall appear a coward, a woman too fond of life' (transl. Collard 1991). The rest of Polyxena's speech suggests that the course of action she chooses is fitting to her noble birth (349–78). Cf. Eur. *IA* 1375–86 (Iphigenia's determination to die). Cf. Sophocles' *Philoctetes*, where the way in which Neoptolemus, Achilles' son as he is repeatedly called (cf. 50, 240–1, 260, 1237), is expected to act in accordance with his noble nature and with what his father stands for, is a central theme. Towards the end of the play, Philoctetes says (1310–13): . . . τὴν φύσιν δ' ἔδειξας, ὦ τέκνον, | ἐξ ἧς ἔβλαστες, οὐχὶ Σισύφου πατρός, | ἀλλ' ἐξ Ἀχιλλέως, ὃς μετὰ ζώντων ὅτ' ἦν | ἥκου' ἄριστα, νῦν δὲ τῶν τεθνηκότων, 'you showed the nature, my son, of the stock you come from, having not Sisyphus for father, but Achilles, who had the greatest fame while he was among the living and has it now among the dead' (transl. Lloyd-Jones 1994). For another context where Neoptolemus is expected to prove himself worthy of both his grandfather Peleus and of his father Achilles, cf. Eur. *Andro.* 342–3.

[19] Translation by West 1987. In a play which problematizes heroic ethos in general, Orestes' words here may have an ironic overtone.

The debate over *arete*

The debate between Amphitryon and Lycus in the course of
the first episode (140–251) raises other issues concerning the
absent Heracles which are relevant when he recovers from
madness.[20] In this confrontation, Lycus and Amphitryon
attack and defend respectively the heroic valour and reputation of Heracles. As Lloyd comments,[21] this debate resembles
an agon-scene, but also has some features which differentiate it
from a typical agon, such as the disparity in length between the
two speeches and the absence of both an introductory dialogue
and a choral comment in between. Lloyd takes this confrontation as an example of the type of scene which may be termed
epideixis, in which a character responds to a provocation by
uttering a long speech. Another *epideixis* speech occurs at the
end of the play, when Heracles, provoked by Theseus, argues
at length that his life is unendurable (1255–1310).

Lycus represents a sceptical and rationalistic approach to
the question of Heracles' divine origin and to the miraculous
character of his deeds. He expresses his disbelief in Zeus's
fatherhood of Heracles, which was the very first thing stated
in this drama in Amphitryon's opening self-identification (τὸν
Διὸς σύλλεκτρον, 1, 'who shared his wife with Zeus'). For
Lycus, the alleged divine origin of Heracles is nothing more
than an empty pretension, as is the claim that Heracles is the
best of men (148–50). Heracles was the traditional ἀνὴρ
ἄριστος.[22] For example, in *Trachiniae*, despite the negative
aspects of his presentation, he is 'the best of men' in the
words of both Deianira (ἀρίστου φωτός, 177) and Hyllus
(ἄριστον ἄνδρα, 811).[23] Lycus' assertion that Heracles is not an
ἀνὴρ ἄριστος is thus meant to be shocking and paradoxical,[24]

---

[20] On debates in Greek tragedy, see Duchemin ²1968; Collard 1975a; Arnott 1989:
   105–31; Lloyd 1992.
[21] Lloyd 1992: 10–11.   [22] Cf. Murray 1946.
[23] Cf. Soph. *Trach.* 1112–13, where the Chorus stress Heracles' distinct worth.
[24] On this and other paradoxical speeches in Euripides and the influence from rhetoric, see Bond 1981: on Eur. *HF* 151–64.

as Amphitryon's reaction shows, when he considers Lycus' accusations 'unspeakable' (174–6).

Despite their seemingly paradoxical nature, and although they are uttered by a figure who is meant to be repulsive, Lycus' rationalizations are effective in casting doubt over the miraculous element in Heracles' exploits and thus in questioning the hero's valour. Also, Lycus' scepticism is not an isolated example of such an attitude but finds parallels in other rationalizing approaches to myth in antiquity. This type of approach towards the myths about Heracles, and more particularly the critique of several factual elements in these myths, is attested for example already in the sixth century BC. Thus Hecataeus rejected the traditional description of Cerberus as a monstrous creature and used etymology to argue that he was merely a snake, albeit a more fearsome one than others.[25] Lycus reduces the fierce hydra which Heracles managed to kill to a mere marsh snake by adding the adjective ἕλειον, 'of the marsh' to the word ὕδραν, 'hydra' (152), and he also says that the verbal similarity between the words βρόχοις, 'nets' and βραχίονος, 'arm' lies behind the fact that, although Heracles caught the Nemean lion in nets, nevertheless he claims to have used his bare hands to strangle it. Lycus is not the only one who uses this kind of argument; other more admirable characters in Euripides use similar types of reasoning, as when Teiresias uses the similarity between the words μηρός, 'thigh', and ὅμηρος, 'hostage', to explain the myth of Dionysus (Eur. *Bacch.* 292–7). Apart from the rationalizing approach to Heracles' exploits, Lycus' attempt to underestimate the importance of such exploits in comparison to warfare (157–61) is also presented in another Euripidean play, when Aethra warns Theseus that he runs the risk of being accused of cowardice, for he may have fought against monsters but now he hesitates to fight in battle (Eur. *Supp.* 314–19).

Amphitryon's defence of Heracles against Lycus' accusation cannot of course provide rational proof of the miraculous element in Heracles' deeds, but instead invokes the divine.

---

[25] *FGrH* 1 F 27. See also Bond 1981 on Eur. *HF* 23 and Galinsky 1972: 23–4.

He leaves the defence of Heracles' divine origin to Zeus (170–1) and calls on divine witnesses in order to refute Lycus' accusation that Heracles is a coward (175–6). Thus he asks Zeus's thunderbolt, and his chariot in which Heracles rode when he helped the gods against the Giants, to testify to Heracles' bravery (177–80). He also asks Lycus to go to Pholoe, the place of Heracles' Centauromachy, and ask the Centaurs whom they would judge to be ἄνδρ᾽ ἄριστον, 'the bravest man' (183). Here the characterization of Heracles as 'the best of men' is almost self-evident.[26] But in the case of Amphitryon's reference to Heracles' Centauromachy, one might also wonder if any of the Centaurs has escaped from the battle to testify to Heracles' strength. The Chorus in the first stasimon (348–441), with their enumeration and celebration of Heracles' labours, will corroborate Amphitryon's defence of the miraculous element in Heracles' deeds, which Lycus provokingly questioned. But Lycus' rationalism should not be taken as an easy target which the lengthy reply of Amphitryon is meant to fully invalidate.[27] Rationalization of myth cannot be refuted by means of an appeal to the validity of myth. Amphitryon's and Lycus' approaches are diametrically opposite, but Lycus' expression of scepticism is enough to raise the question of Heracles' prowess; it is this question after all that is problematized throughout the play, especially with the advent of madness, which turns Heracles' violence towards his own kin.

Heracles and the bow

The main part of the debate between Lycus and Amphitryon, which is in general on the question of Heracles' valour,[28] is devoted to a disparagement and a defence of archery in its

---

[26] Cf. Ar. *Nub.* 1048–50.

[27] Bond 1981, discussing the disparity in length between the speeches by Lycus and Amphitryon, comments that 'Euripides could surely have done better in making the case against Heracles' (102). *Contra* Bond, and for an evaluation of the function of Lycus' provocation, see Barlow 1996: 131.

[28] On this issue in the debate, see e.g. Taragna Novo 1973.

opposition to the hoplite system,[29] as the bow is presented as
the weapon of Heracles *par excellence*. The association of
Heracles with the bow here is pointed if one thinks that in
tradition Heracles was not exclusively an archer. In [Hesiod's]
Shield, he still has his quiver and arrows (129–31) but his
armour is that of a hoplite, as the emphasis on the description
of his shield indicates. In *Trachiniae* too, Heracles is said by the
Chorus to be carrying bow, spears and club: τόξα καὶ λόγχας
ῥόπαλόν τε τινάσσων (512). Interestingly, despite the exclusive
association of Heracles with the bow during the archery
debate, the hero is not presented consistently as an archer
throughout the play. Already in the prologue, Amphitryon
says that the altar of Zeus the Saviour where the suppliants
have taken refuge was set up by his noble son to glorify his
victory after he defeated the Minyans, in a fight which
Amphitryon describes as that of a hoplite: βωμὸν καθίζω τόνδε
σωτῆρος Διός, | ὃν καλλινίκου δορὸς ἄγαλμ᾽ ἱδρύσατο | Μινύας
κρατήσας οὑμὸς εὐγενὴς τόκος, 'I sit here at the altar of Zeus
the Saviour – an altar which my son in his nobility established
to glorify his splendidly conquering spear after he had defeated
the Minyans' (48–50). It is true that the word δόρυ 'spear', may
be used metaphorically to mean 'war',[30] but in this play, where
the weapon discourse is important, the mention of the word in
the prologue is a clear association of Heracles with the spear.

Similarly, when Theseus arrives and asks Amphitryon who
is the man beside the dead bodies, Amphitryon describes his
son as the man who fought as a warrior on the side of the gods
during the Gigantomachy: ἐμὸς ἐμὸς ὅδε γόνος ὁ πολύπονος,
<ὃς> ἐπὶ | δόρυ γιγαντοφόνον ἦλθεν σὺν θεοῖ- | σι Φλεγραῖον
ἐς πεδίον ἀσπιστάς, 'it is my son, my own son, who has
suffered so many labours and <who> came as a warrior with
the gods to the plain of Phlegra to kill the Giants' (1190–4).
The image of Heracles as a hoplite here sharply contrasts with
his portrayal, earlier in the play and again in the words of
Amphitryon, as an archer in the same battle: Διὸς κεραυνὸν

---

[29] On hoplites, see Hanson 1991; van Wees 1992.
[30] See LSJ s.v. δόρυ II 2.

ἠρόμην τέθριππά τε, | ἐν οἷς βεβηκὼς τοῖσι γῆς βλαστήμασιν |
Γίγασι πλευροῖς πτήν᾽ ἐναρμόσας βέλη | τὸν καλλίνικον μετὰ
θεῶν ἐκώμασεν, 'I ask the evidence of Zeus's thunderbolt and
four-horse chariot in which he rode, piercing in the ribs with
winged arrows the Giants, spawn of the earth, and celebrating
glorious victory with the gods' (177–80). The presentation of
Heracles as a bowman in the second example is understandable, as it is part of the speech in which Amphitryon also
defends the heroic valour of Heracles as an archer. The contradiction between the two passages about the status of Heracles
in the Gigantomachy may of course be too slight for an audience to notice,[31] or it may imply carelessness on the part of the
playwright. Instead of charging Euripides with carelessness,
however, one could argue that in a play in which a debate
focuses on the juxtaposition between archers and hoplites,
with Heracles being presented clearly as an archer, references
which also portray Heracles as a hoplite may not be without
significance.

Recent work has attempted to appreciate the cultural registers[32] underlying this debate between Amphitryon and Lycus,
at one time criticized as undramatic, and to trace its thematic
relation to the rest of the play.[33] It is worth examining the
arguments closely.

Lycus marks the bow as the weapon of the coward and
contrasts the archer, who is a coward because he is ready to
run away, with the hoplite, who is brave because he stands
steadfast in his rank and looks face to face at the advancing
troops (158–64). The bow as a cowardly weapon of course may
sound strange if one considers that it was the attribute of two
divinities, Artemis and Apollo, at the hands of whom it was the
manifestation of supreme power, as it was used to cause sudden death.[34] But the context here is different as it applies to
human warfare, so Amphitryon has to use arguments from the
human sphere. His reply to this part of Lycus' accusation is

[31] So Bond 1981 on Eur. *HF* 1194.
[32] See esp. Foley 1985: 167–75; Michelini 1987: 243–6.
[33] See esp. Hamilton 1985; Padilla 1992.
[34] On this, see e.g. Morillo 1995: 31–6.

that the bow, instead of being a cowardly weapon, is a clever invention. Amphitryon in fact shifts the emphasis from bravery itself to the cleverness and effectiveness of the bowman, which are described as the best tactics in warfare. Thus, contrary to the spearman, the archer is self-sufficient because he does not depend on comrades, his endless supply of arrows makes sure that he is never in a state of helplessness, and he always attacks his opponents from a position of safety because he is invisible to his enemies (188–203).

Lycus is of course a repulsive character in the play and his accusations of cowardice against Heracles may at first seem as unacceptable to an audience as they seem to Amphitryon. But does Amphitryon's reply invalidate Lycus' arguments, or are the audience invited to take Lycus' points seriously? Indeed the debate over archery cannot be said to end with a clear refutation of Lycus' arguments by Amphitryon. Rather, the audience are invited to think about the issues raised and the implications that they have for the central theme, that is, Heracles' *arete*. To begin with, the solidarity of the hoplites in their military formation and the hoplite's bravery, which form the core of Lycus' argument, must have been familiar to the Athenian audience of the play, and one might have thought the defence of the hoplite system would have struck them as particularly valid, since it played a significant part in the development of Athenian democracy.[35] But they may have been surprised at the same time, because the defence of the hoplite is actually uttered by a tyrant.

On the other hand, Amphitryon is trying to praise Heracles as an archer, but some of the things he singles out for praise – the archer's isolation and self-sufficiency, for example – may have had negative connotations, recalling for the audience the individualistic ethic of the archaic hero who seeks personal distinction, as opposed to the Athenian communal ethic which values collective action.[36] Besides, in the class-division of fifth-century Athens hoplites were higher up in the hierarchy than

[35] On this issue, see Foley 1985: 169 and n. 41 for further bibliography.
[36] See Foley 1985: 174–5. On Heracles' individualistic ethos, cf. Gregory 1991: 130.

archers.[37] The bow was also associated with slaves and barbarians, especially the Scythians and the Persians respectively.[38] During the Persian Wars in particular, the association of the bow with the Persians was common to the extent that Aeschylus could use the words 'bow' to symbolize the Persians and 'spear' the Greeks (*Pers.* 146–9).

On the other hand, in the course of the fifth century and during the Peloponnesian War in particular, the recognition of the importance of the archers, as of other light troops, in warfare contributed to a rehabilitation of the status of archery.[39] This became more evident for the Athenians after their success at Sphacteria in 425 BC and their failure to employ archers at Delium, where they suffered defeat, in 424 BC. It used to be a commonplace of Euripidean scholars of the so-called historicist school[40] to link the debate between Amphitryon and Lycus with these events of the Peloponnesian War and the changing attitudes towards the status of archery. Representatives of this type of approach treat literary texts in general as sources for historical information and attempt to find correspondences between them and historical events.[41] In the case of *Heracles*, the belief that the play reflects specific events of the Peloponnesian War has also led scholars to speculate that the date of its production was around 423.[42] The

[37] Cf. Bond 1981: 109.

[38] The Scythian bowmen who constituted the police force in Athens were slaves. On Scythians and the Scythian bow, see Snodgrass 1967: 82–4. On various Greek attitudes towards archery, see Snodgrass 1964: 141–56; Morillo 1995, esp. 27–9; in relation also with attitudes to hoplites, see esp. Snodgrass 1967: 48–99; Lissarrague 1990: 13–20.

[39] On archery during the Peloponnesian War, see Goossens 1962: 348–54. On the increased status of the bow during this period, cf. Snodgrass 1967: 98–9.

[40] On this, see Michelini 1987: 28–30.

[41] Cf. Parmentier and Grégoire 1923; Delebecque 1951; Ehrenberg 1954; Goossens 1962; Podlecki 1966. For a recent approach of this type to *Heracles* along with Sophocles' *Trachiniae*, see Vickers 1995.

[42] No date for the play has come down to us from antiquity. An attempt to date it on the basis of metrical evidence brings it close to *Trojan Women* of 415 BC (*c.* 415 BC is the date given by Diggle in his OCT edition of the play; so Bond 1981: xxxi). For general discussion of the date, see Bond 1981: xxx–xxxii. In their discussion of the date of the play Goebel and Nevin 1977: xxix–xxxi, conclude that neither contemporary allusions nor metrical evidence can be said with certainty to be conclusive, and assign the play to the period 424–414 BC. For attempts to use Aristophanes'

tendency, however, to find clear echoes of contemporary history in tragedy has given way to approaches which examine the potential political implications of tragedy in the broadest sense, where evocation of ideology becomes more crucial than references to specific public events.[43]

So far I have argued that for the Athenian audience both the arguments which devalue the role of archery and those of Amphitryon which praise its effectiveness may be said to be grounded in fifth-century beliefs and practices. What emerges, therefore, from the controversy over the importance of archery is a sense of the ambiguous character of the bowman. Accordingly, the implication for the reception of the debate between Amphitryon and Lycus is that both sides give valid arguments, and consequently the overall picture of Heracles' valour becomes ambivalent. The same conclusion may be reached by examining the role of the bow in literature. Indeed the debate over archery in *Heracles* seems to be informed by several examples from the literary tradition of the bowman.

A well-known bowman from tradition was the Homeric Paris-Alexandros. He is described as an archer in *Iliad* 3 (16–20),[44] where he is boastful and imprudent rather than really brave. This becomes clear from the vivid description of his terror at the sight of Menelaus (*Il.* 3.30–7). His withdrawal brings a strong rebuke from Hector (39–57), who questions his brother's courage (45). His lack of ability in fighting is evident in his defeat by Menelaus and his narrow escape only by means

plays as a *terminus ante quem*, see e.g. Delebecque 1951: 131 (the *Clouds* of 423 BC). See also the interesting points made by Beta 1999: 156–7, who argues that an older, different version of the Euripidean *Heracles* (cf. the two Hippolytus plays produced by Euripides) may be alluded to in Aristophanes' *Wasps* of 422 BC. In all these cases, however, the evidence is not conclusive.

[43] Zuntz 1955 is an early representative of this type of balanced approach to Greek tragedy and contemporary history. See also esp. Gregory 1991: 6–12; Pelling 1997, esp. 216–17; Hesk 2000; Matthiessen 2004: 9–35.

[44] Paris also carries a sword and two spears, which may seem a strange accompaniment for a bowman. The two spears here are better understood as light javelins as opposed to the heavy spear normally used by warriors, which Paris himself will later use in his duel with Menelaus. See Kirk 1985: 267–8. In Soph. *Trach.* 512 too, the two spears that Heracles is said to be carrying are rather to be understood as javelins.

of Aphrodite's prompt intervention (380). The rest of book 3, with the scene between Helen and Paris, further elaborates the image of Paris as a warrior of ambiguous valour (esp. 432–6), who is better off inside the 'perfumed chambers' (383), that is, the locus of femininity, than in the battlefield.[45]

The spearman's contempt for archery, as exemplified for example by Diomedes in his scorn for Paris (*Il.* 11.385–95), may be said to be typical in the *Iliad*. Although Pandarus and Teucer, who are also bowmen, are not scorned for cowardice, the norm of fighting in this epic is face to face and not from a distance.[46] With regard to the denigration of Paris as an archer, it is interesting that in the post-Homeric tradition it is Paris who causes Achilles' death by the fatal wound his arrow inflicts on the Greek hero. Thus Diomedes, who is wounded on his foot, may scorn Paris for causing him nothing more than a scratch, but a similar wound on Achilles' foot was to be the most effective and become Paris' most famous exploit.[47]

In the *Odyssey*, with its more 'refined' system of values and its emphasis, as exemplified by Odysseus, on intellectual rather than physical prowess, the bow becomes a symbol of heroic ambivalence. In the hands of Heracles it symbolizes supreme valour, which however is at the same time an older type of defiant and transgressive valour, while in the hands of Odysseus it is a clever weapon that symbolizes an advanced and civilized type of heroic excellence.[48] When Odysseus himself

---

[45] See Lissarrague 1990: 18–19 for associations of the bowmen with femininity.

[46] Cf. Hainsworth 1993 on *Il.* 11.385–95. It must be pointed out that Pandarus' status is not very high; he is the one who wounds Menelaus and violates the truce in *Il.* 4.104–8.

[47] An example from the *Iliad* which illustrates how although archers were considered to be less brave than spearmen, they were nevertheless particularly welcome because of their contribution to the battle, is found in *Il.* 13.712–22. Here it is said that the Locrians were not spearmen but archers, and consequently they lacked the courage to endure close-standing fight; but they were particularly effective, as they caused confusion to the Trojans with their arrows. As for the crucial role of archers in military success, it was by means of Philoctetes' bow that Troy was eventually sacked, a fact which informs the plot of Sophocles' *Philoctetes*, as well as the plots of lost plays by Aeschylus and Euripides.

[48] Cf. Morillo 1995. On Heracles as a foil to Odysseus in the *Odyssey*, see esp. Galinsky 1972: 10–12; Foley 1985: 171. On Heracles in the Homeric epics, see in general Galinsky 1972: 9–15; Bauren 1992.

describes his supreme skill in archery in *Odyssey* 8 (221–8), he is modest in admitting his own inferiority to famous archers such as Heracles and Eurytus, but he dissociates himself from them in that he does not misuse his ability as they did.[49]

Finally, it is worth mentioning two examples from Greek tragedy where the bow is brought to the fore. In the angry confrontation between Menelaus and Teucer in *Ajax*, a juxtaposition is introduced by Menelaus between the archer and the spearman in order to scorn Teucer, a well-known bowman in the *Iliad*: Menelaus looks down on Teucer for being an archer, whereas Teucer asserts that he is braver than Menelaus (1120–3). When in the exodos an equally repulsive Agamemnon succeeds Menelaus in confronting Teucer, the latter speaks in defence of his brother Ajax's heroic valour (1266–88). Here Teucer the bowman praises Ajax's bravery as a spearman and shows that his brother was a greater warrior than Agamemnon. He also mentions in passing his own services on Ajax's side, and in this way he comes back to his self-defence in reply to the accusations uttered against him (1288). Agamemnon scorns Teucer for being barbarian and slave (1228–35; 1259–63), which recalls the common association in antiquity of archery with barbarians and slaves. But the important thing is that Teucer answers Agamemnon's taunts by repeating them sarcastically[50] and returns the same insults to Agamemnon, showing that in fact they apply to Agamemnon and not himself (1289–1307). Overall, the controversy over the status of archery in *Ajax* is constructed in a way which shows that although there is a tendency to denigrate bowmen, they could also be vigorously defended.

The bow is of primary significance in *Philoctetes*, where it is closely associated with heroic achievement. References to it permeate the play, and its visible presence as a stage prop

---

[49] Although the nature of Eurytus' transgression is clearly outlined, that of Heracles is only alluded to. The most famous example was Heracles' use of his bow to attack Hera and Hades in *Iliad* 5 (392 and 395), which seems also to be referred to here in *Odyssey* 8, although the word ἐρίζεσκον at 225 implies not an attack but a challenge. See Heubeck et al. 1988 on *Od.* 8.225.

[50] Cf. Garvie 1998 on Soph. *Aj.* 1289.

places it in a central position in the drama and makes it crucial for the development of the dramatic plot. The bow also closely associates heroism with genuine friendship.[51] Thus Heracles gave it to Philoctetes in recognition of the latter's act of friendship in agreeing to light the funeral pyre for the hero (801–3). Philoctetes recalls this when he allows Neoptolemus to handle the bow (667–70) and when later in his agony he hands it over temporarily to him (776–8). Neoptolemus, following Odysseus' plan, keeps the bow and abandons Philoctetes. The theft of the bow means a breach of the newly established friendship between Philoctetes and Neoptolemus, which was grounded in deception. Conversely, the restoration of genuine friendship between them goes hand in hand with Neoptolemus' change of mind and decision to return the bow to its owner. When Heracles appears in the end as a *deus ex machina*, he foretells that Philoctetes, judged the best in the army, will be chosen to fight against the archer Paris and will thus lead to the capture of Troy. The favourable portrayal of archers and archery is unfailing so far. But Heracles adds an important qualification. The partnership of Philoctetes and Neoptolemus is fundamental for future success (1433–7).[52] The necessity for this partnership reflects the theme of genuine friendship which is stressed throughout the play, but it also shows the importance that the combination of an archer (Philoctetes) and a spearman (Neoptolemus) has in warfare.[53]

I will now go on to show how this issue is raised and clarified in *Heracles* as a whole. It is clear from several references in the play that the spear is the standard weapon of military confrontation.[54] For example, in the parodos, where the

---

[51] On this aspect, see Gill 1993, esp. 95–7. For other discussions of the role of the bow in the play, see e.g. Harsh 1960; Lada-Richards 1997.

[52] The friendship and heroic collaboration of Neoptolemus and Philoctetes is set at the end of Heracles' speech in a context that has troubled many readers (e.g. the warning at 1440–4 about *eusebeia*, 'piety', and the implied reference forward to events at the sack of Troy); see Segal 1995a: ch. 4.

[53] Webster 1970 on Soph. *Phil.* 1436 aptly suggests the similar association of Ajax and Teucer. Cf. also this association in the words of Teucer himself in Soph. *Aj.* 1288.

[54] Cf. 60–1 and 288 (Amphitryon); 65–6 (Megara's father); 224–5 (Greek expedition). Lines 65–6 have been suspected by Diggle as an amendment by a scribe; see Diggle 1994: 90–1 and Barlow 1996 ad loc. For a defence of the lines, see Bond 1981 ad loc.

Chorus come hobbling in, lamenting their old age and weakness,[55] they try to find support in one another (126–30), similar to the solidarity they used to have in battle, which is described by means of an image of hoplite formation:

γέρων γέροντα παρακόμιζ',
ὧι ξύνοπλα δόρατα νέα νέωι
τὸ πάρος ἐν ἡλίκων πόνοις
ξυνῆν ποτ', εὐκλεεστάτας
πατρίδος οὐκ ὀνείδη.

Let the old support the old who once were united in arms in the battles of their youth when they were young together, no disgrace to their country's fame.

This association between youth and spear will be recalled when both Amphitryon (232–5) and the Chorus remember the glorious deeds of their past and lament their present feebleness and helplessness before the tyrant (268–9; 436–41).[56]

On the other hand, it is the bow that predominates throughout the First Stasimon (348–441), where the Chorus sing and glorify Heracles' labours (364–7; 389–93; 419–24).[57] In contrast to the spear, which is the weapon used in organized combat among humans, the bow, which is used in Heracles' labours, is used against creatures that represent the uncivilized world which Heracles' deeds were meant to tame. In this regard, the bow is a weapon that stands in between wildness and civilization. The fact that the literary tradition regularly presented Heracles as both archer and spearman may not be enough to explain the similar presentation of him in the play. Rather, the choice of his equipment each time may be pointed. Thus for example the fight against the Minyans takes place within and not outside the world of civilization, and Heracles

[55] On complaints about old age in Greek tragedy, see Byl 1975.
[56] To continue with the weapon imagery, the mention of the spear that Athena brandishes (κραδαίνουσ' ἔγχος, 1003) when she appears to put an end to Heracles' madness may also be significant in a play where the bow and the spear have been juxtaposed.
[57] On these labours in the ode, see Pralon 1992; on Heracles' exploits in literature and art, see Brommer 1984 and 1986.

here is portrayed as a spearman (49–50).[58] Conversely, the bow is said by Megara to be the weapon with which her husband sacked Oechalia (472–3). In *Trachiniae*, when Lichas recounts this event to Deianira, he says that Heracles led an army of mercenaries against the city (259–60, cf. 74–5, 478; 856–9). What in Sophocles is a victory achieved by collaboration, is described in Megara's words as Heracles' individual heroic exploit. At the same time nothing is said of the circumstances surrounding this exploit, that is, Heracles' passion for Iole and the murder of Iphitus, which must have been well known to the Athenian audience and may have been evoked at the mention of the name Oechalia by Megara.[59] So, the bow in this context is not only symbolic of Heracles' valour but also becomes suggestive of his negative side.

If the bow belongs to the wild world of the labours, the use of it after the completion of these labours and within Thebes seems inappropriate. Thus, when Heracles threatens to kill the treacherous Thebans and fill the river Ismenus with their corpses, the excessive character of his revenge is also coloured by the announcement that his bow will be the instrument of their murders (571). Another weapon he says he will use against the Thebans is his club, again a weapon from the world of his labours. This weapon is given the glorifying epithet 'gloriously conquering': καλλινίκωι (570). This is a standard epithet of Heracles and is recurrent in the play.[60] But its use now for Heracles' weapon outside the labours is not unproblematic. Indeed, the entire context of Heracles' revenge links the past of his labours with the present situation (574–82).

The Chorus will also use the epithet καλλίνικος, 'with glorious victory', to describe the murder of Lycus by Heracles: καλλίνικον ἀγῶνα, 'contest gloriously won' (789). When

---

[58] The fight against the Minyans is also mentioned at 220 and 560. See Bond 1981 on Eur. *HF* 220.

[59] The date of Sophocles' *Trachiniae* is unknown, but Heracles' sack of Oechalia and his association with Iphitus and Iole were treated before the fifth century; see Gantz 1993: 434–47.

[60] See Bond 1981: index i under Heracles as καλλίνικος; it is one of the repeated motifs of the play, for which see Hangard 1976.

147

Heracles uttered his threats against the Thebans he began with his intention to go to Lycus' palace, 'cut off his unholy head and throw it out as dog food', but in the event he followed Amphitryon's suggestion and agreed to wait for the tyrant to arrive at his house. Amphitryon was worried in case Heracles was seen entering the city. Heracles' reply (595–8) begins with what may be said to stress his bravery; he would not care if the whole city had seen him. But immediately afterwards he says that he entered the city secretly in response to a disturbing omen:

ὄρνιν δ' ἰδών τιν' οὐκ ἐν αἰσίοις ἕδραις
ἔγνων πόνον τιν' ἐς δόμους πεπτωκότα,
ὥστ' ἐκ προνοίας κρύφιος εἰσῆλθον χθόνα.

But after seeing a bird of omen in the wrong quarter I knew that there was trouble in the house. And so foreseeing this, I made my approach secretly. (596–8)

His secret entrance here recalls the image of the bowman, familiar from the debate between Amphitryon and Lycus, as the one who acts in secrecy, that is, from a position where he himself detects and explores the situation without being detected.

The plan which Amphitryon then lays out is that of luring Lycus into a trap instead of attacking him directly. The whole plan aims at helping Heracles win safely (604), and this emphasis on safe victory is another element which recalls the image of the bowman.[61] When the revenge plot is put into action and Lycus is lured into the palace where Heracles waits to kill him, Amphitryon describes the trap as one set for hunting animals; in particular, he says that Lycus will be caught in snares of nets, similar to those where animals are trapped and then killed by the sword (729–30).[62] The metaphor of the nets used here recalls Lycus' rationalizing argument in the debate, that Heracles did not fight against the Nemean lion with his bare hands but merely caught it in nets (153–4). Lycus' argument there was intended to scorn Heracles' valour. Amphitryon's use of the metaphor from hunting may have a similar

[61] Cf. Padilla 1992: 4.   [62] See Bond 1981 on Eur. *HF* ad loc.

connotation for the audience, and it may perhaps be recalled when Lycus screams from offstage that he is being killed by guile (ἀπόλλυμαι δόλωι, 754). Lycus' words here make Heracles' revenge lose its heroic element. Lycus' murder is of course justified, and this is the way in which the Chorus answer his words: καὶ γὰρ διώλλυς· ἀντίποινα δ᾽ἐκτίνων | τόλμα, διδούς γε τῶν δεδραμένων δίκην, 'you were a murderer yourself. Resign yourself to paying your debts, taking the penalty for what you did' (755–6). But there is no reply to Lycus' criticism of Heracles' act as the result of treachery; for them the murder of Lycus is 'a contest gloriously won' (789).[63]

When Iris and Lyssa later appear before a terrified Chorus, Iris describes the purpose of their coming in military terms, as an attack directed not against the whole city but against one individual, Heracles (824–5). Lyssa's sudden attack (861–7), the invisibility of the goddess throughout it (874), and the fact that she constantly remains in control of the situation with her victim unable to react, recall the characteristic mode of action of the bowman as it was described in the debate between Amphitryon and Lycus.[64] Also, the goddesses' joint plan against Heracles resembles the revenge plot set up by Amphitryon and Heracles against Lycus. It is Lyssa now who appropriates the role of bowman *par excellence* and makes Heracles her helpless victim. This reversal stresses the change in Heracles' state from invincibility to vulnerability.

Finally, and alarmingly, the ambivalence of the bow as a weapon is stressed during the madness scene, where it becomes the means by which Heracles kills his family. At the beginning of his madness, Heracles asks for his bow and club, the weapons used during his heroic career (942). Thinking that he is attacking Eurystheus' family, he prepares his quiver and

---

[63] Heracles uses treachery also against Iphitus (Soph. *Trach.* 270–3), where treachery further depreciates an atrocious murder. The treachery against the Moliones has negative overtones as Pausanias (5.2.1–2) says that it caused the anger of the Epeians, while Pindar's version (*Ol.* 10.27–34) stresses heroic achievement. (For another example of Heracles' use of ambush, see Ap. Rhod. *Argon.* 2.966–9, where Heracles captures an Amazon.)

[64] Cf. Padilla 1992: 5.

arrows against his own family (969–71). The whole scene of Heracles' madness is full of violent action: he strikes the first son (979), aims his bow at the second and eventually kills him with the bow (984–94), and brings down his wife and third son with a single arrow (995–1000). The phrase used to describe the killing of Megara and the son (δάμαρτα καὶ παῖδ 'ἑνὶ κατέστρωσεν βέλει, 'brought down his wife and child with one arrow', 1000) is reminiscent of the Chorus' description of Heracles' Centauromachy in the First Stasimon: Κενταύρων ποτὲ γένναν | ἔστρωσεν τόξοις φονίοις, 'he laid low with his bloody bow the race of Centaurs' (365–7).

Overall, in his madness Heracles uses the same violence that he exercised during his labours, but with horrific inappropriateness, because he directs it against his own family. His weapons, which are the instruments and thus also the symbols of his supreme heroic valour, become the instruments of kin murder. But since the murder of his family is presented as the result of divinely imposed madness, the unwitting murder of his family is less problematic than his delusion that his victims are Eurystheus' sons, and his use of his heroic weapons to kill them. Eurystheus is of course his enemy and the killing of his sons may have seemed justified, but in a play where Lycus attempts to do the same with Heracles' children, and which abounds in expressions of affection for children, the motivation behind Heracles' action complicates his heroic image, with the bow again used as its symbol. There is the sense that Heracles' violence during the labours is justified and his valour is glorified because of the importance of these labours for mankind. But the use of violence outside this context is not always unproblematic, especially in cases where its motivation and results are brought into question (e.g. the sack of Oechalia or the murder of 'Eurystheus'' children). Thus the bow, which is a civilizing weapon during the labours, proves to be ambivalent when used in inappropriate contexts, and when the world of labours and the world of civilization, especially the domestic sphere, merge.

Finally, what attracts Heracles' attention and puzzlement when he recovers from his mad fit is his weapons scattered

around him: πτερωτὰ δ 'ἔγχη τόξα τ'ἔσπαρται πέδωι, | ἃ πρὶν
παρασπίζοντ'ἐμοῖς βραχίοσιν | ἔσωιζε πλευρὰς ἐξ ἐμοῦ τ'
ἐσώιζετο, 'there scattered on the ground are my bow and
arrows, which have always been like a fighting shield for my
arms and have protected my sides and were protected by me'
(1098–1100). The image of the bow being like a shield which
both protected and was protected by the hero recalls the
hoplite.[65] The likeness of the bow to a shield in the words of
Heracles, if viewed in the light of the earlier juxtaposition
between the archer and the hoplite in the debate between
Lycus and Amphitryon, shows that the function of the metaphor is in fact to evoke the picture of Heracles as both a
bowman and a hoplite. Also, Heracles' first reaction, which
is to wonder whether he is back in Hades, suggests the continuity between his last labour, the descent to Hades to fetch
Cerberus, and his present situation, which is as yet unrealized by
him, that is, his murders. Violence and death characterize both.

The image of Athens in Greek tragedy

I mentioned above, in the context of the archery debate in the
play, how political interpretations of tragedy used to be limited
for the most part to finding correspondences between the texts
and the historical events of the time. On the other hand, the
majority of recent studies have focused on the socio-political
function of Greek tragedy and on its relation to the *polis*; in
particular, they have variously explored Greek tragedy as a
democratic institution, which reaffirmed civic identity and
communal cohesion but also problematized ideological structures and the implications of being a citizen of the fifth-century
Athenian city-state.[66] The association of Greek tragedy with

---

[65] Cf. Eur. *Tro.* 1194–5.
[66] See esp. Goldhill 1986; Euben 1986 and 1990; Vernant and Vidal-Naquet 1988
[their work was originally published in the 1970s]; Winkler and Zeitlin 1990;
Gregory 1991; Meier 1993; Sommerstein et al. 1993; Croally 1994; Goff 1995;
Easterling 1997; Pelling 1997; Zelenak 1998; Rhodes 2003. Seaford 1994 also
stresses the preoccupation with the concerns of the *polis* in Greek tragedy, but his
difference from other approaches is that he sees a development in the plays towards

democracy has also led to studies which examine the relevance
of the political discourse to modern political theory.[67] But
the universal validity of the idea that Greek tragedy was inextricably interwoven with Athenian democracy has also been
challenged in studies which stress that the social character of
tragedy was far wider than the democratic context of its production, a factor which accounts for the continuous popularity
of Greek tragedy after the end of democracy.[68]

There are various ways, then, in which one can approach the
political character of Greek tragedy. My own approach is
concerned with the way in which typically Athenian qualities[69]
are reflected in the plays. It is true that *Heracles* stresses the
friendship between Theseus and Heracles, but Theseus is also
the leader of Athens, and as such, he symbolizes qualities
which are meant to glorify the city. Such qualities include
Athenian independence and willingness to defy any risks in
order to help the weak. Because the presentation of Athens and
the qualities that it stands for are essential for an understanding of the role of Theseus in *Heracles*, in what follows I will
briefly outline the favourable portrayal of Athens in Greek
tragedy.

Athens plays a prominent part in Greek tragedy,[70] under-
standably enough, as tragedy was one of the most significant
creations of Athens and addressed issues which, despite their
mythological distance, were directly relevant to the Athenians.
Athens is a city beloved by the gods, which may be threatened
but which never incurs disasters.[71] References to Athens abound

the communal benefit (of the democratic city-state), following the destruction of the
ruling families and the foundation of cults in the end which strengthen solidarity.
Seaford's approach is particularly insightful, although its universal applicability to
Greek tragedy is questionable, especially because not all plays end with cult or with
the 'happy' prospect of 'democratic' collectivity.

[67] See e.g. Euben 1986: 1–42 and 1990: *passim*; Rocco 1997.
[68] See Griffin 1998 and 1999. Cf. also works on the reception and dissemination of
theatre beyond Athens, e.g. Taplin 1999.
[69] Cf. the praises of Athens in oratory; most famously in Pericles' *Epitaphios* in
Thucydides.
[70] On Athens in Greek tragedy, see e.g. Grossmann 1970: *passim*.
[71] Cf. Parker 1997: 149. In Euripides' *Erectheus*, Eumolpus and his father Poseidon
attack Athens, but Athena intervenes to save the city; on the play, see Collard et al.
1995: 148–94.

and their inclusion often reveals a tendency to glorify the city;[72] to mention one example out of many, the Chorus of the Trojan women in *Trojan Women* wish they could be sent to Athens (208–9).[73] The praise of the city (cf. 218–19) here is intensified because it is uttered by captives for whom Athens and the rest of Greece are their enemy who has enslaved them. Also, if disasters strike royal households in other cities, especially Thebes in extant tragedies, Athens often becomes the city which provides a solution. This is not to say that the plays present a polarity between Thebes and Athens as representing exclusively negative and positive qualities respectively.[74] Thebes as a whole is not without positive characteristics, but whenever a crisis emerges in it or in other cities in the plays, Athens is the city which can ensure that there is a positive development to the plot.

In *Heraclidae*, Athens is glorified for being the only city which offers refuge to Heracles' children. The free and unyielding character of Athens (55–62, 284–7) is matched by another characteristic, that of πολυπραγμοσύνη,[75] which is criticized by the Argive herald (109–10; 139–52). This is a critique of the Athenian policy of interference in the affairs of other states, a policy criticized by her enemies and those states which wanted their autonomy, but defended by the Athenians as a manifestation of their power and often justified as an expression of altruism. *Heraclidae* is a fine example of the latter justification, as what Athens is asked to do in the play is to intervene and

---

[72] There are always of course exceptions to this; thus for example *Ion*, a play which is directly relevant to Athens and glorifies Athenian autochthony, also contains Ion's sceptical remarks about some aspects of life in this city (589–606); on Ion's speech and its relevance in the play, see in brief Lee 1997: 225–6.

[73] The context here is important, as Athens is one of several places they mention; see Easterling 1994.

[74] Zeitlin's view of Thebes as 'anti-Athens' (1990), is particularly insightful, but its universal applicability has also been challenged. See Easterling 1989: 13–14; Taplin 1999: 50–1; more recently, see Angeli Bernardini 2000a and esp. Cerri 2000. Cf. Rehm 2002. A common mistake in following Zeitlin's view uncritically is shown for example in Tyrrell and Bennett 1998, who, in interpreting Sophocles' *Antigone*, often take too much for granted when they hold that for the Athenian audience a Theban character *qua* Theban is expected to act unjustly; see Papadopoulou 2000b.

[75] On πολυπραγμοσύνη, 'officiousness' or 'meddlesomeness' in Athenian politics of the fifth century, see e.g. Ehrenberg 1947; Kleve 1964; Adkins 1976; Allison 1979.

settle a dispute by defending justice. This interference glorifies Athens because the city defies all risks involved in making enemies and starting a war. The city is also praised for adhering to the law regarding prisoners of war; if we allow that something has been lost from the text before 1053, Eurystheus' prophesied protection of Athens after his death comes as a reward for the just way in which he was treated by the city (1026–44).[76]

In Euripides' *Suppliants* and in Sophocles' *Oedipus at Colonus*, Theseus embodies laudable characteristics of the Athenian democracy. Theseus as the representative of Athenian democracy seems to contradict his status as a king, but the combination of democracy and monarchy was a paradox which the plays could turn to their advantage; in the distant heroic past which is dramatized by tragedy, heroes were kings, and the representation of Athenian democracy which was inherent in this genre could thus take concrete form in these kings, especially in Theseus, who was the national hero of Athens.[77]

In *Suppliants*, Theseus is persuaded by his mother Aethra to secure the burial of the seven leaders who died in the war against Thebes. Aethra's concern is the honour of her son and the city (293),[78] and her speech shows the qualities that are to be understood as typically Athenian. Aethra justifies the policy of Athenian interference, the essence of πολυπραγμοσύνη, as that which glorifies the city, for it is through this policy that the city is shown to be upholding a panhellenic law and to be acting according to the will of the gods (301–13). It is this policy that contrasts Athens with other cities which remain quiet and have no glory (320–5). Similarly, the attack on Athenian πολυπραγμοσύνη, 'meddlesomeness',

[76] The acquiescence of the Chorus in the killing of Eurystheus at 1053 is problematic after their apparent mildness earlier. For the abrupt ending and the suspected lacuna, see Wilkins 1993: xxx–xxxi and on l. 1052.

[77] On the problematic relation between 'Theseus the king' and 'Theseus the representative of Athenian democracy', see esp. Davie 1982; Walker 1995.

[78] With regard to the presentation of Theseus in the *Suppliants*, it has often been held that the play is about the character of this hero (see esp. Shaw 1982); but Theseus should rather be understood as the representative of Athens; on this, see e.g. Collard 1975b, vol. i, 30.

though understandable in the words of the herald later (467–75, 576), is immediately followed by praise of this quality by Theseus; for Athens, interference results from Athenian might and contributes to Athenian greatness (577).[79]

Theseus' response to the herald, which is in general informed by Aethra's earlier speech, highlights what Athens stands for and how the city is expected to act. The city cannot be intimidated by threats (cf. 542), is free and consequently will not accept orders from another state (518–21). What is most important is the defence of the panhellenic custom that requires the burial of the dead, which Theseus invites the Thebans to uphold (524–7). Similarly in *Heraclidae*, it was the determination to uphold another sacred institution, that of supplication, which was behind Demophon's response to the herald; when the herald asked him if Athens was a place where criminals could take refuge (259), Demophon asserted the right of supplication (260). Finally, as in the *Heraclidae*, so in this play Athens' benefaction is rewarded at the end of the play (1165–73) by ensuring that the Argives show their gratitude in generations to come.

In *Oedipus at Colonus* it is again Athens and Theseus who provide help by accepting the suppliant Oedipus. Oedipus appeals to the way in which Athens should be expected to act (258–62); he is a suppliant, and driving him away is an unholy crime which would damage the fine reputation of Athens (282–5). Theseus' attitude to Oedipus is that of immediate pity and determination to help despite his terrible destiny that had made the Chorus shriek with fear (σὺ δὲ τῶνδ᾽

---

[79] Defying all risks involved in interfering is of course in accord with an idealized image of Athens. It must be noted, however, that the plays also reflect some uneasiness on the part of the Athenians, concerning the extent or the cost of their interference. The idealized image can co-exist in the plays with sharp awareness of potential discord over policies. For example, in *Heraclidae*, not all the members of the assembly which Demophon has to consult consider the offer of help to Heracles' family to be right (415–19). For readings which argue that irony undermines the patriotic tone of these plays, cf. Fitton 1961; Gamble 1970. A more balanced approach has been put forward by Mills 1997, who stresses the patriotic character of the *Suppliants* and explains the ironies as showing that in the tragic genre, which brings human limitation to the fore, even the Athenian ideal cannot be a panacea for all problems (see ch. 3 and 265–6).

ἑδράνων πάλιν ἔκτοπος | αὖθις ἄφορμος ἐμᾶς χθονὸς ἔκθορε, | μή τι πέρα χρέος | ἐμᾶι πόλει προσάψηις, 'and do you leave this seat and hasten away from my country, for fear you may fasten some heavier burden on my city!', 233–6;[80] cf.254–7). Indeed, the difference between the original reaction of the Chorus, who wanted to drive Oedipus away, and the reaction of Theseus, who is welcoming and eager to help, is meant to highlight the qualities represented by Theseus and, consequently, by Athens.[81]

Theseus feels pity for Oedipus and is willing to grant him whatever request he may have (556–9). He himself has also been an exile (562–4), and he knows that all humans are fragile and thus that compassion for others is essential (566–8). Theseus' insight here into the mutability of human life and the recognition of the importance of human fellowship is reminiscent of a similar situation in *Suppliants*. There for example the fragility of life was used by Adrastus in his attempt to persuade Theseus (176–9). The use of an argument based on the uncertainty of human prosperity is understandable when put into the mouth of a person who asks for help. But the acceptance of the validity of this argument by the person who is prosperous at the time is rare; thus for example, the Thebans in the *Suppliants* were inflexible because they were over confident in their power as if it would last for ever. By contrast, Aethra was moved with pity for the plight of the suppliants and persuaded her son to offer help. The important thing, then, is the recognition of the mutability of life and the value of human fellowship not simply by people who are in need of help, but by those who are prosperous and in a position to either offer or refuse it.[82] Thus, Theseus' readiness to help Oedipus highlights his qualities as a leader, which in turn reflect on his city and its

[80] Translations from *Oedipus at Colonus* will be quoted from Lloyd-Jones 1994.
[81] Cf. Mills 1997: 169, who compares Sophocles' *Oedipus at Colonus* and Euripides' *Suppliants*, and argues that in both plays the principles of the ideal Athens are highlighted by the different approaches by Theseus and the Chorus and by Aethra and Theseus respectively.
[82] On these issues and their effects in Greek tragedy, see Papadopoulou 1999b.

values.[83] Accordingly, Oedipus' gratitude to Theseus for his help against Creon's insolence glorifies Theseus and his city for their unique qualities (καί σοι θεοὶ πόροιεν ὡς ἐγὼ θέλω, | αὐτῶι τε καὶ γῆι τῆιδ'· ἐπεὶ τό γ' εὐσεβὲς | μόνοις παρ' ὑμῖν ηὗρον ἀνθρώπων ἐγὼ | καὶ τοὐπιεικὲς καὶ τὸ μὴ ψευδοστομεῖν, 'And may the gods grant you what I desire, for yourself and for this country, since I have found in you alone among mankind piety and fairness and the absence of lying speech!', 1124–7; cf. 1552–5).[84]

Heracles and Theseus

I turn now to an examination of how Heracles responds to his circumstances and how this response is informed by the presentation of Theseus and Athens. Heracles' question ποῦ ποτ' ὢν ἀμηχανῶ; 'wherever am I that I can be at a loss?' (1105) is the culmination of his reversed situation, from the hero of the labours to complete helplessness, the very opposite of his normal state.[85] The reference to his bonds is also important. It was first made by the Messenger (1009), and then, when the *skene* doors open and the *ekkyklema*[86] reveals Heracles tied to the pillar among the corpses of his children and wife,[87] the Chorus describe what the audience can now see (1032–8). The strong image of a passive Heracles tied to a pillar stresses the hero's vulnerability and weakness, a state so strange to Heracles that it bewilders him when he wakes up (1094–7). The strange image of Heracles in bonds may also be said to recall

---

[83] Theseus is aware of the dangers of faction at Athens; cf. 1031–3.

[84] This can be taken seriously by an Athenian audience even when the speaker is himself a liar, as Creon is shown to be.

[85] Cf. Pind. *Nem.* 7.96–7, where it is said that Heracles often delivers mortals from helplessness. In Aeschylus' *Prometheus Unbound* (fr. 199.6–9 Radt), Prometheus predicts that Heracles will be in a state of helplessness in his fight against the Ligurians, but Zeus will eventually help him; on the fragment, see Griffith 1983: 299–300.

[86] For the use of the *ekkyklema* here, see e.g. Bond 1981 on Eur. *HF* 1028 ff.; Halleran 1988: 6–7; Barlow 1996: on Eur. *HF* 1029.

[87] This picture of Heracles among corpses is the culmination of a series of images relating to death in the play; on this, see Petre 1985: 23–5.

Prometheus being tied to a rock in *Prometheus Bound*. In both cases the greatness of the heroes is sharply contrasted with their immobility and vulnerabilty. The rest of the play will offer a kind of answer to Heracles' helplessness in a way that will recall similar issues which Amphitryon and Megara were faced with at the beginning.

Heracles' first reaction upon learning about the murders he has committed is to decide to kill himself (1146–52). His wish to die is motivated by three factors;[88] his grief for the loss of his children (1147), his wish to avenge their murder (1150) and his fear of dishonour (1152). The sight of Theseus makes Heracles veil his head, fearing that he will pollute Theseus and in shame for what he has done (1159–62). Upon arriving and seeing Amphitryon, Theseus declares that he has come with an army to help Heracles' family against Lycus, and mentions his earlier rescue by Heracles in Hades (1163–71). This rescue was earlier mentioned by Heracles himself in answer to Amphitryon's asking what was the reason for his delay (619). The reference there is made in passing and the mention of Theseus (619–21) may serve to foreshadow the role that Theseus will play later. But what is important now with Theseus' arrival is that Athens turns out to be the only city which is willing to help Heracles' family and show gratitude to the hero. From the beginning of the play the theme of ingratitude, both of individuals and of cities, has been heard several times. Already in the prologue Amphitryon remarks that true *philia* is tested in times of unhappiness (55–9, cf. Megara's remark: ἄφιλον, ἵν' αὖθίς σοι λέγω, τὸ δυστυχές, 'I repeat, trouble means an absence of friends' 561). The Chorus make an implied accusation of the Greeks' inactivity when they end their first song with an impassioned reference to what the loss of the children will mean ('Ελλὰς ὦ ξυμμάχους | οἵους οἵους ὀλέσασα | τούσδ' ἀποστερήσηι, 'O Greece, what allies, what allies you will lose if you are deprived of these boys!', 135–7). Amphitryon later lashes out against the ingratitude of both Thebes and Greece towards his son's services to them (217–28).

---

[88] See Adkins 1966: 214.

The ingratitude of the Thebans in particular (cf. 560) will make Heracles utter threats against them (568–73).

Thus, the emphasis on the ingratitude of everyone else gives prominence to the readiness of Theseus and his city to interfere and to start a war if necessary (1163–5) in defence of Heracles' family. But Theseus comes too late, as he himself immediately realizes when he sees the corpses on the ground. If Theseus has not arrived in time to save the family, he will now offer help to Heracles. The prolonged period during which Heracles sits veiled and silent while Amphitryon explains the situation to Theseus stresses Heracles' passivity and the helplessness of his state, which had driven him to suicidal despair. The intensity of the scene (1178–1213) is conveyed by means of the metrical pattern, which is an exchange between Amphitryon's sung lyrics (mainly dochmiacs) and Theseus' spoken trimeters, where the use of *antilabē* underlines the urgency of the situation. As Amphitryon explains to Theseus, Heracles has veiled his head αἰδόμενος τὸ σὸν ὄμμα | καὶ φιλίαν ὁμόφυλον | αἷμά τε παιδοφόνον, 'he is ashamed that you might look at him, ashamed before your friendship of kin and at the blood of his murdered children' (1199–1201).[89] The emotional intensity is deepened in the supplication scene between Amphitryon and Heracles (1203–13). Amphitryon's words contain a comment on Heracles' previous intention to kill himself, which is now presented as the result of inflexibility and as an unholy murder which would add to the present misfortunes (1210–13). The lion image used to describe Heracles' inflexible character (1211) encapsulates the problem that Theseus faces in trying to dissuade his friend from suicide.

Theseus does not fear pollution (1214–19). As he said to Amphitryon earlier (1202), he is determined to help Heracles in his trouble; by contrast with people who do not want to share

---

[89] The veiling of the head is a reaction generated by the feeling of αἰδώς, 'shame'; see Cairns 1993: 292; cf. Bond 1981 on Eur. *HF* 1160–2. The peculiarity of Heracles' αἰδώς here is that the phrase αἷμά τε παιδοφόνον, 'the blood of his murdered children' (1201) introduces a retrospective sense to the notion of αἰδώς, which comes very close to the notion of guilt (cf. 1160). This is interesting, for αἰδώς is usually inhibitory, not retrospective; on this, see Cairns 1993: 295–6.

other people's troubles and to help their friends, Theseus stresses his willingness to help his friend in his misfortunes (1220–5). Thus, if Theseus earlier, by bringing his army to Thebes, proved his superiority to others who did not try to help Heracles' family, now he is again unique in his determination to help Heracles in his troubles. Theseus does not hesitate to help the polluted Heracles, nor to bring him to Athens.[90] His urging of Heracles to uncover his head[91] and look at those around him (1226–7) is also an invitation to his friend to live, and as it is immediately followed by a gesture with which Theseus himself removes the veil from his friend's head (cf. 1231), it foreshadows the active and crucial role that Theseus will play in persuading Heracles to live. Theseus argues that the truly noble man must bear the misfortunes sent by the gods (1227–8). This stress on the value of endurance as an alternative to suicide, and its association with nobility, bring to the fore and problematize the central issue after Heracles' attack of madness, that is, whether Heracles should kill himself or live. There is an echo here of a similar issue at the beginning of the play, as exemplified by the different attitudes of Amphitryon and Megara before the desperate situation they had to face.

Theseus' role as Heracles' helper, which shifts the focus from Heracles to Theseus, is not without significance if one considers the relation between these two heroes in Athens.[92] Theseus' heroic career was modelled upon that of Heracles, and in his *Life of Theseus* (29.3), Plutarch calls the Athenian hero ἄλλος ʽΗρακλῆς, 'another Heracles'. Heracles was also a

[90] On the danger of pollution in general, see Parker 1983. It is the magnanimity of Athens which is emphasized when the city dares to accept a polluted person; in this respect, see Mills 1997: 151 and n. 102, against Tarkow 1977, who held that Athens' rash acceptance of dangerous murderers (as in the case of Medea) is problematic; cf. Wolff 2001: 15.

[91] In Eur. *Supp.* 111, Theseus urges Adrastus to uncover his head and stop his weeping. In this play too Aethra covers her head (286). In both cases, veiling of the head is due to grief. Cf. Iolaus in Eur. *Heracl.* 604. On the stage history of this gesture, see Arnott 1989: 62–3.

[92] On Theseus in antiquity, see Dugas and Flacelière 1958; Ward 1970; Calame 1990. On his role in Greek tragedy in relation to his role in Greek society, see Walker 1995; Mills 1997.

popular figure during the tyranny of Peisistratus,[93] and although the advent of democracy shifted the emphasis from Heracles to Theseus, Heracles remained popular, and his traditional association with Athena, which was still strong and not eliminated after Theseus also became her protégé, is a factor which may partly explain his popularity.[94] But the modelling of Theseus upon Heracles was not enough for the Athenians. Thus, the tendency in Athens during the fifth century was to give Theseus a more eminent role than Heracles.[95] This process is characteristic of Athens, where Theseus was the national hero, although outside Athens Heracles was a greater hero still; Theseus was essentially a local hero and never reached the panhellenic status that Heracles had.[96] The story of Heracles' rescue of Theseus, when the latter went to Hades with Peirithous, was well known, but its effect was rather to glorify Heracles, since thereafter Theseus was indebted to him.[97] By contrast, the development of the plot in *Heracles*, with Theseus' help to Heracles in turn, is meant to glorify Theseus.

Another subtle element that shows the tendency to move from Heracles to Theseus is seen in the ode, which is meant to glorify Heracles by enumerating his labours (348–424). The description of the labours here has often been compared with their depiction on the metopes of the temple of Zeus in Olympia (*c.* 460 BC).[98] However, critics have also noted that the Euripidean description is very similar to the portrayal of Heracles' labours on the sculptures of the Hephaesteum ('Theseum') (*c.* 450–440), facing the Athenian agora, where

[93] On the association between Peisistratus and Heracles, and the popularity of Heracles during the Peisistratid tyranny, see esp. Boardman 1972; 1975; 1984; 1989. For a more sceptical view, see Huttner 1997: 25–42.

[94] See Walker 1995: 49–53 and n. 132. On the popularity of Heracles in Attic cult, see esp. Woodford 1971; cf. Kearns 1989: 35–6, 166.

[95] For example, by the first quarter of the fifth century, Theseus' appearances on vase-paintings increase, whereas those of Heracles decrease. On this, and other examples, see Mills 1997: 27–9.

[96] For the changes in the relation between Heracles and Theseus in Athens, see Walker 1995: 50–5; Mills 1997, esp. 27–9.

[97] Cf. Mills 1997: 11–12, 136. In Sophocles' *Oedipus at Colonus* the Theseus/Peirithous descent is alluded to (1593–4) without bringing in Heracles, and Heracles does not figure among the protective divinities of the play.

[98] Cf. Bond 1981: 154; Barlow 1996: 139.

in fact there were depictions of both Heracles' and Theseus' exploits.[99] This is significant, because the description of Heracles' labours in the ode might then be intended to evoke Theseus at this early point in the drama, and thus to foreshadow his important role later.

There is also a contradiction in the Chorus' description which may not be without significance. They place Heracles' fight against the Centaurs in Thessaly (373), whereas Amphitryon stated earlier that it took place in Arcadia (182). This contradiction has usually been played down as insignificant because it refers to a detail in myth.[100] But the placement of Heracles' fight against the Centaurs specifically in Thessaly may evoke another famous Centauromachy, that of Theseus, which was well known to have taken place there.[101] Theseus' Centauromachy was in fact one of his exploits which were depicted in the Hephaesteum.[102] It may be that the connection between Heracles and Theseus, which is of primary importance later in the play, is prepared for at this early stage, and later when Theseus promises Heracles 'stone monuments' (1331) there may have been an evocation for the audience of the Hephaesteum with its depictions of Heracles' labours.[103] Finally, the description of Heracles' labours in the ode, as has often been observed,[104] plays down his Peloponnesian associations and instead emphasizes his panhellenic status. So the early evocation of Theseus in this ode foreshadows the glory that Athens will attain, when she alone among all cities of Greece will help accept, and consequently appropriate, the one truly panhellenic hero.[105]

---

[99] Carrière 1975.

[100] Cf. Bond 1981 on Eur. *HF* 182: 'Euripides, writing before the codification of mythology, could be casual about details.'

[101] Angeli-Bernardini 1978 notes this, but takes it that for Heracles' Centauromachy to take place where Theseus had fought is an appropriation which would have been considered by the Athenian audience as offensive to their national hero.

[102] Carrière 1975: 19.   [103] Cf. Bond 1981 on Eur. *HF* 1331–3.

[104] E.g. Bond 1981: 154; Barlow 1996: 139.

[105] Heracles may be said to be predominantly a Dorian hero, and thus his appropriation by Athens may be not without significance for a play produced while Athens was at war with Sparta. But Heracles was above all a panhellenic hero, and this

An important element added in *Heracles* is the connection between Heracles' rescue of Theseus from Hades and his own initiation into the Eleusinian Mysteries. As he says to Amphitryon in the play, he fought with Cerberus in battle, but it was his experience of the Mysteries which helped him accomplish his task (612–13). The initiation of Heracles into the Great as well as the Lesser Mysteries was one way in which the Athenians associated their city, which controlled the Mysteries in the fifth century, with the great hero.[106] At the same time, the mention of the help that the Eleusinian Mysteries provided to Heracles serves a specific purpose in the play by making clear that he already received benefits from Athens in Hades. This help is the first in the reciprocal relation which continues with Heracles' rescue of Theseus from Hades and then with his own rescue in turn by the Athenian hero.

There is another element which presents Theseus as a more advanced or enlightened hero than Heracles in the play. Heracles veiled his head so that he should not pollute Theseus. Theseus now, by unveiling his friend himself, asserts that there is no fear of pollution:

Θη. τί δ'; οὐ μιαίνεις θνητὸς ὢν τὰ τῶν θεῶν.
Ηρ. φεῦγ', ὦ ταλαίπωρ', ἀνόσιον μίασμ' ἐμόν.
Θη. οὐδεὶς ἀλάστωρ τοῖς φίλοις ἐκ τῶν φίλων. (1232–4)

THESEUS: How? You a mere mortal cannot pollute what is divine.
HERACLES: My poor friend, keep away from my unholy defilement.
THESEUS: No avenging spirit can cross from friend to friend.

Theseus' view of pollution, contrary to Heracles' traditional one, is rationalistic.[107] This view was expressed by Creon in *Antigone*, where however the tone was different. There, following

may be all the more important for a play produced while Athens aspired to achieve panhellenic pre-eminence. On Heracles as the one truly panhellenic hero, see esp. Farnell 1921; Galinsky 1972: 3. The civilizing mission of Heracles' labours was also similar to the mission that Periclean Athens claimed for herself; see Bond 1981: xxvii.

[106] On Heracles and Eleusis as well as on the association between Heracles' descent into Hades and his initiation into the Mysteries, see Woodford 1966: 49–53; Lloyd-Jones 1967; Keuls 1974: 161–3; Boardman 1975; Robertson 1980.

[107] Cf. Bond 1981 on Eur. *HF* 1232–4.

the hyperbole (1040–3) that Polyneices will not be buried, not even if the eagles of Zeus carry him as prey to the throne of the god, Creon justifies what he has said by using a maxim: εὖ γὰρ οἶδ᾿ ὅτι | θεοὺς μιαίνειν οὔτις ἀνθρώπων σθένει, 'I know well that no human is able to defile the gods' (1043–4). The idea is essentially the same in both contexts, but the difference in its purpose could not be greater; Creon's purpose is to justify an impious action, while Theseus attempts to encourage his friend. Theseus' enlightened attitude will become apparent also at the end of the play, when he gives his hand to Heracles and raises him from the ground (1398). Also, the emphasis is on the power of friendship (1234),[108] which no avenging spirit resulting from pollution can harm. Heracles is again terrified that Theseus will incur pollution, this time by touching, but Theseus shows no hesitation:

Θη. παῦσαι· δίδου δὲ χεῖρ᾿ ὑπηρέτηι φίλωι.
Ἡρ. ἀλλ᾿ αἷμα μὴ σοῖς ἐξομόρξωμαι πέπλοις.
Θη. ἔκμασσε, φείδου μηδέν· οὐκ ἀναίνομαι. (1398–1400)

THESEUS: Enough. Give your hand to a friend who wants to help you.
HERACLES: Be careful that the blood of my pollution does not wipe off on
                       your clothes.
THESEUS: Wipe away! As much as you like! I do not reject it.

The image of the blood of Heracles' family being wiped away on Theseus, with total disregard for the contamination involved, is strong, and its effect is to lay emphasis on the enlightened Theseus and on the power of his friendship towards Heracles. A similar situation is presented by Sophocles in his *Oedipus at Colonus*, but treated differently. There Oedipus, grateful to Theseus for his help, wishes to embrace the Athenian king, but refrains (1130–5). Like Heracles, so

---

[108] The Greek word φιλία is wider than the English word friendship, in that it is a bond which creates a co-operative relationship and which is meant to be expressed in mutually benefiting behaviour in work or family; see Blundell 1989. But a more emotional bond which could correspond more to the modern definition 'friendship' was also possible (see Konstan 1997), and *Heracles* shifts the emphasis to the importance of the friendship between Heracles and Theseus. On aspects of φιλία in Euripides, see e.g. Scully 1973; Konstan 1985; Schein 1988; Stanton 1990; Perdicoyianni 1996. On friendship in *Heracles*, see esp. Johnson 2002.

Oedipus fears the ritual pollution that Theseus can incur. The dramatic focus is all on Oedipus; he is overcome with relief and wants to show his profound gratitude, but holds back because he still *feels* polluted, despite his earlier protestations of innocence. Contrary to the Euripidean Theseus, his Sophoclean counterpart makes no attempt to touch the afflicted hero, or to assert Oedipus' ritual purity.[109] The difference between the two attitudes of Theseus may be due to the somehow more complicated status of Oedipus,[110] but it can also be due to the relation between Theseus and Heracles, which is closer than that between Theseus and Oedipus. Theseus meets Oedipus for the first time, whereas Heracles and Theseus are related through ties of both kinship and long friendship (*HF* 1154). It is thus the intimacy between two friends which Theseus' gesture and disregard for ritual contamination stresses, and in this respect, Theseus here is similar to Pylades in *Orestes* 792–4, where he does not hesitate to touch his friend and thus to defy the risk of contagion.[111]

Heracles' decision to die is based on the extremity of his sufferings, but Theseus counterargues that in wishing to kill himself Heracles speaks like an ordinary man: εἴρηκας ἐπιτυχόντος ἀνθρώπου λόγους (1248). Theseus' attempt in general is to remind his friend of his heroic past and the many labours he had to endure, in order to persuade him to show endurance also in the present misfortune. Theseus' taunt is followed by an accusation of ἀμαθία, 'ignorance' or 'stupidity': οὐκ ἄν <σ'> ἀνάσχοιθ᾽ Ἑλλὰς ἀμαθίαι θανεῖν, 'Greece will not allow <you> to die through your own stupidity (1254). It was also ἀμαθία of which Amphitryon in his debate with Lycus had accused the tyrant (172).[112] Theseus is here presented as a more enlightened figure than Heracles, in the sense that his role is clearly to show Heracles that his decision to kill himself is wrong.

---

[109] But the Sophoclean Theseus' attitude towards ritual is also enlightened; thus, he does not hesitate to interrupt a sacrifice to Poseidon (*OC* 887–90) and rush when an urgent situation asks for his help.

[110] So Mills 1997: 177.   [111] Cf. Barlow 1996 on Eur. *HF* 1400.

[112] On ἀμαθία, see Bond 1981 on Eur. *HF* 172 and 1354.

Suicide in Greek tragedy[113]

The different attitudes of Heracles and Theseus towards suicide have a prominent part in the play, as the development of the plot is based on how the debate over suicide will be decided. Suicide is a recurrent motif in Greek tragedy; the way the tragedians portray it, with grief, despair and dishonour as the predominant motives, echoes contemporary Greek society and ethics. Thus, before the influence of Christianity, which prohibited suicide altogether, suicide was also absolutely condemned by the Pythagoreans and a certain uneasiness was also evident in the treatment of the bodies of suicides.[114] But in a society in which shame and honour were important values, suicide could be viewed in favourable terms, and distinctions were indeed also made between acceptable and unacceptable suicides.[115] In Plato, for example, although suicide is taken in general to be wrong (e.g. *Phd.* 62 b–c; *Leg.* 9, 873 c–d), a distinction is also made between suicides which are motivated by unendurable misfortune (περι ωδύνωι ἀφύκτωι προσπεσούσηι τύχηι ἀναγκασθείς) or dishonour (αἰσχύνης τινὸς ἀπόρου καὶ ἀβίου μεταλαχών), which are justifiable, and suicides motivated by laziness (ἀργία) and cowardice (ἀνανδρίας δειλία), which are not acceptable.

The great majority of examples of suicide from Greek tragedy seem designed to intensify the pathos and are not explicitly criticized on the grounds that suicide is unacceptable in principle. Whether grief (e.g. Sophocles' Eurydice and Haimon), disgrace (e.g. Sophocles' Ajax or Euripides' Phaedra) or extreme suffering (e.g. Aeschylus' Io or Sophocles' Philoctetes) are the main drives which cause characters to contemplate suicide and sometimes to carry it out, the thought of killing oneself is presented as an understandable solution on the part of the dramatic characters. The way, however, in which the suicide

---

[113] On suicide in Greek tragedy, see esp. Faber 1970; Katsouris 1976; Garrison 1995.
[114] On the pollution attached to suicides, see Parker 1983, esp. 42. But see also Garrison 1995: 11–32, with some modifications to Parker's thesis.
[115] See also the overview by Yoshitake 1994.

motif is used is dependent on dramatic circumstances, and this means that there is no unique line of approach to suicide in Greek tragedy; the issue of suicide is never detached from each dramatic situation in all its complexity, and no single, clear-cut attitude can be inferred from these scenes.

A couple of examples will make this evident. In *Trojan Women* (1010–14) suicide is clearly described in favourable terms when Hecuba argues that the noble course of action prescribed for a woman[116] in the situation which Helen only falsely claims to be in is suicide (1010–14). However, under different circumstances, suicide may be criticized. In *Orestes*, Menelaus thinks that Orestes has death in mind when he mentions a recourse from his madness, and he responds with an answer similar to the one used by Theseus to Heracles: μὴ θάνατον εἴπῃς· τοῦτο μὲν γὰρ οὐ σοφόν, 'do not say death; for this is not wise' (415). Similarly, in fr. 1070 K[117] it is said that suicide οὐκ ἐν σοφοῖσιν ἔστιν, 'is not amongst the wise'. In both cases, suicide is not considered an intelligent course of action. Amphitryon's description of Heracles' plan to kill himself as ἀνόσιον, 'unholy' (*HF* 1212) also registers strong criticism.[118]

Heracles' decision to commit suicide and his subsequent change of mind have often recalled a similar situation which, however, ended differently: in *Ajax* the protagonist finally kills himself.[119] Theseus' taunting of Heracles concerning his wish to kill himself might seem odd when applied to Ajax; could Ajax also be considered to be ἐπιτυχών, 'ordinary', and ἀμαθής, 'ignorant' or 'stupid'?[120] It is worth comparing the two cases more closely.

There are several similarities between Ajax and Heracles. To begin with, they both became cult heroes. Also, in myth they were both afflicted with madness sent by a goddess

---

[116] Here the gender is clearly crucial.

[117] For Kannicht's numbering (*TrGF* 5, still forthcoming), see the preface in the Budé edition by Jouan and van Looy 1998.

[118] For the religious attitude, cf. Philostr. *Her.* 35. 14–15, interpreting what is said in the *Little Iliad* about the burial of Ajax in a coffin, as a ritual prohibition on cremation of suicides, rather than a mark of dishonour.

[119] For comparisons, see James 1969; Barlow 1981; Furley 1986; de Romilly 1995.

[120] Cf. Furnell 1986: 110.

(Athena and Hera), suffered similar delusions during which they misidentified their victims, and had to face the dishonour of their acts upon recovering. As in the case of Heracles, the heroic valour of Ajax is stressed throughout the Sophoclean play.[121] The sympathetic Chorus, for example, stress Ajax's greatness in the parodos (134–200) and later lament the reversal in Ajax's fortune by referring to his past 'greatest excellence' (617). It is this reversal that is deplored by Ajax himself when he recovers (430–79), and it is his excellence too that makes him think of suicide as the only means by which he can show his father that he is not a coward and the only way also to avoid disgrace:

πεῖρά τις ζητητέα
τοιάδ᾽ ἀφ᾽ ἧς γέροντι δηλώσω πατρὶ
μή τοι φύσιν γ᾽ ἄσπλαγχνος ἐκ κείνου γεγώς.
αἰσχρὸν γὰρ ἄνδρα τοῦ μακροῦ χρήιζειν βίου,
κακοῖσιν ὅστις μηδὲν ἐξαλλάσσεται.
τί γὰρ παρ᾽ ἦμαρ ἡμέρα τέρπειν ἔχει
προσθεῖσα κἀναθεῖσα πλὴν τοῦ κατθανεῖν;
οὐκ ἂν πριαίμην οὐδενὸς λόγου βροτὸν
ὅστις κεναῖσιν ἐλπίσιν θερμαίνεται.
ἀλλ᾽ ἢ καλῶς ζῆν ἢ καλῶς τεθνηκέναι
τὸν εὐγενῆ χρή. (*Aj.* 470–80)

I must seek some such enterprise that from it I shall show my aged father that I, his son, am not naturally a coward. It is shameful for a man to wish for his life to be long, if he experiences no alternation in his misfortunes. For what pleasure can day after day provide as it brings one near to or moves one back from death? I would not buy at any valuation the mortal who warms himself on empty hopes. The noble man should either live well or die well.[122]

Ajax's words here are remarkably similar to Megara's attitude in *Heracles*. She too criticized the trust in vain hope and the prolongation of life, as exemplified by Amphitryon, and she suggested voluntary death as the noble solution, and as the means to uphold reputation and avoid dishonour. Suicide is also the first thought of Heracles when he realizes what he has

---

[121] Despite the stress on Ajax's heroic value, the unacceptability of his murderous attack on his comrades problematizes Ajax's overall portrayal in the play.
[122] Translation by Garvie 1998.

done in his madness, and his reaction also follows the kind of heroic code which is represented by Ajax as well as Megara.[123]

But despite the similarities, Ajax is different from Heracles. Contrary to Heracles, who was pious towards the gods before his madness, Ajax is reported by the Messenger to have disregarded the gods. Thus, when his father advised him to win victories but always with the help of the gods, he replied boastfully that he did not need divine help (766–70). This is immediately followed by the account of another past occasion where Ajax was arrogant towards Athena and thus incurred her hatred (770–7). These are serious offences against gods and reveal that Ajax's heroism, however admirable, can also be transgressive.[124] A similar attitude towards the gods is shown in the scene where Athena appears to the deluded Ajax. Ajax there is glad to have Athena as an ally (91–3, 116–17), but when the goddess asks him not to torture what he thinks is the captured Odysseus (111), Ajax says that although he is willing to let her have her way in other things, with this particular one he will not comply (112–13); this is refusal towards a divinity and implies that Ajax is placing himself almost on the same level with the goddess.

Another occasion where Ajax's attitude towards the gods is problematized occurs when to Tecmessa's entreaty to him by their son but also by the gods (587–8), he replies: ἄγαν γε λυπεῖς. οὐ κάτοισθ' ἐγὼ θεοῖς | ὡς οὐδὲν ἀρκεῖν εἴμ' ὀφειλέτης ἔτι; 'you irritate me too much. Don't you realize that I am no longer obliged to serve the gods?' (589–90). Ajax had earlier stated that Athena destroyed him (401–3), and that he was hated by the gods (457–8), both statements underscoring his isolation. But at 589–90, his belief that he owes no service to the gods because he has been abandoned by them, conveys

---

[123] In Heracles' case, of course, the situation is more complex since Heracles comes to realize that he is the murderer of his own family.

[124] Garvie 1998 on Soph. *Aj.* 758–61 is not persuasive in attempting to undermine the importance of Ajax's arrogant behaviour towards the gods. The same applies to his attempt to dissociate Ajax from Athena's advice against human arrogance towards the divine in the prologue (127–33; see Garvie 1998 ad loc.). Athena's remarks are maxims, but they also apply directly to Ajax in the play.

169

something more than mere despair. Ajax repudiates the gods and distances himself from them in the same way as he feels himself destroyed or abandoned by them. In this sense, Ajax's attitude here contains in seminal form the kind of full-scale repudiation of the gods by Heracles. The difference is that Ajax's relation with the gods was arrogant even before his madness, as the Messenger makes clear, whereas Heracles' attitude before madness was consistently meant to be pious; this makes his repudiation of the gods and re-definition of divinity all the more drastic, especially if one thinks that he is a son of Zeus and that an important question of the play is whom he accepts as his 'real' father.

Ajax strictly adheres to the heroic principle of 'helping one's friends and harming one's enemies',[125] but this adherence becomes problematic when the Atreids fail him in the allocation of arms and are therefore regarded by him as enemies. Ajax then attempts to murder them, and it is only by the intervention of Athena, directing his violence against animals, that the Greek leaders are saved. Ajax never of course regrets his intention; on the contrary, he is angry because his madness prevented him from carrying out his revenge and because this failure has exposed him to ridicule (457–80).

It is true that Athena's own description of her intervention in the prologue stresses her wish to protect the Atreids, but does not say, at least explicitly, that the goddess intended to punish Ajax for doing something wrong.[126] But no matter how understandable Ajax's intention to murder the Argive leaders may be, when considered as revenge against enemies, it is still presented as extraordinary and problematic. Thus, it causes surprise to Odysseus (cf. 44, 46). Ajax's intended revenge was also a manifestation of the type of individualism which defies hierarchy, disobeys authority and thus endangers the solidarity and safety of the community, as Menelaus points out to

---

[125] On this principle, see esp. Blundell 1989. In *Heracles*, it is expressed by Amphitryon: τοῖς φίλοις <τ᾽> εἶναι φίλον | τά τ᾽ ἐχθρὰ μισεῖν, 'to love your friends and hate your enemies' (585–6).

[126] On this view, and for a tendency to take Ajax's revenge as justifiable and unproblematic, see Garvie 1998: 11–12.

Teucer (1052–88). Now, the presentation of Menelaus as a whole, like that of Agamemnon later, is meant to portray him in unfavourable terms, as becomes evident by his arrogant treatment of Teucer; his arguments too, which praise discipline in both the city and the army, are the kind of sophistic points also made by Creon in *Antigone* (663–776);[127] but, although there too the overall portrayal of Creon is made in unfavourable terms, yet the specific arguments carry weight.

Ajax's rigid behaviour is also evident in his treatment of his family. Like the Euripidean Heracles, Ajax also has a family who support him, but the overall domestic portrayal of Heracles is very different from that of Ajax. It is not only intimacy that Tecmessa asks for and Ajax does not show.[128] In her attempt to dissuade her husband from killing himself (485–524), Tecmessa says that if Ajax kills himself, he will incur the shame of abandoning his family, and this is contrary to what a noble person should do (αἴδεσαι 'feel shame', 506 and 507, οὐκ ἂν γένοιτ' ἔθ' οὗτος εὐγενὴς ἀνήρ, 'he could no longer be regarded as a noble man', 524). The use of the vocabulary of nobility and shame by Tecmessa seems to be the only means she can find to influence Ajax, as he is preoccupied with the heroic ethos. Accordingly, Tecmessa's words are meant to show that Ajax's concern strictly with his own personal honour, although understandable and justifiable, clashes with his duty, again part of the heroic ethos, to protect his family. But at this point Ajax remains distant and isolated; he cannot consider anything else apart from his own personal honour (594–5, cf. 372–91).

Already in her first utterance, Tecmessa calls Ajax δεινός, 'awesome' or 'terrible', μέγας, 'great', ὠμοκρατής, 'fierce in his might' (205), epithets which summarize the double-edged character of Ajax's heroism. Especially the compound epithet ὠμοκρατής, from ὠμός, 'raw', conveys the kind of fierceness which is close to savagery. Ajax himself uses the word ὠμός, when he addresses his son (548). This address recalls Hector's

---

[127] See Garvie 1998 on Soph. *Aj.* 1073–6.
[128] For the rhetoric of the scene between Ajax and Tecmessa, see Easterling 1984.

farewell to his own son in *Iliad* 6 (466–84). But the difference in tone is great. Hector laughed when his son shrank back in fear from the crest of his father's helmet, whereas Ajax begins by saying that his son will show no fear at the blood (545–7). Hector also prayed for his son to equal or surpass his father in glory. Ajax on the other hand hopes that his son may become as fierce as his father, and his words also imply that he wishes his son to take revenge on his father's enemies (556–7).[129]

It is the same fierceness that will again be mentioned in association with Ajax's unyielding character (885, 930). In the so-called 'deception speech' (646–92) Ajax too, while contemplating the principle of alternation, likens himself to hard iron, a simile which well illustrates how inflexibility was always a feature of his character. But the principle of alternation also applies to his case, and Ajax, who twice objected to Tecmessa's appeals to soften his attitude (371, 594–5), now admits that he has been affected (650–3). Whether in this speech Ajax deliberately deceives those around him without ever abandoning his decision to commit suicide, or seriously considers the principle of alternation but eventually decides not to follow it,[130] the fact remains that he abides by his decision to kill himself. But Ajax's thoughts on alternation, which also outline an alternative to suicide, have implications for Heracles' change of mind. Heracles too originally considers suicide, but eventually his change takes a concrete form when he decides to live, whereas in the case of Ajax this change is implied but rejected when Ajax commits suicide.

Suicide to avoid disgrace was the result of Ajax's unshaken belief in the notion of 'harming one's enemy', a notion which became all the more complicated in his case once his former friends (the Greek leaders) became his enemies. Odysseus on the other hand represents a more flexible attitude towards the question of enmity. This is evident in the prologue and his response to Athena's invitation to laugh at the fall of Ajax, now turned into his enemy (74–80). Odysseus refrains because

---

[129] Cf. Garvie 1998 on Soph. *Aj.* 556–7. Ajax's wish for revenge will later be expressed in his curses against the Greek leaders (835–44).

[130] For an overview of several approaches to Ajax's speech, see Garvie 1998: 184–6.

in the changed fortune of Ajax he sees the vulnerability of himself as well as the fragility of human life in general. When he reappears towards the end of the play (1318), where the central issue is that of Ajax's burial, he confronts Agamemnon, defends Ajax's valour and argues in favour of granting him burial (1332–45). Odysseus argues for flexibility of attitude (1361) and says to Teucer that Ajax, who was his enemy, is now his friend (1377). But despite the favourable presentation of Odysseus, Ajax remains at the centre of the drama throughout. The issue of his burial shifts the focus back to the hero and vindicates his heroic status. The paradox in Ajax is that the rigidity and inflexibility which are his flaws are at the same time the qualities that make him a great hero. For this reason, the impression is that it would be inconceivable for Ajax to do what Heracles does, that is, to change his mind and decide to live.

Heracles' decision to live

I turn now to the motivation behind Heracles' decision to live, a decision which is presented as the outcome of a tragic dilemma. Theseus' taunts are particularly effective in provoking a response from Heracles, who utters a long speech to demonstrate why his life is unendurable,[131] and it remains to be seen from the course and outcome of the debate if Theseus' view against suicide was right, and what contribution he has made to his friend's final choice. Heracles argues that his misfortunes started even before he was born, as Amphitryon killed Alcmena's father and married her while still polluted by the murder (1258–62, cf. 16–17). This introduces the idea of inherited guilt and pollution to intensify the despair of Heracles' life (1261–2). Heracles also had to endure Hera's enmity from the time he was at his mother's breast, and when he came of age he had to endure a series of labours (1263–78). But now his present misfortune is the peak of all his previous troubles, and is also described as a labour: τὸν λοίσθιον δὲ τόνδ᾽

---

[131] On this speech as an *epideixis*, see Lloyd 1992: 10.

ἔτλην τάλας πόνον, | παιδοκτονήσας δῶμα θριγκῶσαι κακοῖς, 'now in my misery I have endured my last labour of all. I have crowned the troubles of my household by murdering my own children' (1279–80). The helplessness of his present situation is described in a series of questions, which stress Heracles' isolation and lack of alternative (1281–90).[132]

The reference to ἀνάγκη at 1281 (ἥκω δ᾽ ἀνάγκης, 'the pitch of necessity to which I have come'),[133] that is, the power of necessity, recalls Megara's earlier mention of a person's attitude to necessity, when she said that whoever fights against it is a fool: τῶι δ᾽ ἀναγκαίωι τρόπωι | ὃς ἀντιτείνει σκαιὸν ἡγοῦμαι βροτῶν (282–3). There voluntary death was the solution, and it is the same solution that Heracles considers here. Pollution, fear of mockery and isolation are the core of Heracles' despair, which is further intensified by a reference to the cosmic scale (1295–7). His conclusion then is that life is pointless (1301–2). But contemplating his helplessness also causes a reaction against Hera, whom he considers responsible for his downfall, along with an assertion of his own valour and innocence (1303–10). This reaction is significant, for it contributes to Heracles' eventual decision to live.

Theseus' reply to Heracles is a consolation divided into two parts.[134] The first part is a response to Heracles' despair at his extreme misfortune, and here Theseus uses the *non tibi hoc soli* (cf. Cic. *Tusc.* 3.33.79) line of argumentation. Heracles is not the only one to suffer, but because his suffering is indeed enormous, Theseus strengthens his argument by saying that even the gods who are powerful suffer misfortunes (1314–19), to conclude: καίτοι τί φήσεις, εἰ σὺ μὲν θνητὸς γεγὼς | φέρεις ὑπέρφευ τὰς τύχας, θεοὶ δὲ μή; 'so what is your defence then, if you, a mere mortal, complain excessively about fate when the gods do not?' (1320–1).[135] In the second part of his reply

---

[132] For the rhetorical pattern here, see Bond 1981 on Eur. *HF* 1281–90.

[133] On the term ἀνάγκη, see Schreckenberg 1964.

[134] On Theseus' role as comforter, see also Michelini 1987: 258–62. On *topoi* of consolation in Greek tragedy, see Ciani 1975.

[135] In the *Iliad* (18.117–19), Achilles recognizes that he faces death, recalling that even Heracles had to die.

(1323–37) he promises purification as well as gifts and honours to Heracles both during his lifetime and after his death, claiming that the Athenians will win praise from the Greeks for their actions:

καλὸς γὰρ ἀστοῖς στέφανος Ἑλλήνων ὕπο
ἄνδρ' ἐσθλὸν ὠφελοῦντας εὐκλείας τυχεῖν. (1334–5)

It will be a fine crown for my citizens to have got glory for helping a noble man.

Theseus' offer, in particular, to his friend of his own gifts of land, which will thereafter be called after Heracles, seems to be an attempt to explain Heracles' association with Athens,[136] by linking him and Theseus, although his labours never actually brought him there. Whether this was already established before Euripides or whether it is a Euripidean invention,[137] the fact remains that the linking of Heracles with Theseus is made in a way which glorifies the national hero of Athens. Thus, Theseus' intervention, which is based on pity and companionship, also reflects the qualities of Athens as these were represented in the Euripidean *Heraclidae* and *Suppliants* or later in Sophocles' *Oedipus at Colonus*.

Theseus interferes by virtue not only of his past readiness to confront Lycus but also of his active support to the suffering Heracles. He exemplifies the quality of πολυπραγμοσύνη, 'meddlesomeness' to practical effect, especially in the present situation, where Heracles is most in need of friends (1337). The sympathetic Chorus had also spoken in similar terms when, at the same time as condemning Lycus, they defended interference on behalf of friends:[138] κἄπειτα πράσσω πόλλ' ἐγώ φίλους ἐμοὺς | θανόντας εὖ δρῶν, οὗ φίλων μάλιστα δεῖ; 'and yet am I accounted a meddler if I help my dead friends when they most need allies?' (266–7). But whereas the Chorus were willing but unable to help, Theseus is in a position, as the leader and representative of Athens, to offer active help. And although

---

[136] On this association, see esp. Woodford 1966: 9–35 (Heracles' cults); 36–48 (Heracles' relation with Theseus); 49–53 (Eleusinian Mysteries); 131–261 (Heracles in Athenian art).
[137] See Bond 1981 on Eur. *HF* 1326–33.   [138] On this, see Mills 1997: 143.

Theseus' offers are a repayment of Heracles' past favour in rescuing him, it is clear that this is not simply a matter between two friends. Thus, the city of Athens is helping a great hero who has now fallen into despair, and it is Athens which, by rehabilitating Heracles, will be glorious in Greece (1334–5).

Heracles' response to Theseus' speech begins with his famous assertion that divinity has nothing to do with the kind of imperfect gods that Theseus used as his examples for the universality of suffering (1340–6). This is followed by an expression of his change of mind, and his decision to endure life:[139]

ἐσκεψάμην δὲ καίπερ ἐν κακοῖσιν ὢν
μὴ δειλίαν ὄφλω τιν' ἐκλιπὼν φάος·
ταῖς συμφοραῖς γὰρ ὅστις οὐχ ὑφίσταται
οὐδ' ἀνδρὸς ἂν δύναιθ' ὑποστῆναι βέλος.
ἐγκαρτερήσω βίοτον· εἶμι δ' ἐς πόλιν
τὴν σήν, χάριν τε μυρίαν δώρων ἔχω. (1347–52)

But even in my present despair I have been thinking that I might incur the reputation of cowardice if I kill myself. The man who is unable to sustain adversity could never sustain an opponent's weapons. I shall have the courage to endure life. I shall come to your city and I thank you for the immense favour of your gifts.

Heracles gives two motives for his change of mind, that is, the fear of cowardice,[140] and his gratitude to Theseus. The mention of cowardice and the use of the vocabulary of battle suggest that Heracles refers to the type of courage displayed in warfare; this might then be said to imply that there is no change in his notion of valour because it is the traditional kind of *arete*

[139] For changes of mind in Greek tragedy, see in general Knox 1979; Gibert 1995. Heracles' state of mind here recalls Odysseus' deliberations, in the midst of despair, whether to kill himself or to endure life; endurance of life is what the famous πολύτλας, 'much-enduring', Homeric hero chooses (*Od.* 10.49–53). For the reading βίοτον, 'life', instead of the manuscript's θάνατον, 'death', in Eur. *HF* 1351, see Barlow 1981: 112 and n. 1. The correction βίοτον gives better meaning with the verb ἐγκαρτερήσω. On the other hand, in favour of the manuscript's reading and its meaning, see e.g. Ebener 1981, and more recently Gibert 1997. But the reading βίοτον makes better sense as it stresses Heracles' courage to endure a life which is unbearable following the death of his family.
[140] Fitzgerald 1991: 94 is certainly mistaken in arguing that Heracles' decision to live is in fact a manifestation of cowardice.

which motivates his actions.[141] This is corroborated by the fact that when Theseus earlier argued that suicide would be the option of an ordinary man (1248), and referred to Heracles' heroic past as incompatible with resignation (1250), he was obviously alluding to traditional excellence and the courage shown in battle. But Heracles' extreme misfortune, which Theseus, although sympathetic, has not experienced himself (cf. 1249), has taught him for the first time that he is vulnerable. The use of the vocabulary of battle is also telling, for it describes Heracles facing this new kind of adversity as a warrior facing his opponent's weapons.

The interesting thing here is that, in the context of the weapon vocabulary used in the play so far, Heracles is portrayed as a hoplite, vulnerable and courageous at the same time. His vulnerability is also evident in his phrase νῦν δ', ὡς ἔοικε, τῆι τύχηι δουλευτέον, 'but, as it is, it appears I must let fortune dominate me' (1357); when Amphitryon praised the efficiency of the archer, who, unlike the spearman, remains invisible and consequently invulnerable, he also used the phraseology of fortune: τοῦτο δ' ἐν μάχηι | σοφὸν μάλιστα, δρῶντα πολεμίους κακῶς | σώιζειν τὸ σῶμα, μὴ 'κ τύχης ὡρμισμένον, 'this is the most sensible tactic in battle, to preserve yourself and hurt your enemy without being dependent on chance' (201–3).[142] Being slave to fortune in both the hoplite's and Heracles' case is an indication of vulnerability. Heracles' acceptance of his vulnerability is also closely related to his deliberate dissociation of himself from the traditional gods and his definition of divinity as flawless. His *vivamus* comes as a result of his repudiation of the kind of gods similar to

---

[141] Against Chalk 1962, who held that after his madness Heracles displays a new kind of heroic excellence, Adkins 1966 argued that Heracles' valour is traditional throughout, and went further to say that, after his fall, Heracles cannot even be said to have any *arete*, but only that he tries to salvage the remnants of his old valour. Some of Adkins' arguments against Chalk are valid (e.g. friendship cannot be said to replace *arete* at the end of the play), but his overall approach to the play is restrictive and eventually does no justice to it, for it completely misses the new insight that Heracles gains after his recovery; for criticisms of Adkins, see also Furley 1986: *passim*.

[142] Cf. Hamilton 1985: 23.

Hera, who has destroyed him. This repudiation is Heracles' own 'revenge' on the agents of his fall. If his urge was to commit suicide because he had been destroyed by Hera, now, by asserting that Hera is no divinity, he treats his misfortune as a chance event (τύχη, 1357) and decides to live. By deliberately rejecting the traditional gods that Theseus had described, and by attributing his misfortune to random τύχη, he also shows the courage to assume full responsibility for his crimes, whereas the admission of Hera's responsibility would partly exonerate him.

Committing suicide, as an act which would remove his disgrace, would be a courageous and noble solution, as Heracles himself originally thought, but only if he believed that he had been abandoned by the gods.[143] What has changed now is that Theseus' reference to the imperfect gods as examples has provoked Heracles' radical redefinition of his relation with divinity. His death would mean that he accepted his defeat at the hands of the gods whom he now chooses to reject; it would also please Hera, whom Heracles imagined celebrating his disaster (1303-7), whereas his decision to live is also his victory over her, following that of his own refusal to call her a proper divinity. If the gods who have destroyed him are not gods in his view because gods are perfect, then suicide is pointless. At the same time, Theseus' offers provide him with a bearable alternative to death, and Athens becomes the place which can receive Heracles. The practical solution offered to Heracles is also an element which was not available to the Sophoclean Ajax, who was also isolated and helpless, but was never offered the kind of alternative that Theseus can give to Heracles.

Heracles' vulnerability also means that his experience and knowledge of life are now enlarged. This becomes evident in his emotional address to his weapons (1376-85), the symbols of his heroic valour but also the reminders of his murder of his wife and children. Deciding whether to keep them or not is too difficult (ἀμηχανῶ, 'I do not know', 1378), but eventually he decides to keep them: ἀθλίως δὲ σωστέον, 'I must keep them,

---

[143] Cf. Yoshitake 1994: 148.

painful though it is' (1385). His decision is the result of his affirmation of his heroic past, but also of the vulnerability and grief he has experienced after murdering his kin.

In the context of the weapon vocabulary of the play, his keeping of his bow and club does not mean that Amphitryon's defence of the archer has finally and suddenly prevailed; rather, the weapons become symbolic of the gradual change in Heracles. He used to be the kind of self-sufficient bowman Amphitryon praised. But in the play he was also described in contexts which associated him with the spear (49, 1194), that is, in contexts where the vulnerability of the warrior was stressed. In this sense Amphitryon's and Lycus' exclusive description of Heracles as archer emphasizes the image of an invulnerable Heracles. The picture of the archer Heracles is different now, however, as here his weapons clearly stress his vulnerability. And at the same time they are also the instruments of courage, not simply the kind displayed in battle, but also the kind displayed in Heracles' endurance of life.

Also, although he was not always an isolated warrior – for example he is said to have co-operated with other warriors in his expedition against the Amazons (411–18)[144] – he never experienced the kind of solidarity and fellowship that he now experiences with Theseus. As he himself describes their friendship when Theseus supports him, they are ζεῦγός γε φίλιον, 'a yoke of friendship indeed' (1403). He also adds that he follows his friend like a small boat in tow: Θησεῖ πανώλεις ἑψόμεσθ' ἐφολκίδες, 'I shall follow Theseus like a small boat in tow' (1424). Heracles had earlier used this metaphor for the dependence of his children upon him: ἄξω λαβών γε τούσδ' ἐφολκίδας χεροῖν, | ναῦς δ' ὣς ἐφέλξω, 'I shall take these children by the hand and draw them after me like a ship with its little boats in tow' (631–2). In both cases, the image is not of someone simply offering help to a passive person, but one of structural interdependence, as becomes evident from the word ἐφολκίς, which

---

[144] Iolaus (e.g. Hes. *Theog.* 317; Eur. *Heracl.* 8) accompanied Heracles in some of his labours, but in *Heracles* no mention is made of him; the play focuses instead on the bond between Heracles and Theseus. Already in Homer (*Il.* 5.640–2) Heracles is said to have been accompanied by other warriors when he sacked Troy.

means a boat not separate from the main ship but part of it.[145]
Thus, Heracles depends on Theseus but Theseus also depends
on his friend; their friendship is reciprocal, as became evident
when Heracles helped him in Hades and now he helps him
in turn. He will also help Theseus and his city again when his
cult is established in the city. So in the case of Heracles'
children before they died, they depended on their father but
he also depended on them, because in the future they would
continue the lineage and reputation of the family (cf. 462–79,
1367–70).[146]

Theseus is even asked by Heracles to help him carry
Cerberus to Argos: ἔν μοί τι, Θησεῦ, σύγκαμ᾽ · ἀγρίου κυνὸς |
κόμιστρ᾽ ἐς" Ἀργος συγκατάστησον μολών, | λύπηι τι παίδων μὴ
πάθω μονούμενος, 'bear with me, Theseus, in one more thing.
Come to Argos and help me convey the savage dog [from
Hades]. I am afraid I might suffer on my own, deprived of
my children' (1386–8). Heracles is not asking for help in carrying out the labour; as he told Amphitryon earlier (611–17), he
had already subdued Cerberus in battle and left the beast at the
city of Hermion, in Demeter's grove, before coming to Thebes
to find out what the situation was at his home.[147]

The notion of Theseus helping Heracles deal with Cerberus
is raised in another play, the fragmentary *Peirithous*, written
either by Euripides or by Critias, which dramatized Heracles'
rescue of Theseus and Peirithous from the Underworld.[148]
Theseus offers to help Heracles in his labour, which is presented as yet unaccomplished (ἆθλον ... ἀνήνυτον, fr. 1. 13–14
Diggle). The context of Theseus' offer there could be Heracles'
rescue of Peirithous, Theseus' friend,[149] and Theseus' offer of

[145] See Torr 1895: 103. On the idea of interdependency here, cf. Griffiths 2002: 654.
[146] For parents' hopes in their children, see e.g. Golden 1988.
[147] Wilamowitz ²1895 on Eur. *HF* 1386 interpreted Heracles' request for help in
fetching Cerberus as evidence that the Cerberus labour had not been completed
already. He also argued (109) that Heracles would not engage in further exploits;
this view is in accord with Wilamowitz's overall interpretation of Heracles in the
play as the mighty Dorian hero, who eventually repudiates this type of heroism.
Wilamowitz's approach has long been rejected; see e.g. Chalk 1962: *passim*.
[148] On *Peirithous*, see Mette 1983; Collard 1995; Mills 1997: 257–62.
[149] See Mette 1983: 17.

help serves to glorify his valour, as the Athenian hero is presented as capable of matching the supreme valour of Heracles.
The glorification of Theseus extends to praise of his city,
which is expressed in Heracles' own words. Heracles thanks
Theseus for his offer, saying that it is in accord with Athenian
willingness always to help the unfortunate. But he refuses to
accept help in an as yet unaccomplished labour, saying that
Eurystheus would not approve:

σαυτῶι τε], Θησεῦ, τῆι τ᾽ ᾿Αθηναίων πό[λει
πρέπουτ᾽ ἔλεξας· τοῖσι δυσ[τυ]χοῦσι γὰρ
ἀεί ποτ᾽ εἶ σὺ σύμμαχος· σκῆψιν δ᾽[ἐμ]οὶ
ἀεικές ἐστ᾽ ἔχοντα πρὸς πάτραν μολεῖν.
Εὐρυσθέα γὰρ πῶς δοκεῖς ἂν ἄσμενον,
εἴ μοι πύθοιτο ταῦτα συμπράξαντά σε,
λέγειν ἂν ὡς ἄκραντος ἤθληται πόνος; (Fr. III 4–10 Diggle)[150]

[HERACLES:] What you have said is worthy of yourself and of the city of the
Athenians. For you are always an ally of the unfortunate. But it is shameful
for me to go home with this pretence. How do you think Eurystheus would
gladly say that the endless labour was accomplished if he learned that you
had helped with it?[151]

The difference between the two contexts is obvious. In
Peirithous, Theseus' offer does credit to himself and his city,
but for Heracles to accept Theseus' help in carrying out this
labour would detract from his *arete*. In *Heracles*, the labour
has already been accomplished and Heracles asks his friend to
accompany him to Argos lest he suffer on his own, deprived of
his children; the collaboration that Heracles asks for here
stresses his emotional and psychological state.

As becomes evident from *Peirithous*, Athens and her representative have the qualities which were even more stressed in
plays such as *Oedipus at Colonus*, or in Euripides' *Heraclidae*,
Suppliants and *Heracles*. Athens is the city which shows compassion and which does not hesitate to take action and face
danger in order to help the suffering. In doing so, the city
upholds both human and divine laws. In *Heracles*, Athens

---

[150] Text as printed in Diggle 1998: 176.
[151] Translation by Mills 1997: 260.

gives Heracles the active support that both mortals and immortals refused to give him. There is no explicit indication that when Theseus is helping Heracles he is facing any risks; nevertheless, the risk is implicitly raised by Heracles' own words (1281–98), which stress his isolation when he imagines himself in exile and not only excluded from people but even rejected by natural elements, such as the earth and the waters, which will forbid him to touch them. This part of Heracles' speech is full of pathos and culminates in his desperate τί δῆτά με ζῆν δεῖ; τί κέρδος ἕξομεν | βίον γ᾿ ἀχρεῖον ἀνόσιον κεκτημένοι;, 'Why then should I live? What advantage would I gain, now that my life is both useless and accursed?' (1301–2). The word ἀνόσιον, 'accursed', 'not holy', picks up the phrase οὔτ᾿ ... ὅσιον, 'not permitted by divine law', 'not holy', at 1281–2, where Heracles says that he will no longer be allowed to stay in Thebes after his crimes. So, there is the idea that Heracles is some sort of miasma and will be doomed to complete isolation. But Theseus and his city are not deterred by this and are exalted as the only ones to give Heracles refuge. A determining factor in this is the friendship between Theseus and Heracles. When Heracles praises Theseus as an exemplary friend (ὦ πρέσβυ, τοιόνδ᾿ ἄνδρα χρὴ κτᾶσθαι φίλον, 'this is the sort of man one should have for a friend, father', 1404), Amphitryon's reply, which mentions the city of Athens, is telling: ἡ γὰρ τεκοῦσα τόνδε πατρὶς εὔτεκνος, 'the land that nurtured him is blessed in its sons' (1405).

This intimacy is in accord with the general tone of the play, which puts the emphasis on humanity and human solidarity before the gods. The change in Heracles' approach to the gods and his determination to dissociate himself from them leads him eventually to a rejection of the fatherhood of Zeus (1263–5). Consequently, Heracles also refuses his semi-divine self, which means that he, the conqueror of death, will eventually die, or so Theseus has indicated (1331). Traditionally it was the Athenians, in particular the Marathonians, who took pride in claiming to have been the first to worship Heracles as a god.[152]

---

[152] Paus. I.15.3, 32.4. See also Farnell 1921: 95.

Here there is no allusion to Heracles' apotheosis or to his worship as a god, as Euripides focuses on the human Heracles;[153] Athenians however are again given special distinction for being the first to offer Heracles worship after his death. Athenian altruism will be rewarded; apart from winning renown in Greece (1334–5), the establishment of cult in honour of Heracles implies that the city will receive benefits from Heracles in future.

Heracles' refusal to accept Zeus as his father also has consequences for the conception of nobility in the play, for it is now no longer based on his divine origin. When Heracles came back from Hades to help his family, the Chorus had spoken of his nobility in terms of his divine origin, but also stressed that the greatness of Heracles' exploits was such as to surpass this nobility (Διὸς ὁ παῖς· τᾶς δ᾽εὐγενίας | πλέον ὑπερβάλλων <ἀρετᾶι> | μοχθήσας τὸν ἄκυμον | θῆκεν βίοτον βροτοῖς | πέρσας δείματα θηρῶν, 'it is Zeus's son. He has far surpassed the reputation of his birth <by his courage> and he has worked to bring about for men their peaceful life by destroying the monsters which terrified them', 697–700). Now, after he rejects his divine paternity, he shows that the nobility of his divine lineage is again surpassed, this time not through his heroic exploits, but through his endurance. When Theseus asks his friend to uncover his head, for the noble endure their god-sent misfortunes (1226–8), the notion of nobility does not simply depend upon lineage but also upon character. Heracles' reputation, which he had achieved during his labours, has not been eliminated because of his madness,[154] but after he recovers from madness the notion of Heracles' *arete* as heroic

---

[153] There is, of course, a reference to the worship of Heracles (1331–3), but this seems to suggest a worship of Heracles as a hero, not as a god. Cf. Bond 1981 on Eur. *HF* 1331–3: 'The language is deliberately vague (Wilamowitz). Theseus is thinking of the honours paid to a dead hero; no apotheosis is here envisaged.' On the cults of Heracles, see Gruppe 1918: 910–1000; for those in Attica, see Woodford 1966: 9–35 and 1971: 211–25. On Heracles' apotheosis, see Stinton 1987; *LIMC* v.1 1990: 121–32; Holt 1992. On Heracles' worship as a hero and as a god, see Shapiro 1983; Lévêque and Verbanck-Piérard 1992.

[154] See Bond 1981 on Eur. *HF* 1335 against Adkins 1966.

valour is enriched by the notion of endurance in suffering (1347–57).[155]

The glorification of Theseus and Athens never detracts from Heracles' central role in the drama. Theseus, of course, plays an important role in the rehabilitation of Heracles with his offers. He is also presented as more enlightened when he argues against suicide. But, despite Theseus' contribution, Heracles' decision is ultimately his own. With his references to the imperfections of the gods, Theseus shows traditional piety, and he reacts against Heracles' outburst against them (1244). Also, when he invites Heracles to Athens, he describes his city as πόλισμα Παλλάδος, 'the city of Pallas', (1323), echoing the Athenians' reverence for the divine. Theseus' essential contribution to Heracles' decision to live turns out to be that he provokes his redefinition of his relation with divinity. Theseus is finally successful because Heracles decides not to kill himself, but this decision is the result not of Theseus' persuasion of Heracles to resign himself to his god-sent misfortune, but of Heracles' revolt against the divine.

There is another element which shows that, despite the importance of Theseus' role, this is not a drama about Theseus but the tragedy of Heracles till the end. When Heracles leans on his friend for support, he is still so overwhelmed with grief over his sufferings that Theseus becomes impatient:

Θη. οὕτω πόνων σῶν οὐκέτι μνήμην ἔχεις;
Ηρ. ἅπαντ᾽ ἐλάσσω κεῖνα τῶνδ᾽ ἔτλην κακά.
Θη. εἴ σ᾽ ὄψεταί τις θῆλυν ὄντ᾽ οὐκ αἰνέσει.
Ηρ. ζῶ σοι ταπεινός; ἀλλὰ πρόσθεν οὐ δοκῶ.
Θη. ἄγαν γ᾽· ὁ κλεινὸς Ἡρακλῆς οὐκ εἶ νοσῶν.
Ηρ. σὺ ποῖος ἦσθα νέρθεν ἐν κακοῖσιν ὤν;
Θη. ὡς ἐς τὸ λῆμα παντὸς ἦν ἥσσων ἀνήρ.
Ηρ. πῶς οὖν†ἔτ᾽ εἴπης†ὅτι συνέσταλμαι κακοῖς;
Θη. πρόβαινε. (1410–18)

---

[155] On changes in the notion of nobility at the end of the play, see Gregory 1991, esp. 143–7. On similar tendencies in Greek tragedy, see Gregory 1991: 123–4, who focuses especially on Euripides, and cf. Mantziou 2002: 238–41 for a perceptive discussion of the relevant vocabulary in Sophocles. For the notion of nobility in antiquity in general, see Rose 1992.

THESEUS: Do you no longer have any memory of your labours?
HERACLES: All those labours I endured were less than this.
THESEUS: If anyone sees you behaving like a woman, he will condemn you.
HERACLES: Am I now so low in your eyes? You did not think so once.
THESEUS: Yes, you are. For in your sickness you are not the famous
             Heracles of old.
HERACLES: Think what you were like when you were in trouble in Hades.
THESEUS: Yes, I was defeated in spirit then.
HERACLES: How then+can you say+that I have been brought to
             collapse by my suffering?
THESEUS: You must begin to go.

Theseus here cannot tolerate Heracles' excessive weeping
and wants to put an end to it by saying that such an attitude
carries the stigma of effeminacy and is inappropriate to the
kind of valour Heracles always displayed in his labours.[156]
This scene is the climax of Heracles' grief, which was expressed
earlier when Heracles commented on his state: ἀτὰρ πόνων δὴ
μυρίων ἐγευσάμην, | ὧν οὔτ᾽ ἀπεῖπον οὐδέν᾽ οὔτ᾽ ἀπ᾽ ὀμμάτων |
ἔσταξα πηγάς, οὐδ᾽ ἂν ὠιόμην ποτὲ | ἐς τοῦθ᾽ ἱκέσθαι, δάκρυ᾽ ἀπ᾽
ὀμμάτων βαλεῖν. | νῦν δ᾽, ὡς ἔοικε, τῆι τύχηι δουλευτέον, 'I
have experienced countless trials. I did not refuse a single one
of them nor did I ever shed tears and I never thought I should
ever come to this that I should actually weep now. But, as it is,
it appears I must let fortune dominate me' (1353–7).

We need to set this passage against a wider background.
Bacchylides has Heracles shed tears for what is said to be the
first time in the hero's life, in pity for Meleager's early death
(5.155–8).[157] The juxtaposition here between the strong epithet
'fearless in battle' (ἀδεισιβόαν, 155) and the image of Heracles
shedding tears is effective; the mighty hero who had fearlessly
encountered troubles in his life is affected by the feeling of
pity, an emotion not experienced before, which also marks a

[156] Since an aspect of Heracles' ambivalence was his crossing of the poles of virility
and femininity, Theseus' words here recall this ambivalence, highlight the difficulty of Heracles' state, and create suspense as to Heracles' reaction.
[157] On this famous ode by Bacchylides, see esp. Lefkowitz 1969; Burnett 1985; Cairns
1997. The Homeric Heracles also weeps when he finds himself in a helpless
situation (Il. 8.364); this, as Galinsky 1972: 15 aptly remarks, is a Homeric attempt
to humanize the otherwise violent epic hero. In Soph. Trach. 1070–5, Heracles says
that he is weeping for the first time, and describes weeping as effeminate.

change in Heracles as well as preparing for his own future experiences, for the fate of Meleager and that of Heracles are intertwined in the poem. Despite all the compassion that Heracles feels, which obviously marks a change in him, the hero can only be an observer of Meleager's suffering; he has not yet experienced the suffering itself. This is also shown by his address to Meleager (159–64), where he does not let himself be carried away by emotion, but shows that he is still a man of action.

In Greek tragedy, weeping can be regarded as beneficial and may cause pity in a listener, but it can also be criticized as futile.[158] Thus in *Trojan Women*, the Chorus remark that those who are in trouble find relief in tears (608–9).[159] But in Sophocles' *Electra* the Chorus say to Electra that she will not bring back her father from Hades by weeping (137–9).[160] The association of tears and weeping with women, however, often causes some tension when applied to men. Men weep when they feel pity for someone or when they themselves suffer misfortunes, and weeping occurs several times in association with old men apart from women;[161] but there is a sense that male weeping should not be excessive and also that it would be better done in private. Excessive weeping on the contrary could be criticized as a sign of unmanly weakness and feminization.[162]

Theseus' exhortation to Heracles to stop weeping is similar to that of Creon to Oedipus (*OT* 1515), or to Theseus' interruption

[158] On tears and weeping in Greek tragedy, with particular reference to *Alcestis*, see Segal 1993. On weeping in Greek literature in general, see also Arnould 1990.

[159] Cf. Aesch. *PV* 637–9, where Prometheus says to Io that indulging in weeping is worthwhile when one is likely to cause tears in the listener.

[160] So the Chorus in *Alcestis* tell Admetus that weeping does not bring the dead back (986–8). In the *Trojan Women* too, Hecuba urges Andromache to stop lamenting, for tears will not save her (698).

[161] E.g. Peleus in *Andro.* 1201; Amphitryon in *HF* 528, 1111, 1114, 1181.

[162] In *Trachiniae* Hyllus weeps at the suffering of his father (796), and the suffering Heracles himself says that he cries like a woman for the first time in his life (1070–5). Like the Euripidean Heracles, then, the Sophoclean hero has never shed tears before, and his shame at being shown to be like a woman is similar to Theseus' accusation of his friend that he is behaving like a woman. In both cases where the accusation of feminization occurs, the context is not simply excessive weeping but also being seen weeping by others. Thus the Sophoclean Heracles says that he was never seen weeping (*Trach.* 1072–3). He also urges his son to try and hold back his tears when he lights the funeral pyre, thus acting as the true son of his brave father (*Trach.* 1199–1201). In *Orestes*, Orestes asks his sister to stop the

of Adrastus' lamenting in order to ask him to focus on the funeral speech (Eur. *Supp.* 839–40). But the closest parallel is in *Alcestis*, where it is Heracles in fact who has the role of Theseus. Heracles there urges Admetus, who had not managed to restrain his weeping in front of Heracles before (530, 826), to endure his suffering, saying that prolonging his weeping is futile (1077–83). Here Heracles is reminded by Admetus that it is easy for someone to advise and console when he stands outside misfortune (1078) but at least he eventually shows some understanding for Admetus' prolonged weeping.

In *Heracles*, Theseus does not explicitly show understanding, although Heracles' reaction to his scorn (1410–17) seems to be effective in making Theseus implicitly admit that his attitude was unjustified; thus, Heracles has the last word (1417), and his question is answered simply by Theseus' urging him to start moving (πρόβαινε, 1418). Another Theseus was also impatient with another suffering hero, Oedipus in *Oedipus at Colonus*. There he checked Oedipus for clinging to his anger (592); his intention was good, that is, excessive anger is dangerous, but he rushed to conclusions about Oedipus without first knowing the reasons for his behaviour. When Oedipus pointed this out to him, Theseus admitted his mistake (593–4). In both plays, although Theseus is the glorified representative of Athens and has the distinctive qualities of this city, he cannot overshadow Oedipus and Heracles. It is the suffering character who remains at the centre of each drama throughout.

Conclusion

In this chapter I have examined issues regarding Heracles' *arete* and the presentation of Athens in the play. I began with an investigation of the way in which the part of the drama up to Heracles' return foreshadows important issues concerning

'womanish weeping' (γυναικείους γόους, 1022), and criticizes tears as unmanly (1031–2). In *Ajax* too, Tecmessa says that Ajax's lamentations were in sharp contrast to his belief that weeping was the sign of the cowardly man (317–20). Ajax in turn asks his wife to stop weeping, saying that wailing is characteristic of women (579–80).

arete, which Heracles addresses after his recovery from madness. Megara's decision to choose voluntary death in order to save the reputation of the family is repeated at the end of the play, when Heracles decides to kill himself because of his shame and his despair. But eventually, and contrary to Megara's earlier attitude, he decides to live. Heracles' change of mind implies a change also in the notion of nobility and heroic excellence. Enduring life now becomes the equivalent of courage instead of cowardice.

Heracles' decision to endure life is directly associated with his redefinition of divinity, which means that he dissociates himself now from the kind of gods who brought him down. Such a radical attitude to divinity belongs throughout to Heracles alone. Although other characters and the Chorus complain about the gods' behaviour towards Heracles, none of them reaches his radical position towards divinity. The extremity of Heracles' reaction against the gods, which matches the extremity of his suffering, turns out to be a catalyst for his assertion of his wish to live. Heracles' radical attitude towards the gods, although a positive factor for his decision to live, is also crucially relevant to what I have called his ambivalence in the play. He is both a suffering human being and a son of Zeus, and the play dramatizes the fundamental problems that his story presents. His final understanding of his story is that it needs to be totally revised, and he does not hesitate to claim his right to redefine the very notion of divinity.

I have also discussed how the presentation of Heracles as a bowman in the debate between Lycus and Amphitryon highlights ways in which his *arete* can be defined or challenged, and how the issue is eventually dealt with in the movement of the plot towards Athens, and in Heracles' combination of both the valour of the archer and the vulnerability of the hoplite. Athens becomes the only city which actively helps Heracles, and her appropriation of the great panhellenic hero is all the more crucial for a city which aspired to pre-eminence. But despite the importance of both Athens and Theseus, the tragedy remains that of Heracles, and the play shows him acquiring a new mentality, based on the recognition of the vulnerability of human life, the importance of human fellowship, and the need for endurance. Finding the courage to persevere, to take action and to recognize at least the possibility of reshaping one's life, introduces a sense of order and direction and constitutes a response to a seemingly chaotic and meaningless world of arbitrariness and violent disjunction.

CONCLUSION

In this book I have argued that *Heracles* is a far more complex tragedy than many critics have thought. Euripides exploits the conflicting views of ancient tradition about Heracles' nature and *arete*. The superlative strength that Heracles exhibited during his labours is laudable, but its transference from wildness into civilization becomes problematic. The play suggests that the solution is provided by the civic (and Athenocentric) context, where individuality and the archaic type of heroic excellence give way to solidarity and the value of community.

The drama is of central significance for an understanding of the religious universe of Euripidean tragedy. The extent to which in this play the divine imposition of madness upon Heracles questions the role of the gods, their justice and their concern for humans, is almost unique in the extant Euripidean corpus. Even in plays which portray vindictive gods, the dramatist attempts at least to show some justification for divine action. In *Hippolytus*, Aphrodite punishes Hippolytus because he refused to worship her, and she explicitly says that, when she receives honours from mortals, she reciprocates. In *Bacchae*, Pentheus is destroyed by Dionysus, but his death is presented as the result of his impiety towards the god. In both cases, to be sure, human suffering is enormous for all mortals involved in the dramatic action, but the gods are not left without serious motives for their actions. Even in the *Trojan Women*, a play which is permeated by grief, caused to some extent by divine involvement in the Trojan War, the seeming callousness and arbitrariness of the gods are given their motivation, when the audience hear in the prologue that the transgressions of the Greeks will not be left unpunished by the gods.

In *Heracles*, however, all attempts to find some justification or to make sense of divine motivation prove to be futile. The play has often been considered as the one Euripidean drama in which the gap between gods and humans is left completely unbridgeable. Even more, Heracles in his negation of the traditional gods has even been considered the mouthpiece of a rationalist Euripides who erases anthropomorphic gods. Euripides indeed opens wide the gap between humans and gods in this play, but he does not deny the existence of the traditional gods; rather, he presents gods as incomprehensible to such a degree that he ultimately shows the limits of human potential and knowledge. This is not a play where gods are erased, but a play where the human understanding of the divine is called into question.

Heracles is brought down because of Hera's jealousy, as all characters accept and as the audience must also have understood, since Hera's persecution of Heracles was a datum of myth. But at the same time, Iris complicates the divine motivation behind Heracles' destruction, by introducing the notion of justice and punishment. The exact motivation and the degree of its justification is further complicated by the absence of Zeus as well as by Lyssa's unwillingness to destroy Heracles. Zeus's absence may be explained by Iris' words (827–9) that destiny and Zeus did not allow anyone to harm Heracles before the completion of his labours. The implication is that even the king of the gods cannot interfere to save a mortal, or has to give in, when it is the will of another divinity to destroy him. Whether in our play it is merely the will of Hera to destroy Heracles, or this destruction is the result of wider divine workings, including destiny, is left unclear. What is clear, however, is that the gods have absolute power over humans, and that divine reciprocation for human piety is something that humans cannot demand but only hope for.

The building of an entire scene between Iris and Lyssa, where the former orders the destruction of Heracles but the latter expresses her unwillingness to destroy the pious hero, is a device which aptly shows that the divine universe is not entirely devoid of gods who show concern for humans and want to reciprocate human piety. Also, the intervention of the goddess Athena, the traditional agent of Zeus in protecting Heracles, to put an end to the hero's madness, shows that the divine framework of the play is more complex, and in particular, that humans are not totally abandoned. Athena's intervention to save Heracles, or at least to prevent him from adding to his murders that of his own father, is also important, for Athena is the patron goddess of Athens, and thus she foreshadows the role that her city will play in dissuading Heracles from suicide as his last deed of violence. Thus, although the play seems to be moving along secular lines after Heracles' recovery, it seems that the divine framework is also present and runs parallel to the orientation of the play towards an Athenian context; it will be to the 'city of Pallas' that Theseus invites Heracles to come (1323).

The fact that the play also has some place for divinities who care for humans is important in a context where the role of the gods is questioned throughout by mortals. The development of the plot indeed goes hand in hand with the development of the views that the characters and the Chorus have about their gods, to the extent, in fact, that each reversal in the plot causes a change in these views. Amphitryon is hopeful for the family's rescue insofar as his belief in Zeus is unshaken, but when all hope seems to have vanished he rebukes the god. Conversely, when the situation is reversed and Heracles appears, both Amphitryon and the Chorus reaffirm their belief in divine reciprocation, a belief which is in turn shaken when Heracles is afflicted with madness. Mortals think that they know their gods too well, but the events prove them wrong.

The culmination of the characters' ever-changing views of the gods is Heracles' criticism of the imperfections of the traditional gods and his own view of a faultless divinity. It is important here that Heracles does not deny the existence of imperfect gods. Rather, he holds that gods who are imperfect should not be considered to be proper gods by humans, in other words, they do not deserve the name 'god', and consequently they do not deserve human worship. Although the description of a faultless divinity may have been influenced by philosophical discussions current in Euripides' time, there is no need to think that Heracles here advocates an abstract notion of divinity which has nothing to do with the kind of anthropomorphic gods presented in the play.

In other words, Heracles has not suddenly turned into a philosopher. It is worth noticing something that has usually escaped critical comment: Heracles says clearly (1343) that his notion of a perfect divinity is not new, but one he has always held. This should not be dismissed as a mere 'rhetorical' saying. It means that he always had an 'idealized' view of the gods, which further implies that even in the past whenever gods behaved in an 'inappropriate' way according to the standards that he himself had set for his gods, he found them lacking. What has changed now, and has caused him to go one step further and refuse to call them gods, is that he has experienced a new kind of suffering; in other words, it is the first time that he cannot see even a trace of divine reciprocity, or the first time that he finds himself completely abandoned by the gods.

Heracles' 'idealized' notion of divinity must have sounded appealing to the audience, if one accepts that the hope for divine reciprocation lies behind worship. But no matter how appealing it may have sounded, and no matter how justified it seems to be when expressed by the suffering Heracles, the fact is that it remains ultimately irrelevant. Heracles may refuse to regard traditional gods as divinities, but gods with all their imperfections will continue to exist, and their behaviour cannot be determined by human standards. In a way, Heracles' 'idealized' view of the gods is the kind of radical behaviour one would expect from a figure of his stature. What is interesting in his reaction to his suffering is that it essentially expresses not impiety, but rather some sort of extreme piety. In other words, Heracles reacts not by saying that he no longer believes in gods, but by asserting his belief in perfect gods; he is not content with opting to live in a godless universe, but his assertion is rather a desperate cry for gods who would be considered faultless by human standards. I have used the term 'extreme piety' to indicate that Heracles' notion of divinity is idealized and idiosyncratic, if one assumes that gods cannot be judged by human standards, and that it is their divinity *per se*, not their behaviour, which is the prerequisite for their worship by mortals.

Heracles' view of divinity as faultless is significant, in that it contributes to his eventual decision not to commit suicide, but it remains ultimately his own. On the other hand, Theseus, the representative of Athens, accepts the traditional gods, their imperfections and their power to destroy humans, which means that he and his city show traditional piety. The help that Theseus gives to Heracles shows that friendship and human solidarity can empower mortals who have been brought down by gods; but he never expresses this empowerment in terms of an attack against gods. Athens is glorified for his willingness and ability to help the weak, but the city does not question the divine.

Heracles may have been brought down by Hera, but Athens can purify him from his present pollution, and rehabilitate him with the offer of refuge and future cult. Athens is glorified for being the only city to help Heracles, but despite the Athenocentric emphasis or the patriotic tone of the drama, it is Heracles who remains the focus of the drama throughout. The insight into human life that his suffering has given him is an experience that Theseus cannot fully grasp, no matter how enlightened he is. Heracles discovers his own vulnerability and the importance of human solidarity, and now sees his past heroic career in an enlarged perspective. The play makes the hero face challenges which are far more difficult than the opponents he had to fight during his labours. The labours are still important, but the development of the plot shifts the focus to an internalized Heracles and the way in which he responds to his suffering. The self-sufficiency, invulnerability and bravery he showed during the labours are now redefined. Their validity is never questioned, but Heracles' misfortune is also an experience that makes him regard courage in terms of dealing with suffering and deciding to endure life. The development of the image of Heracles, from the invincible hero of the labours to the courageous bearer of suffering, gives the play an important place in the tradition of Heracles, as a telling example of the humanization and moralization of this figure especially in the later fifth century BC.

BIBLIOGRAPHY

Adkins, A. W. H. (1960) *Merit and Responsibility: A Study in Greek Values.* Oxford.

(1966) 'Basic Greek Values in Euripides' *Hecuba* and *Hercules Furens'*, *CQ* 16: 193–219.

(1976) '*Polypragmosynê* and "Minding One's Business": A Study in Greek Social and Political Values', *CPh* 71: 301–27.

Aélion, R. (1983) *Euripide: Héritier d' Eschyle* (2 vols.). Paris.

Alford, C. F. (1992) *The Psychoanalytical Theory of Greek Tragedy.* Yale.

Allison, J. W. (1979) 'Thucydides and Πολυπραγμοσύνη', *AJAH* 4: 10–22.

Amburger, E. (1949) *Athena und Herakles in der Kunst.* Diss. Berlin.

Angeli Bernardini, P. (1978) 'Eracle e i centauri in Euripide, *Herc.* 364–74', *QUCC* 29: 63–70.

(ed.) (2000a) *Presenza e funzione della città di Tebe nella cultura greca.* Rome.

(2000b) 'La città di Tebe nell' *Eracle* di Euripide', in Angeli Bernardini (2000a): 219–32.

Angiò, F. (1989) 'Il quinto stasimo dell' *Eracle* di Euripide', *Sileno*: 191–6.

Aretz, S. (1999) *Die Opferung der Iphigeneia in Aulis. Die Rezeption des Mythos in antiken und modernen Dramen.* Stuttgart.

Arnott, P. D. (1989) *Public and Performance in Greek Theatre.* London.

Arnott, W. G. (1973) 'Euripides and the Unexpected', *G & R* 20: 49–64.

(1978) 'Red Herrings and Other Baits. A Study in Euripidean Techniques', *MPhL* 3: 1–24.

Arnould, D. (1990) *Le Rire et les larmes dans la littérature grecque d' Homère à Platon.* Paris.

Aronen, J. (1992) 'Notes on Athenian Drama as Ritual Myth-telling within the Cult of Dionysus', *Arctos* 26: 19–37.

Arrighetti, G. (ed.) (1964) *Satiro: Vita di Euripide.* Pisa.

Arrowsmith, W. A. (1954) *The Conversion of Heracles: An Essay in Euripidean Tragic Structure.* Diss. Princeton.

(1956) 'Introduction to *Heracles'*, in *The Complete Greek Tragedies: Euripides*, eds. D. Grene and R. Lattimore vol. II. Chicago.

Assaël, J. (1994) 'L' *Héraclès* d' Euripide et les ténèbres infernales', *LEC* 62: 313–26.

(1996) ' Le Choeur de 'vieux cygnes' de l' *Héraclès* d' Euripide', *CGITA*, 9: 69–91.

Babut, D. (1974) 'Xénophane critique des poètes', *AC* 43: 83–117.

Bárberi-Squarotti, G. (1993) *"La Rete mortale": caccia e cacciatore nelle tragedie di Euripide*. Rome.

Barlow, S. A. (1971) *The Imagery of Euripides: A Study in the Dramatic Use of Pictorial Language*. London.

(1981) 'Sophocles' *Ajax* and Euripides' *Heracles*', *Ramus* 10: 112–28.

(ed.) (1986) *Euripides: Trojan Women*. Warminster.

(1993) 'Structure and Dramatic Realism in Euripides' *Heracles*', in McAuslan and Walcot (1993): 193–203.

(ed.) (1996) *Euripides: Heracles*. Warminster.

Barrett, W. S. (ed.) (1964) *Euripides: Hippolytos*. Oxford.

Bartosiewiczová, J. (1987–8) 'Zum *Herakles* des Euripides: Ein Beitrag zur Interpretation', *GLO* 19–20: 3–11.

Bates, W. N. (1930) *Euripides: A Student of Human Nature*. Philadelphia.

Baudy, G. J. (1993) 'Die Herrschaft des Wolfes: Das Thema der "Verkehrten Welt" in Euripides' *Herakles*', *Hermes* 121: 159–80.

Bauren, C. (1992) 'Héraclès dans l' épopée Homerique', in Bonnet and Jourdain-Annequin (1992): 67–109.

Beckel, G. (1961) *Götterbeistand in der Bildüberlieferung griechischer Heldensagen*. Waldsassen.

Becroft, S. J. (1972) *Personal Relationships in the Heracles of Euripides*. Diss. Yale.

Beta, S. (1999) 'Madness on the Comic Stage: Aristophanes' *Wasps* and Euripides' *Herakles*', *GRBS* 40: 135–57.

Bierl, A. F. H. (1991) *Dionysos und die griechische Tragödie*. Tübingen.

Billerbeck, M. (ed.) (1999) *Seneca: Hercules Furens*. Leiden.

Blaiklock, E. M. (1945) 'The Epileptic', *G & R* 14: 48–63.

(1952) *The Male Characters of Euripides: A Study in Realism*. Wellington.

Blank, D. L. (ed.) (1998) *Sextus Empiricus: Against the Grammarians (Adversus Mathematicos I)*. Oxford.

Blundell, M. W. (1989) *Helping Friends and Harming Enemies: A Study in Sophocles and Greek Ethics*. Cambridge.

Boardman, J. (1972) 'Herakles, Peisistratos and Sons', *RA* 1972: 59–72.

(1975) 'Herakles, Peisistratos and Eleusis', *JHS* 95: 1–12.

(1984) 'Image and Politics in Sixth Century Athens', in *Ancient Greek and Related Pottery: Proceedings of the International Vase Symposium in Amsterdam*, ed. H. A. G. Brijder. Amsterdam: 239–47.

(1989) 'Herakles, Peisistratos and the Unconvinced', *JHS* 109: 158–9.

Boardman, J. et al. (1988) 'Herakles', in *LIMC* iv.1. Zurich: 728–838.

(1990) 'Herakles', in *LIMC* v.1. Zurich: 1–192.

Bond, G. W. (ed.) (1981) *Euripides: Heracles*. Oxford.

Bond, R. S (1996) 'Homeric Echoes in *Rhesus*', *AJPh* 117: 255–73.

Bonnechère, P. (1994) *Le Sacrifice humain en Grèce ancienne*. Liège.

Bonnet, C. and Jourdain-Annequin, C. (eds.) (1992) *Héraclès: d'une rive à l'autre de la Méditerranée. Bilan et perspectives*. Brussels.

Bowie, E. L. (1993) 'Lies, Fiction and Slander in Early Greek Poetry', in Gill and Wiseman (1993): 1–37.

Bowra, C. M. (1938) 'Xenophanes on Songs and Feasts', *CPh* 33: 353–67.

Braden, G. (1993) 'Herakles and Hercules: Survival in Greek and Roman Tragedy (with a Coda on *King Lear*), in Scodel (1993): 245–64.

Brelich, A. (1958) *Gli eroi greci: un problema storico-religioso*. Rome.

Bremer, J. M. (1972) 'Euripides' *Heracles* 581', *CQ* 22: 236–40.

Brommer, F. (1984) *Herakles II: Die Unkanonischen Taten des Helden*. Darmstadt.

(1986) *Heracles. The Twelve Labors of the Hero in Ancient Art and Literature*, trans. and enlarged by S. J. Schwarz. New York. [Münster 1979.]

Brown, A. L. (1978) 'Wretched Tales of Poets: Euripides, *Heracles* 1340–6', *PCPhS* 24: 22–30.

(1983) 'The Erinyes in the *Oresteia*: Real Life, the Supernatural, and the Stage', *JHS* 103: 13–34.

Bruni, A. and Piccitto, L. (1991) *Follia e realtà nella letteratura tragica*. Milan.

Burian, P. (1972) 'Supplication and Hero Cult in Sophocles' *Ajax*', *GRBS* 13: 151–6.

(1974) 'Suppliant and Saviour: Oedipus at Colonus', *Phoenix* 28: 408–29.

(ed.) (1985) *Directions in Euripidean Criticism: a Collection of Essays*. Durham.

Burkert, W. (1966) 'Greek Tragedy and Sacrificial Ritual', *GRBS* 7: 87–121.

(1987) *Ancient Mystery Cults*. Cambridge, Mass.

Burnett, A. P. (1971) *Catastrophe Survived. Euripides' Plays of Mixed Reversal*. Oxford.

(1973) 'Medea and the Tragedy of Revenge', *CPh* 68: 1–24.

(1985) *The Art of Bacchylides*. Cambridge, Mass.

(1998) *Revenge in Attic and Later Tragedies*. Berkeley.

Busch, G. (1937) *Untersuchungen zum Wesen der TYXH in den Tragödien des Euripides*. Heidelberg.

Buxton, R. G. A. (1988) 'Bafflement in Greek Tragedy', *Métis* 3: 41–51.

(1994) *Imaginary Greece: the Contexts of Mythology*. Cambridge.

Byl, S. (1975) 'Lamentations sur la vieillesse dans la tragédie grecque', in *Le monde grec: Pensée, littérature, histoire, documents. Hommages à Claire Préaux*, eds. J. Bingen et al. Brussels: 130–9.

Cairns, D. (1993) *Aidôs: The Psychology and Ethics of Honour and Shame in Ancient Greek Literature*. Oxford.

(1997) 'Form and Meaning in Bacchylides' Fifth Ode', *Scholia* 6: 34–48.

Calame, C. (1990)*Thésée et l' imaginaire athénien: Légende et culte en Grèce antique*. Lausanne.

Calder, W. M. (1960) Review of LOBEL, E. et al. (eds.) (1957) *The Oxyrhynchus Papyri, Part XXIV*. London, *CPh* 55: 127–8.

Carpenter, T. H. and Faraone, C. A. (eds.) (1993) *Masks of Dionysus*. Ithaca.

Carrière, J. (1952) 'La Composition de l' *Héraclès* d' Euripide', *AFLT* 2: 2–14.

(1972) 'L' Apparition d' Athéna dans l' *Héraclès* d' Euripide', in *Studi classici in onore di Quintino Cataudella*, eds. C. U. Crimi et al. vol. I. Catania: 233–6.

(1975) 'Art et lyrisme: une galerie de métopes dans un choeur tragique', *Pallas* 11: 13–22.

Casabona, J. (1966) *Recherches sur le vocabulaire des sacrifices en Grec des origines à la fin de l' époque classique*. Aix-en-Provence.

Cerri, G. (2000) 'L' etica di Simonide nell' *Eracle* di Euripide: l' opposizione mitica Atene-Tebe', in Angeli-Bernardini (2000a): 233–66.

Chalk, H. H. O. (1962) '*Arete* and *Bia* in Euripides' *Herakles*', *JHS* 82: 7–18.

Ciani, M. G. (1974) 'Lessico e funzione della follia nella tragedia greca', *BIFG* 1: 70–110.

(1975) 'La *consolatio* nei tragici greci: elementi di un topos', *BIFG* 2: 89–129.

Clinton, C. (1992) *Myth and Cult: the Iconography of the Eleusinian Mysteries*. Stockholm.

Colakis, M. (1986) 'The Laughter of the Suitors in *Odyssey* 20', *CW* 79: 137–44.

Collard, C. (1975a) 'Formal Debates in Euripides' Drama', *G & R* 22: 58–71.

(ed.) (1975b) *Euripides: Supplices*. Groningen.

(ed.) (1991) *Euripides: Hecuba*. Warminster.

(1995) 'The Pirithous Fragments', in *De Homero a Libanio*, ed. J. A. López Férez. Madrid: 183–93.

Collard, C. et al. (eds.) (1995) *Euripides: Selected Fragmentary Plays*. Warminster.

Collinge, N. E. (1962) 'Medical Terms and Clinical Attitudes in the Tragedians', *BICS* 9: 43–56.

Conacher, D. J. (1967) *Euripidean Drama: Myth, Theme, and Structure*. Toronto.

(1998) *Euripides and the Sophists: Some Dramatic Treatments of Philosophical Ideas*. Duckworth.

Connor, W. R. (1985) 'The Razing of the House in Greek Society', *TAPhA* 115: 79–102.

Conradie, P. J. (1958) *Herakles in die Griekse Tragedie*. Groningen.

Craik, E. (ed.) (1988) *Euripides: Phoenician Women*. Warminster.

(2001) 'Medical Reference in Euripides', *BICS* 45: 81–95.

Croally, N. T. (1994) *Euripidean Polemic: The Trojan Women and the Function of Tragedy*. Cambridge.

Cropp M. J. (1975) *A Stylistic and Analytical Commentary on Euripides' Herakles 1–814, with an Introduction to the Play as a whole*. Diss. Toronto.

(1986) 'Heracles, Electra and the Odyssey', in Cropp et al. (1986): 187–99.

(ed.) (1988) Euripides: Electra. Warminster.

(ed.) (2000) Euripides: Iphigenia in Tauris. Warminster.

Cropp, M. et al. (eds.) (1986) Greek Tragedy and its Legacy: Essays Presented to D.J. Conacher. Calgary.

(2000) Euripides and Tragic Theatre in the Late Fifth Century, Champaign, Illinois (ICS 1999–2000).

Danforth, L. M. (1982) The Death Rituals of Rural Greece. Princeton.

Davie, J. N. (1982) 'Theseus the King in Fifth-century Athens', G & R 29: 25–34.

Davis, M. (1986) 'Politics and Madness', in Euben (1986): 142–61.

Defradas, J. (1962) 'Le Banquet de Xénophane', REG 75: 344–65.

Delebecque, E. (1951) Euripide et la guerre du Péloponnèse. Paris.

Denniston, J. D. (ed.) (1939) Euripides: Electra. Oxford.

Desch, W. (1986) 'Der Herakles des Euripides und die Götter', Philologus 130: 8–23.

Detienne, M. (1996) The Masters of Truth in Archaic Greece, trans. J. Lloyd. New York. [Paris 1973.]

Devereux, G. (1970) 'The Psychotherapy Scene in Euripides' Bacchae', JHS 90: 35–48.

Dieterich, A. (1891) 'Schlafszenen auf der attischen Bühne', RhM 46: 25–46.

Diggle, J. (1994) Euripidea: Collected Essays. Oxford.

(1996) 'P. Petrie 1.1–2: Euripides, Antiope (fr. 223 (Nauck) Kannicht, XLVIII Kambitsis)', PCPS 42: 106–26.

(ed.) (1998) Tragicorum Graecorum Fragmenta Selecta. Oxford.

(1999) 'Euripides the Psychologist', in Patsalidis and Sakellaridou (1999): 287–96.

Dillon, M. (1991) 'Tragic Laughter', CW 84: 345–55.

Dodds, E. R. (1929) 'Euripides the Irrationalist', CR 43: 97–104.

(ed.) (²1960) Euripides: Bacchae. Oxford.

Douglas, M. (1966) Purity and Danger. London.

Downing, E. (1990) 'Apate, Agon, and Literary Self-Reflexivity in Euripides' Helen', in Essays on Classical and Comparative Literature in Honor of T.G. Rosenmeyer, eds. M. Griffith and D. Mastronarde. Atlanta: 1–16.

Drexler, H. (1943/9) 'Zum Herakles des Euripides', NAWG: 311–43.

Drew Griffith, R. (1993) 'Oedipus pharmakos? Alleged Scapegoating in Sophocles' Oedipus the King', Phoenix 47: 95–114.

Duchemin, J. (1967) 'Le Personnage de Lyssa dans l' Héraclès Furieux d' Euripide', REG 80: 130–9.

(²1968) L' AΓΩN dans la tragédie grecque. Paris.

Dugas, C. and Flacelière, R. (1958) Thésée: images et récits. Paris.

Dumézil, G. (1969) Heur et malheur du guerrier. Paris.

Dumortier, J. (²1975) Le Vocabulaire médical d' Eschyle et les écrits Hippocratiques. Paris.

Dunn, F. M. (1996) *Tragedy's End: Closure and Innovation in Euripidean Drama*. Oxford.

(1997) 'Ends and Means in Euripides' *Heracles*', in *Classical Closure: Reading the End in Greek and Latin Literature*, eds. D. H. Roberts et al. Princeton: 83–111.

(2000) 'Euripidean Aetiologies', *CB* 76: 3–27.

Durand, J.-L. (1986) *Sacrifice et labour en Grèce ancienne: essai d' anthropologie religieuse*. Paris.

Easterling, P. E. (ed.) (1982) *Sophocles: Trachiniae*. Cambridge.

(1984) 'The Tragic Homer', *BICS* 31: 1–8.

(1987) 'Putting Together the Pieces: a Passage in the *Bacchae*', *Omnibus* 14: 14–16.

(1988) 'Tragedy and Ritual', *Métis* 3: 87–109.

(1989) 'City Settings in Greek Poetry', *PCA* 86: 5–17.

(1993a) 'Tragedy and Ritual', in Scodel (1993): 7–23.

(1993b) 'Gods on Stage in Greek Tragedy', in *Religio Graeco-Romana, Festschrift für Walter Pötscher*, eds. J. Dalfen et al. *Grazer Beiträge* Suppl. V. Graz: 77–86.

(1994) 'Euripides Outside Athens: a Speculative Note', *ICS* 19: 73–80.

(ed.) (1997) *The Cambridge Companion to Greek Tragedy*. Cambridge.

Ebener, D. (1966) *Rhesos: Tragödie eines unbekannten Dichters*. Berlin.

(1981) 'Selbstverwirklichung des Menschen im euripideischen *Herakles*', *Philologus* 125: 176–80.

Effe, B. (1980) 'Der Funktionswandel des Herakles-Mythos in der griechischen Literatur', *Poetica* 12: 145–66.

(1990) 'Die Grenzen der Aufklärung: zur Funktion des Mythos bei Euripides', in *Mythos: Erzählende Weltdeutung im Spannungsfeld von Ritual, Geschichte und Rationalität*, eds. G. Binder and B. Effe. Trier: 56–74.

Ehrenberg, V. (1946) 'Tragic Heracles', in V. Ehrenberg, *Aspects of the Ancient World*. Oxford: 144–66.

(1947) '*Polypragmosynê*: a Study in Greek politics', *JHS* 67: 46–67.

(1954) *Sophocles and Pericles*. Oxford.

Eisenstadt, M. (1974) 'Xenophanes' Proposed Reform of Greek Religion', *Hermes* 102: 142–50.

Eisner, R. (1979) 'Euripides' Use of Myth', *Arethusa* 12: 153–74.

Elliott-Sorum, C. (1978) 'Monsters and the Family: the Exodos of Sophocles' *Trachiniae*', *GRBS* 19: 59–73.

Erbse, H. (1984) *Studien zum Prolog der euripideischen Tragödie*. Berlin.

Euben, J. P. (ed.) (1986) *Greek Tragedy and Political Theory*. Berkeley.

(1990) *The Tragedy of Political Theory: the Road not Taken*. Princeton.

Faber, M. D. (1970) *Suicide in Greek Tragedy*. New York.

Farnell, L. R. (1921) *Greek Hero Cults and Ideas of Immortality*. Oxford.

Feder, L. (1980) *Madness in Literature*. Princeton.

Fenik, B. (1964) *Iliad X and the* Rhesus. Brussels.

Ferguson, J. (1969) 'Tetralogies, Divine Paternity, and the Plays of 414', *TAPhA* 100: 109–17.

Ferrini, F. (1978) 'Tragedia e patologia: lessico Ippocratico in Euripide', *QUCC* 29: 49–62.

Fisher, R. K. (1992) 'The "Palace Miracles" in Euripides' *Bacchae*: a Reconsideration', *AJPh* 113: 179–88.

Fitch, J. G. (ed.) (1987) *Seneca's Hercules Furens*. Ithaca.

Fitton, J. W. (1961) 'The *Suppliant Women* and the *Heraklidai* of Euripides', *Hermes* 89: 430–61.

Fitzgerald, G. I. (1991) 'The Euripidean Heracles: an Intellectual and a Coward?', *Mnemosyne* 44: 85–95.

Flashar, H. (1966) *Melancholie und Melancholiker in der medizinischen Theorie der Antike*. Berlin.

Foley, H. P. (1985) *Ritual Irony: Poetry and Sacrifice in Euripides*. Ithaca.

Fontenrose, J. (1968) 'The Hero as Athlete', *CSCA* 1: 73–104.

Franzino, E. (1995) 'Euripides' *Heracles* 858–73', *ICS* 20: 57–63.

Friedrich, R. (1996) 'Everything to do with Dionysus? Ritualism, the Dionysiac, and the Tragic', in *Tragedy and the Tragic: Greek Theatre and Beyond*, ed. M. S. Silk. Oxford: 257–83.

Furley, D. (1986) 'Euripides on the Sanity of Heracles', in *Studies in Honour of T.B.L. Webster*, eds. J. H. Betts et al. vol. 1. Bristol: 102–13.

Galinsky, G. K. (1972) *The Herakles Theme: The Adaptations of the Hero in Literature from Homer to the Twentieth Century*. Oxford.

Gamble, R. B. (1970) 'Euripides' *Suppliant Women*: Decision and Ambivalence', *Hermes* 98: 385–405.

Gantz, T. (1993) *Early Greek Myth: A Guide to Literary and Artistic Sources* vol. 1. Baltimore.

Garrison, E. P. (1995) *Groaning Tears: Ethical and Dramatic aspects of Suicide in Greek Tragedy*. Leiden.

Garvie, A. F. (ed.) (1986) *Aeschylus: Choephori*. Oxford.

(ed.) (1998) *Sophocles: Ajax*. Warminster.

Gasparri, C. et al. (1986) 'Dionysos', in *LIMC* III.1. Zurich: 414–566.

Gasti, H. [Ε. Γκαστή] (1998) 'Σοφοκλέους Αίας: Η Τραγωδία της Όρασης', *Dodone* 27: 165–204.

Gennep, A. van (1960) *The Rites of Passage*, trans. M. B. Vizedom and G. L. Caffee. London. [Paris 1909.]

Gentili, B. (1977) 'Eracle "omicida giustissimo": Pisandro, Stesicoro e Pindaro', in Gentili and Paioni (1977): 299–305.

Gentili, B. and Paioni, G. (eds.) (1977) *Il mito greco: atti del convegno internazionale (Urbino 7–12 Maggio 1973)*. Rome.

George, D. P. (1994) 'Euripides' *Heracles* 140–325: Staging and the Stage Iconography of Heracles' Bow', *GRBS* 35: 145–57.

Georgoudi, S. (1999) 'À propos du sacrifice humain en Grèce ancienne: remarques critiques', *Archiv für Religionsgeschichte* 1: 61–82.

Gerber, D. E. (ed.) (1982) *Pindar's Olympian One: A Commentary*. Toronto.

Gernet, L. (1953) 'Dionysos et la religion dionysiaque: eléments hérités et traits originaux', *REG* 66: 377–95.

Giannakis G. K. [Γ. Κ. Γιαννάκης] (1998) 'Το ποιητικό μοτίβο "γάμος-θάνατος" στην αρχαία ελληνική και την ινδοευρωπαϊκή', *Dodone* 27: 93–113.

Giannopoulou, V. (2000) 'Divine Agency and *Tyche* in Euripides' *Ion*: Ambiguity and Shifting Perspectives', in Cropp et al. (2000): 257–71.

Gibert, J. (1995) *Change of Mind in Greek Tragedy*. Göttingen.

(1997) 'Euripides' *Heracles* 1351 and the Hero's Encounter with Death', *CPh* 92: 247–58.

(2003) 'Apollo's Sacrifice: the Limits of a Metaphor in Greek Tragedy', *HSCP* 101: 159–206.

Giles, P. (1916) 'Some Greek Medical Terms and Euripides' Conception of the Madness of Heracles', *PCPhS* 103–5: 14–16.

Gill, C. (1993a) 'Plato on Falsehood – not Fiction', in Gill and Wiseman (1993): 38–87.

(1993b) 'Bow, Oracle, and Epiphany in Sophocles' *Philoctetes*', in McAuslan and Walcot (1993): 95–103.

(1996) 'Mind and Madness in Greek Tragedy', *Apeiron* 29: 249–67.

Gill, C. and Wiseman, T. P. (eds.) (1993) *Lies and Fiction in the Ancient World*. Exeter.

Girard, R. (1977) *Violence and the Sacred*, trans. P. Gregory. Baltimore. [Paris 1972.]

Goebel, G. H. and Nevin, T. R. (eds.) (1977) *Euripides: Heracles*. Madison.

Goff, B. (ed.) (1995) *History, Tragedy, Theory: Dialogues on Athenian Drama*. Austin.

Golden, M. (1988) 'Did the Ancients Care when their Children Died?', *G & R* 35: 152–63.

Goldhill, S. (1986) *Reading Greek Tragedy*. Cambridge.

(1990) 'The Great Dionysia and Civic Ideology', in Winkler and Zeitlin (1990): 97–129.

(1991) 'Violence in Greek Tragedy', in *Violence in Drama*, ed. J. Redmond. Cambridge: 15–33.

(1993) 'Reading Performance Criticism', in McAuslan and Walcot (1993): 1–11.

(1997) 'Modern Critical Approaches to Greek Tragedy', in Easterling (1997): 324–47.

Goossens, R. (1962) *Euripide et Athènes*. Brussels.

Gordon, R. L. (1979) 'Reason and Ritual in Greek Tragedy: on René Girard, *Violence and the Sacred* and Marcel Detienne, *The Gardens of Adonis*', *Comparative Criticism Yearbook* 1: 279–310.

Gould, J. P. (1973) *'Hiketeia'*, *JHS* 93: 74–103.

(1985) 'On Making Sense of Greek Religion', in *Greek Religion and Society*, eds. P. E. Easterling and J. V. Muir. Cambridge: 1–33.

Graf, F. (1974) *Eleusis und die Orphische Dichtung Athens in vorhellenistischer Zeit*. Berlin.

(1993) 'Euripides, Myth, and the Gods', in F. Graf, *Greek Mythology: an Introduction*, trans. T. Marier. Baltimore: 168–75. [Munich 1987.]

(ed.) (1998) *Ansichten griechischer Rituale*. Geburtstags-Symposium für Walter Burkert. Stuttgart.

Grassby, R. M. R. (1969) *The Religious Content of the Heracles of Euripides*. Diss. Yale.

Greenwood, L. H. G. (1953) *Aspects of Euripidean Tragedy*. Cambridge.

Gregory J. (1974) *Madness in the Heracles, Orestes and Bacchae: A Study in Euripidean Drama*. Diss. Harvard.

(1977) *'Euripides' Heracles'*, *YCS* 25: 259–75.

(1991) *Euripides and the Instruction of the Athenians*. Michigan.

(ed.) (1999) *Euripides: Hecuba*. Atlanta.

(2000) 'Comic Elements in Euripides', in Cropp et al. (2000): 59–74.

Griffin, J. (1998) 'The Social Function of Attic Tragedy', *CQ* 48: 39–61.

(1999) 'Sophocles and the Democratic City', in *Sophocles Revisited: Essays Presented to Sir Hugh Lloyd-Jones*, ed. J. Griffin. Oxford: 73–94.

Griffith, M. (ed.) (1983) *Aeschylus: Prometheus Bound*. Cambridge.

(ed.) (1999) *Sophocles: Antigone*. Cambridge.

Griffiths, E. M. (2002) *'Euripides' Herakles* and the Pursuit of Immortality'. *Mnemosyne* 55: 641–56.

Grossmann, G. (1968) 'Das Lachen des Aias', *MH* 25: 65–85.

(1970) *Promethie und Orestie*. Heidelberg.

Grube, G. M. A. (1941) *The Drama of Euripides*. London.

Grummond, W. W. de (1983) 'Heracles' Entrance: an Illustration of Euripidean Method', *Eranos* 81: 83–90.

Gruppe, O. (1918) 'Herakles', in W. Kroll (ed.), *RE* Supplement III. Stuttgart: 910–1000.

Guépin, J. P. (1968) *The Tragic Paradox. Myth and Ritual in Greek Tragedy*. Amsterdam.

Hainsworth, B. (ed.) (1993) *The Iliad: A Commentary, vol. III: Books 9–12*. Cambridge.

Hall, E. (1989) *Inventing the Barbarian: Greek Self-definition through Tragedy*. Oxford.

(2003) 'Introduction', in R. Waterfield transl. *Euripides: Alcestis, Heracles, Children of Heracles, Cyclops*. Oxford: vii–xli.

(ed.) (forthcoming) *The Rhesus attributed to Euripides*. Warminster.

Halleran, M. R. (1986) 'Rhetoric, Irony and the Ending of Euripides' *Herakles'*, *CA* 5: 171–81.

(1988) *The Heracles of Euripides: Introduction, Notes and Interpretative Essay*. Cambridge, Mass.

(ed.) (1995) *Euripides: Hippolytus*. Warminster.

Hallett, C. A. and Hallett, E. S. (1980) *The Revenger's Madness: A Study of Revenge Tragedy Motifs*. Lincoln.

Hamilton, R. (1985) 'Slings and Arrows: the Debate with Lycus in the *Heracles*', *TAPhA* 115: 19–25.

Hangard, J. (1976) 'Remarques sur quelques motifs répétés dans l' *Héraclès* d' Euripide', in *Miscellanea Tragica in honorem J.C. Kamerbeek*, eds. J. M. Bremer et al. Amsterdam: 125–46.

Hanson, V. D. (ed.) (1991) *Hoplites: the Classical Greek Battle Experience*. London.

Hardin, R. F. (1983) '"Ritual" in Recent Criticism: the Elusive Sense of Community', *PMLA* 98: 846–62.

Harris, W. V. (2001) *Restraining Rage: the Ideology of Anger Control in Classical Antiquity*. Cambridge, Mass.

Harsh, P. W. (1960) 'The Role of the Bow in the *Philoctetes* of Sophocles', *AJPh* 81: 408–14.

Hartigan, K. (1987) 'Euripidean Madness: Herakles and Orestes', *G & R* 34: 126–35.

(1997) 'Male Sacrifice/Female Revenge in a Godless World: Euripides' *Hekabe*', *Colby Quarterly* 33: 26–41.

HELIOS 17, 1 (1990) special issue on R. Girard and Western Literature.

Hendrickson, G. L. (1919) 'The Heracles Myth and its Treatment by Euripides', in *Classical Studies in Honor of Charles Forster Smith*. Madison: 11–29.

Henrichs, A. (1979) 'Greek and Roman Glimpses of Dionysos', in *Dionysos and his Circle: Ancient Through Modern*, ed. C. Houser. Cambridge, Mass.: 1–11.

(1981) 'Human Sacrifice in Greek Religion', in J. Rudhardt and O. Reverdin, *Le sacrifice dans l' antiquité*. Geneva: 195–242.

(1982) 'Changing Dionysiac Identities', in *Jewish and Christian Self-Definition*, eds. B. F. Meyer and E. P. Sanders. London: 137–60.

(1984) 'Loss of Self, Suffering, Violence: the Modern View of Dionysus from Nietzsche to Girard', *HSCP* 88: 205–40.

(1986) 'The Last of the Detractors: Friedrich Nietzsche's Condemnation of Euripides', *GRBS* 27: 369–97.

(1993) '"He has a God in him": Human and Divine in the Modern Perception of Dionysus', in Carpenter and Faraone (1993): 13–43.

(1995) '"Why Should I dance?" Choral Self-referentiality in Greek Tragedy', *Arion* 3: 56–111.

(1996a) 'Dancing in Athens, Dancing on Delos: some Patterns of Choral Projection in Euripides', *Philologus* 140: 48–62.

(1996b) 'Dionysus', in *Oxford Classical Dictionary*, eds. S. Hornblower and A. Spawforth, 3rd edn. Oxford: 479–82.

BIBLIOGRAPHY

(2000) 'Drama and *drōmena*: Bloodshed, Violence, and Sacrificial Metaphor in Euripides', *HSCP* 100: 173–88.

Hershkowitz, D. (1998) *The Madness of Epic: Reading Insanity from Homer to Statius*. Oxford.

Hesk, J. (2000) *Deception and Democracy in Classical Athens*. Cambridge.

Heubeck, A. et al. (1988) *A Commentary on Homer's Odyssey*, vol. I. Oxford.

Higgins, W. E. (1984) 'Deciphering Time in the *Heracles* of Euripides', *QUCC* 47: 89–109.

Holt, P. (1992) 'Herakles' Apotheosis in Lost Greek Literature and Art', *AC* 61: 38–59.

Hose, M. (1990) *Studien zum Chor bei Euripides*, 1st vol. Stuttgart.

(1991) *Studien zum Chor bei Euripides*, 2nd vol. Stuttgart.

Hourmouziades, N. C. (²1984) *Satyrika*. Athens.

Howie, J. C. (1983) 'The Revision of Myth in Pindar *Olympian* One: the Death and Revival of Pelops (25–27, 36–66)', in *Papers of the Liverpool Latin Seminar* 4: 277–313.

Hughes, D. D. (1991) *Human Sacrifice in Ancient Greece*. London.

Huttner, U. (1997) *Die politische Rolle der Heraklesgestalt im griechischen Herrschertum*. Stuttgart.

Jaekel, S. (1972) 'Der euripideische *Herakles* als ein Drama der Wende', *Gymnasium* 79: 50–61.

Jakob, D. I. [Δ. Ι. Ιακώβ] (1998) *Η Ποιητική της Αρχαίας Ελληνικής Τραγωδίας*. Athens.

(2000) 'Σεισμός και κεραυνός στις Βάκχες του Ευριπίδη. Μια αναψηλάφηση του θαύματος του παλατιού', in *Κτερίσματα. Φιλολογικά Μελετήματα αφιερωμένα στον Ιωάννη Σ. Καμπίτση (1938–1990)*, eds., G. M. Sifakis et al. Herakleion: 61–71.

James, C. (1969) '"Whether 'tis Nobler...". Some Thoughts on the Fate of Sophocles' Ajax and Euripides' Heracles, with Special Reference to the Question of Suicide', *Pegasus* 12: 10–20.

Jameson, M. H. (1988) 'Sacrifice and Ritual: Greece', in *Civilization of the Ancient Mediterranean: Greece and Rome* vol. II, eds. M. Grant and R. Kitzinger. New York: 959–79.

Johnson, J. F (2002) 'Compassion and Friendship in Euripides' *Herakles*', *CB* 78: 115–29.

Jong, I. J. F. de (1991) *Narrative in Drama: The Art of the Messenger's Speech*. Leiden.

Jouan, F. (1966) *Euripide et les Chants Cypriens*. Paris.

(1970) 'Le *Prométhée* d' Eschyle et l' *Héraclés* d' Euripide', *REA* 72: 317–31.

Jouan, F. and van Looy, H. (1998) *Euripide. Fragments, 1re partie*. Paris.

Jouanna, J. (1992) 'Rite et spectacle dans la tragédie grecque: remarques sur l' utilization dramatique des libations et des sacrifices', *Pallas* 38: 47–56.

Jourdain-Annequin, C. (1989) *Héraclès aux portes du soir*. Paris.

Kambitsis, J. (ed.) (1972) *Euripides: Antiope*. Athens.

Kamerbeek, J. C. (1966) 'Unity and Meaning of Euripides' *Heracles*', *Mnemosyne* 19: 1–16.

Kannicht, R. (ed.) (1969) *Euripides: Helena* (2 vols.). Heidelberg.

Karabela, H. I (E. I. Καράμπελα) (2003) Σκοτεινὸν φάος. Δραματολογική Προσέγγιση στον Ηρακλή του Ευριπίδη. Herakleion.

Katsouris, A. (1976) 'The Suicide Motif in Ancient Drama', *Dioniso* 47: 5–36.

Kearns, E. (1989) *The Heroes of Attica*, *BICS* Suppl. 57. London.

Keuls, E. (1974) *The Water Carriers in Hades: A Study of Catharsis through Toil in Classical Antiquity*. Amsterdam.

Kirk, G. S. (1977) 'Methodological Reflexions on the Myths of Heracles', in Gentili and Paioni (1977): 285–97.

    (1985) *The Iliad: A Commentary*, *vol. I: books 1–4*. Cambridge.

Kirkpatrick, J. and Dunn, F. (2002) 'Heracles, Cercopes, and Paracomedy', *TAPhA* 132: 29–61.

Kitto, H. D. F. (³1961) *Greek Tragedy: A Literary Study*. London.

Kleve, K. (1964) '*Apragmosynê* and *Polypragmosynê*: Two Slogans in Athenian Politics', *SO* 39: 83–8.

Knox, B. M. W. (1964) *The Heroic Temper: Studies in Sophoclean Tragedy*. Berkeley.

    (1979) 'Second Thoughts in Greek Tragedy', in B. Knox, *Word and Action: Essays on the Ancient Theatre*. Baltimore: 231–49.

Komornicka, A. M. (1972) 'Quelques remarques sur la notion d' ΑΛΑΘΕΙΑ et de ΨΕΥΔΟΣ chez Pindare', *Eos* 60: 235–53.

    (1981) 'Termes déterminant le vrai et le faux chez Pindare', in *Aischylos und Pindar: Studien zu Werk und Nachwirkung*, ed. E. Schmidt. Berlin: 81–9.

Konstan, D. (1985) '*Philia* in Euripides' *Electra*', *Philologus* 129: 176–85.

    (1997) *Friendship in the Classical World*. Cambridge.

    (1999) 'What we Must Believe in Greek Tragedy', *Ramus* 28: 75–88.

Kopperschmidt, J. (1967) *Die Hikesie als Dramatische Form*. Tübingen.

Kossatz-Deissmann, A. (1992) 'Lyssa', in *LIMC* VI.1. Zurich: 322–9.

Kovacs, D. (ed. and trans.) (1995) *Euripides: Children of Heracles, Hippolytus, Andromache, Hecuba*. Cambridge, Mass.

Kraus, C. S. (1998) 'Dangerous Supplements: Etymology and Genealogy in Euripides' *Heracles*', *PCPS* 44: 137–57.

Kroeker, E. (1938) *Der Herakles des Euripides*. Diss. Leipzig.

Krummen, E. (1990) Pyrsos Hymnon: *Festliche Gegenwart und Mythisch-Rituelle Tradition als Voraussetzung einer Pindarinterpretation (Isthmie 4, Pythie 5, Olympie 1 und 3)*. Berlin.

    (1998) 'Ritual und Katastrophe: Rituelle Handlung und Bildersprache bei Sophokles und Euripides, in Graf (1998): 296–325.

Kullmann, W. (1987) 'Deutung und Bedeutung der Götter bei Euripides', in *Mythos: Deutung und Bedeutung*, eds. S. Posch et al. Innsbruck: 7–22.

Kunstler, B. (1991) 'The Werewolf Figure and its Adoption into the Greek Political Vocabulary', *CW* 84: 189–205.

Kuntz, M. (1994) 'The Prodikean Choice of Herakles: a Reshaping of Myth', *CJ* 89: 163–81.

Lada-Richards, I. (1997) 'Neoptolemus and the Bow: Ritual *Thea* and Theatrical Vision in Sophocles' *Philoctetes*', *JHS* 118: 179–83.

  (1998) 'Staging the *Ephebeia*: Theatrical Role-playing and Ritual Transition in Sophocles' *Philoctetes*', *Ramus* 27: 1–26.

  (1999) *Initiating Dionysus: Ritual and Theatre in Aristophanes' Frogs.* Oxford.

Lattimore R. (1964) *Story Patterns in Greek Tragedy.* London.

Laurens, J.-L. (1986) 'Busiris', in *LIMC* III.1. Zurich: 147–52.

Lawrence, S. E. (1998) 'The God that is Truly God and the Universe of Euripides' *Heracles*', *Mnemosyne* 51: 129–46.

Leach, E. (1976) *Culture and Communication.* Cambridge.

Lee, K. H. (ed.) (1976) *Euripides: Troades.* London.

  (1980) 'Human and Divine in Euripides' *Heracles*', in *Vindex Humanitatis: Essays in Honour of J.H. Bishop*, ed. B. Marshall. Armidale: 34–45.

  (1982) 'The Iris-Lyssa Scene in Euripides' *Heracles*', *Antichthon* 16: 44–53.

  (ed.) (1997) *Euripides: Ion.* Warminster.

Lefkowitz, M. (1969) 'Bacchylides' *Ode* 5: Imitation and Originality', *HSCP* 73: 45–96.

  (1987) 'Was Euripides an Atheist?', *SIFC* 5: 149–66.

  (1989) '"Impiety" and "Atheism" in Euripides' Dramas', *CQ* 39: 70–82.

Lévêque, P. and Verbanck-Piérard, A. (1992) 'Héraclès héros ou dieu?', in Bonnet and Jourdain-Annequin (1992): 43–65.

Liapis, V. (2003) Ἄγνωστος Θεός. Ὅρια τῆς ἀνθρώπινης γνώσης στους προσωκρατικούς καὶ στον Οἰδίποδα Τύραννο. Athens.

Lincoln, B. (1975) 'Homeric λύσσα: "Wolfish Rage"', *IF* 80: 98–105.

Lissarrague, F. (1980) 'L' Iconographie de Dolon le loup', *RA*: 3–30.

  (1990) *L' Autre guerrier: archers, peltastes, cavaliers dans l' imagerie attique.* Paris.

Lloyd, M. (1992) *The* Agon *in Euripides.* Oxford.

  (ed.) (1994) *Euripides: Andromache.* Warminster.

Lloyd-Jones, H. (1967) 'Heracles at Eleusis: *P.Oxy.* 2622 and *PSI* 1391', *Maia* 19: 206–29. [= Lloyd-Jones, H. (1990) *Greek Epic, Lyric, and Tragedy: The Academic Papers of Sir Hugh Lloyd-Jones.* Oxford: 167–87. Oxford. (With a note on later relevant literature, p. 187).]

  (ed. and trans.) (1994) *Sophocles: Antigone, The Women of Trachis, Philoctetes, Oedipus at Colonus.* Cambridge, Mass.

  (1998) 'Ritual and Tragedy', in Graf (1998): 271–95.

Long, A. A. (1968) *Language and Thought in Sophocles: A Study of Abstract Nouns and Poetic Technique.* London.

Loraux, N. (1990) 'Herakles: the Super-male and the Feminine', in *Before Sexuality: The Construction of Erotic Experience in the Ancient World*, eds. D. M. Halperin et al. Princeton: 21–52.

(1995) *The Experiences of Tiresias: The Feminine and the Greek Man*, trans. P. Wissing, Princeton. [Original: Paris 1989.]

Luschnig, C. (1988) *Tragic Aporia: A Study of Euripides' Iphigenia at Aulis*. Victoria.

Maio, D. P. (1977) *The First Part of Euripides' Herakles*. Diss. Berkeley.

Mantziou, M. (2002) 'Ἐπαναλαμβανόμενα θέματα καὶ ἐκφράσεις στις τραγωδίες του Σοφοκλή', *Dodone* 31: 229–45.

Masqueray, P. (1906) 'Euripide et les enfants', *REA* 8: 85–92.

Mastrocinque, A. (1993) *Ercole in occidente*. Trento.

Mastronarde, D. J. (1986) 'The Optimist Rationalist in Euripides: Theseus, Jocasta, Teiresias', in Cropp et al. (1986): 201–11.

(1990) 'Actors on High: the Skene Roof, the Crane, and the Gods in Attic Drama', *ClAnt* 9: 247–94.

(ed.) (1994) *Euripides: Phoenissae*. Cambridge.

(2000) 'Tragedy and Other Genres', in Cropp et al. (2000): 17–39.

Mattes, J. (1970) *Der Wahnsinn im griechischen Mythos und in der Dichtung bis zum Drama des fünften Jahrhunderts*. Heidelberg.

Matthiessen, K. (1964) *Elektra, Taurische Iphigenie und Helena: Untersuchungen zur Chronologie und zur dramatischen Form im Spätwerk des Euripides*. Göttingen.

(2004) *Euripides und sein Jahrhundert*. Munich.

McAuslan, I. and Walcot, P. (eds.) (1993) *Greek Tragedy*. Oxford.

McDonald, M. (1978) *Terms for Happiness in Euripides*. Göttingen.

Meagher, R. (1989) *Mortal Vision: The Wisdom of Euripides*. New York.

Meier, C. (1993) *The Political Art of Greek Tragedy*, trans. A. Webber. Cambridge. [Munich 1988.]

Meijering, R. (1987) *Literary and Rhetorical Theories in Greek Scholia*. Groningen.

Menu, M. (1992) 'L' enfant chez Euripide: affectivité et dramaturgie, *Pallas* 38: 239–58.

Mercier, C. A. (1990) *Suppliant Ritual in Euripidean Tragedy*. Diss. Columbia.

Meridor, R. (1983) 'The Function of Polymestor's Crime in the *Hecuba* of Euripides', *Eranos* 81: 13–20.

(1984) 'Plot and Myth in Euripides' *Heracles* and *Troades*', *Phoenix* 38: 205–15.

Mette, H. (1983) 'Peirithous, Theseus, Herakles bei Euripides', *ZPE* 50: 13–19.

Metzger, H. (1995) 'Le Dionysos des images Eleusiniennes du ive siècle, *RA*: 3–22.

Michelakis, P. (2002) *Achilles in Greek Tragedy*. Cambridge.

Michelini, A. (1987) *Euripides and the Tragic Tradition*. Wisconsin.

Mikalson, J. (1986) 'Zeus the Father and Heracles the Son in Tragedy, *TAPhA* 116: 89–98.

(1991) *Honor Thy Gods: Popular Religion in Greek Tragedy*. Chapel Hill.

Miller, H. W. (1944) 'Medical Terminology in Tragedy, *TAPhA* 75: 156–67.

Mills, S. (1997) *Theseus, Tragedy and the Athenian Empire*. Oxford.

Mirto, M. S. (1980) 'Il sacrificio tra metafora e *mechanema* nell' *Elettra* di Euripide', *CCC* 1: 299–329.

(ed.) (1997) *Euripide: Eracle*. Milan.

Mitchell-Boyask, R. N. (1993) 'Sacrifice and Revenge in Euripides' *Hecuba*', *Ramus* 22: 116–34.

Morillo, S. R. (1995) El simbolismo del arco de Odisseo', *Gerión* 13: 27–45.

Morwood, J. (1997) (trans.) *Euripides: Medea and other Plays*. Oxford.

Mossman, J. (1995) *Wild Justice: A Study of Euripides' Hecuba*. Oxford.

(ed.) (2003) *Oxford Readings in Classical Studies: Euripides*. Oxford.

Moulinier, L. (1952) *Le Pur et l' impur dans la pensée des Grecs jusqu' à la fin du IVe siècle avant J.-C.* Paris.

Mullens, H. G. (1939) '*Hercules Furens* and *Prometheus Vinctus*', *CR* 53: 165–6.

(1941) 'The Aeschylean Interpretation of *Hercules Furens*', *CJ* 36: 229–32.

Murray, G. (1946) 'Herakles, the Best of Men', in *Greek Studies*, ed. G. Murray. Oxford: 106–26.

Musitelli, S. (1968) 'Riflessi di teorie mediche nelle *Baccanti* di Euripide', *Dioniso* 42: 93–114.

Mylonas, G. (1961) *Eleusis and the Eleusinian Mysteries*. Princeton.

Nesselrath, H.-G. (1997) 'Herakles als tragischer Held in und seit der Antike', in *Tragödie: Idee und Transformation*, ed. H. Flashar. Stuttgart: 307–31.

Nikolakakis, E. D. [Η. Δ. Νικολακάκης] (1993) *Η ιδέα περί θεού στις τραγωδίες του Ευριπίδη. Συμβολή στην μελέτη της αρχαίας ελληνικής θρησκείας.* Thessaloniki.

Norwood, G. (1954) *Essays on Euripidean Drama*. London.

Nussbaum, M. C. (1986) *The Fragility of Goodness: Luck and Ethics in Greek Tragedy and Philosophy*. Cambridge.

O'Brien-Moore, A. (1924) *Madness in Ancient Literature*. Weimar.

O'Bryhim, S. (2000) 'The Ritual of Human Sacrifice in Euripides', *CB* 76: 29–37.

O' Connor-Visser, E. A. M. E. (1987) *Aspects of Human Sacrifice in the Tragedies of Euripides*. Amsterdam.

Otto, W. F. (1965) *Dionysus: Myth and Cult*, trans. R. B. Palmer. Bloomington. [Frankfurt 1933.]

Pachet, P (1972) 'Le Bâtard monstrueux', *Poétique* 12: 531–43.

Padel, R. (1981) 'Madness in Fifth-century Athenian Tragedy', in *Indigenous Psychologies: The Anthropology of the Self*, eds. P. Heelas and A. Lock. London: 105–31.

(1992) *In and Out of the Mind: Greek Images of the Tragic Self*. Princeton.

(1995) *Whom Gods Destroy: Elements of Greek and Tragic Madness.* Princeton.

Padilla, M. (1992) 'The Gorgonic Archer: Danger of Sight in Euripides' *Heracles*', *CW* 86: 1–12.

(1994) 'Heroic Paternity in Euripides' *Heracles*', *Arethusa* 27: 279–302.

Page, D. L. (ed.) (1938) *Euripides: Medea.* Oxford.

Papadopoulou, Th. (1998) 'Tradition and Invention in the Greek Tragic Scholia: some Examples of Terminology', *SIFC* 16: 202–32.

(1999a) 'Literary Theory and Terminology in the Greek Tragic Scholia: the Case of *Plasma*', *BICS* 43: 203–10.

(1999b) 'Subjectivity and Community in Greek Tragedy: the Example of Euripides' *Heracles*', in Patsalidis and Sakellaridou (1999): 297–307.

(2000a) 'Cassandra's Radiant Vigour and the Ironic Optimism of Euripides' *Troades*', *Mnemosyne* 53: 513–27.

(2000b) Review of Tyrrell and Bennett (1998), *JHS* 120: 154–5.

(2001a) 'Revenge in Euripides' *Heracles*', in *Homer, Tragedy and Beyond: Essays in Honour of P.E. Easterling*, eds. F. Budelmann and P. Michelakis. London: 113–28.

(2001b) 'The Prophetic Figure in Euripides' *Phoenissae* and *Bacchae*', *Hermes* 129: 21–31.

(2001c) 'Representations of Athena in Greek Tragedy', in *Athena in the Classical World*, eds. S. Deacy and A. Villing. Leiden: 293–310.

(2001d) Review of Burnett (1998), *JHS* 121: 193.

(2004) 'Herakles and Hercules: the Hero's Ambivalence in Euripides and Seneca', *Mnemosyne* 57: 257–83.

Parker, R. (1983) *Miasma: Pollution and Purification in Early Greek Religion.* Oxford.

(1997) 'Gods Cruel and Kind: Tragic and Civic Ideology', in Pelling (1997): 143–60.

Parmentier, L. and H. Grégoire (eds.) (1923) *Euripide:* Héraclès, Budé Edition, vol. III. Paris.

Parry, H. (1965) 'The Second Stasimon of Euripides' *Heracles* (637–700)', *AJPh* 86: 363–74.

Patsalidis, S. and Sakellaridou, E. (eds.) (1999) *(Dis)Placing Classical Greek Theatre.* Thessaloniki.

Pelling, C. (ed.) (1997) *Greek Tragedy and the Historian.* Oxford.

Perdicoyianni, H. (1996) '*Philos* chez Euripide', *RBPh* 74: 5–26.

Petre, Z. (1985) 'La Représentation de la mort dans la tragédie grecque', *StudClas* 23: 21–35.

Piccaluga, G. (1968) *Lykaon: un tema mitico.* Rome.

Pigeaud, J. (1981) *La Maladie de l' âme: Étude sur la relation de l' âme et du corps dans la tradition médico-philosophique antique.* Paris.

(1987) *Folie et cures de la folie chez les médecins de l' antiquité gréco-romaine: la manie.* Paris.

(1988) *Aristote. L'homme de génie et la mélancholie: problème XXX, 1*. Paris.

Pike, D. L. (1978) 'Hercules Furens: some Thoughts on the Madness of Heracles in Greek Literature', *PACA* 14: 1–6.

Podlecki, A. J. (1966) *The Political Background of Aeschylean Tragedy*. Ann Arbor.

(ed.) (1989) *Aeschylus: Eumenides*. Warminster.

Pohlenz, M. (²1954) *Die griechische Tragödie*. Göttingen.

Porter, D. (1987) *Only Connect: Three Studies in Greek Tragedy*. New York.

Pralon, D. (1992) 'Les Travaux d' Héraclès dans l' *Héraclès Furieux* d' Euripide (Eur. *H.F.* 348–441)', *L' initiation: actes du colloque international de Montpellier*, 11–14 Avril 1991, 2nd. vol., ed. A. Moreau. Montpellier: 5–17.

Pratt, L. H. (1993) *Lying and Poetry from Homer to Pindar: Falsehood and Deception in Archaic Greek Poetics*. Ann Arbor.

Pucci, P. (1980) *The Violence of Pity in Euripides' Medea*. Ithaca.

Rehm, R. (1988) 'The Staging of Suppliant Plays', *GRBS* 29: 263–307.

(1994) *Marriage to Death: The Conflation of Wedding and Funeral Rites in Greek Tragedy*. Princeton.

(2000) 'The Play of Space: Before, Behind, and Beyond in Euripides' *Heracles*', in Cropp et al. (2000): 363–75.

(2002) *The Play of Space: Spatial Transformation in Greek Tragedy*. Princeton.

Reinhardt, K. (1961) *Die Ilias und ihr Dichter*, ed. U. Hölscher. Göttingen.

(2003) 'The Intellectual Crisis in Euripides', in Mossman (2003), 16–46. [Original 1960.]

Rhodes, P. (2003) 'Nothing to do with Democracy: Athenian Drama and the *Polis*', *JHS* 123: 104–19.

Ritchie, W. (1964) *The Authenticity of the Rhesus of Euripides*. Cambridge.

Rivier, A. (²1975) *Essai sur le tragique d' Euripide*. Paris.

Robert, C. (1921) *Die Griechische Heldensage* vol. II. Berlin.

Robertson, D. S. (1938) 'Euripides *H.F.* 499 sqq.', *CR* 52: 50–1.

Robertson, N. (1980) 'Heracles' "Catabasis"', *Hermes* 108: 274–300.

Rocco, C. (1997) *Tragedy and Enlightenment: Athenian Political Thought and the Dilemmas of Modernity*. Berkeley.

Romilly, J. de (1960) *L' Évolution du pathetique, d' Eschyle à Euripide*. Paris.

(1995) 'Le Refus du suicide dans l' *Héraclès* d' Euripide', in J. de Romilly, *Tragédies grecques au fil des ans*. Paris: 159–69.

Rose, P. W. (1992) *Sons of the Gods, Children of the Earth: Ideology and Literary Form in Ancient Greece*. Ithaca.

Rosivach, V. J. (1983) 'On Creon, Antigone, and Not Burying the Dead', *RhM* 126: 193–211.

(1987) 'Execution by Stoning in Athens', *ClAnt* 6: 232–48.

Ruck, C. A. P. (1976) 'Duality and the Madness of Herakles', *Arethusa* 9: 53–75.

Rutherford, I. (1995) 'Apollo in Ivy: the Tragic Paean', *Arion* 3: 112–35.

Rutherford, R. B. (1982) 'Tragic Form and Feeling in the *Iliad*', *JHS* 102: 145–60.

Schamun, M. C. (1997) 'Significaciones de τάραγμα (perturbación) en *Heracles* de Euripides', *Synthesis* 4: 99–112.

Schein, S. L. (1988) 'Φιλία in Euripides' *Alcestis*', *Métis* 3: 179–206.

Schlesier, R. (1985a) 'L' *Héraclès* et la critique des dieux chez Euripide', *ASNSP* 15: 7–40.

(1985b) 'Der Stachel der Götter: Zum Problem des Wahnsinns in der Euripideischen Tragödie', *Poetica* 17: 1–45.

(1986) 'Götterdämmerung bei Euripides?', in *Der Untergang von Religionen*, ed. H. Zinser. Berlin: 35–50.

(1993) 'Mixtures of Masks: Maenads as Tragic Models', in Carpenter and Faraone (1993): 89–114.

Schmid, W. and O. Staehlin (1929–48) *Geschichte der griechischen Literatur*. (5 vols.). Munich.

Schmidt, J. W. (1987) 'Die Götter – Wirklichkeit oder menschliche Erfindung? Überlegungen zum Herakles-Drama des Euripides', *Theologie und Glaube* 77: 443–59.

Schreckenberg, H. (1964) Anankê: *Untersuchungen zur Geschichte des Wortgebrauchs*. Munich.

Scodel, R. (1980a) 'Hesiod Redivivus', *GRBS* 21: 301–20.

(1980b) *The Trojan Trilogy of Euripides*. Göttingen.

(ed.) (1993) *Theater and Society in the Classical World*. Ann Arbor.

Scullion, S. (2000) 'Tradition and Invention in Euripidean aitiology', in Cropp et al. (2000): 217–33.

Scully, S. E. (1973) *Philia and Charis in Euripidean Tragedy*. Diss. Toronto.

Seaford, R. (1993) 'Dionysus as Destroyer of the Household: Homer, Tragedy, and the *Polis*', in Carpenter and Faraone (1993): 115–46.

(1994) *Reciprocity and Ritual: Homer and Tragedy in the Developing City-State*. Oxford.

(ed.) (1996) *Euripides: Bacchae*. Warminster.

Segal, C. (1971) *The Theme of the Mutilation of the Corpse in the Iliad*. Leiden.

(1981) *Tragedy and Civilization: An Interpretation of Sophocles*. Cambridge, Mass.

(1982) *Dionysiac Poetics and Euripides' Bacchae*. Princeton.

(1986a) 'Literature and Interpretation: Conventions, History, and Universals', in C. Segal, *Interpreting Greek Tragedy: Myth, Poetry, Text*. Ithaca: 359–75.

(1986b) 'The Two Worlds of Euripides' *Helen*', in C. Segal, *Interpreting Greek Tragedy: Myth, Poetry, Text*. Ithaca: 222–67.

(1990a) 'Sacrifice and Violence in the myth of Meleager and Heracles: Homer, Bacchylides, Sophocles', *Helios* 17: 7–24.

(1990b) 'Violence and the Other: Greek, Female, and Barbarian in Euripides' *Hecuba*', *TAPhA* 120: 109–31.

(1993) 'Female Death and Male Tears', in C. Segal, *Euripides and the Poetics of Sorrow: Art, Gender, and Commemoration in Alcestis, Hippolytus, and Hecuba*. Durham: 51–72.

(1995a) *Sophocles' Tragic World: Divinity, Nature, Society*. Cambridge, Mass.

(1995b) 'Drama and Perspective in *Ajax*', in C. Segal, *Sophocles' Tragic World: Divinity, Nature, Society*. Cambridge, Mass.: 16–25.

(1997) *Dionysiac Poetics and Euripides' Bacchae*. Princeton. [Expanded edition of C. Segal (1982).]

(2000) 'Lament and Recognition: a Reconsideration of the Ending of the *Bacchae*', in Cropp et al. (2000): 273–91.

Seidensticker, B. (1979) 'Sacrificial Ritual in the *Bacchae*', in *Arktouros: Hellenic Studies Presented to Bernard M. W. Knox on the Occasion of his 65th Birthday*, eds. G. W. Bowersock et al. Berlin: 181–90.

(1982) *Palintonos Harmonia: Studien zu komischen Elementen in der griechischen Tragödien*. Göttingen.

Shapiro, H. A. (1983) 'Hêrôs Theos: the Death and Apotheosis of Heracles', *CW* 77: 7–18.

Shaw, M. (1982) 'The ἦθος of Theseus in the *Suppliant Women*', *Hermes* 110: 3–19.

Shelton, J. (1979) 'Structural Unity and the Meaning of Euripides' *Herakles*', *Eranos* 77: 101–10.

Sheppard, J. T. (1916) 'The Formal Beauty of the *Hercules Furens*', *CQ* 10: 72–9.

Sifakis, G. M. (1967) *Studies in the History of Hellenistic Drama*. London.

(1979) 'Children in Greek Tragedy', *BICS* 26: 67–80.

Silk, M. (1993) 'Heracles and Greek Tragedy', in McAuslan and Walcot (1993): 116–37.

Simon, B. (1978) *Mind and Madness in Ancient Greece*. Ithaca.

Simon, E. (1990) 'Iakchos', in *LIMC* v.1. Zurich: 612–14.

Smith, W. D. (1967) 'Disease in Euripides' *Orestes*', *Hermes* 95: 291–307.

Snodgrass, A. M. (1964) *Early Greek Armour and Weapons from the End of the Bronze Age to 600 BC*. Edinburgh.

(1967) *Arms and Armour of the Greeks*. London.

Sommerstein, A. H. (ed.) (1989) *Aeschylus: Eumenides*. Cambridge.

Sommerstein, A. H. et al. (eds.) (1993) *Tragedy, Comedy and the Polis. Papers from the Greek Drama Conference, Nottingham, 18–20 July 1990*. Bari.

Sourvinou-Inwood, C. (1997) 'Medea at a Shifting Distance: Images and Euripidean Tragedy', in *Medea: Essays on Medea in Myth, Literature, Philosophy, and Art*, eds. J. J. Clauss et al. Princeton: 253–96.

(2003) *Tragedy and Athenian Religion*. Lanham.

Staden, H. von (1992) 'The Mind and Skin of Heracles: Heroic Diseases', in *Maladie et maladies: histoire et conceptualisation*, ed. D. Gourevitch. Geneva: 131–50.

Stanton G. R. (1990) '*Philia* and *Xenia* in Euripides' *Alkestis*', *Hermes* 118: 42–54.

Starobinski, J. (1974) *Trois fureurs*. Paris.

Stevens, P. T. (ed.) (1971) *Euripides: Andromache*. Oxford.

Stinton T. C. W. (1965) *Euripides and the Judgement of Paris*. London. [=Stinton, T. C. W. (1990) *Collected Papers on Greek Tragedy*. Oxford: 17–75.]

(1976) '"*Si credere dignum est*": Some Expressions of Disbelief in Euripides and Others', *PCPhS* 22: 60–89. [=Stinton, T. C. W. (1990) *Collected Papers on Greek tragedy*. Oxford: 236–64.]

(1987) 'The Apotheosis of Heracles from the Pyre', in *Papers Given at a Colloquium on Greek Drama in Honour of R.P. Winnington-Ingram*, ed. L. Rodley. London: 1–16. [=Stinton, T. C. W. (1990) *Collected Papers on Greek Tragedy*. Oxford: 493–507.]

Straaten, F. T. van (1995) *Hiera Kala: Images of Animal Sacrifice in Archaic and Classical Greece*. Leiden.

Sutton, D. F. (1980) *The Greek Satyr Play*. Meisenheim.

Szlezák, T.A. (1986) '*Mania* und *Aidôs*: Bemerkungen zur Ethik und Anthropologie des Euripides', *A & A* 32: 46–59.

Taplin, O. (1977) *The Stagecraft of Aeschylus: The Dramatic Use of Exits and Entrances in Greek Tragedy*. Oxford.

(1999) 'Spreading the Word through Performance', in *Performance Culture and Athenian Democracy*, eds. S. Goldhill and R. Osborne. Cambridge: 33–57.

Taragna Novo, S. (1973) 'L' *APETH* di Eracle e la sorte dell' uomo nel contrasto tra Lico e Anfitrione (Eur. *H.F.* 140–239)', *RIFC* 101: 45–69.

Tarkow, T. A. (1977) 'The Glorification of Athens in Euripides' *Heracles*', *Helios* 5: 27–35.

Temkin, O. (²1971) *The Falling Sickness: A History of Epilepsy from the Greeks to the Beginnings of Modern Neurology*. Baltimore.

Theodorou, Z. (1993) 'Subject to Emotion: Exploring Madness in *Orestes*', *CQ* 43: 32–46.

Torr, C. (1895) *Ancient Ships*. Cambridge.

Turner, V. (1969) *The Ritual Process: Structure and Anti-Structure*. Ithaca.

(1974a) *Dramas, Fields and Metaphors: Symbolic Action in Human Society*. Ithaca.

(1974b) 'Metaphors of Anti-structure in Religious Culture', in *Changing Perspectives in the Scientific Study of Religion*, ed. A. W. Eister. New York: 63–84.

Tyrrell, W. B. and Bennett, L. J. (1998) *Recapturing Sophocles' Antigone*. Lanham.

Tzanetou, A. (2000) 'Almost Dying, Dying Twice: Ritual and Audience in Euripides' *Iphigenia in Tauris'*, in Cropp et al. (2000): 199–216.

Valk van der, M. (1958) 'On Apollodorus' *Bibliotheca'*, *REG* 71: 100–68.

Vasquez, P. R. (1972) *Literary Convention in Scenes of Madness and Suffering in Greek Tragedy*. Diss. Columbia.

Vellacott, P. (1963) trans. *Euripides: Medea and Other Plays (Medea, Hecabe, Electra, Heracles)*. Harmondsworth.

(1975) *Ironic Drama: A Study of Euripides' Method and Meaning*. Cambridge.

Vernant, J.-P. (1985) *La Mort dans les yeux: figures de l' autre en Grèce ancienne*. Paris.

(1991a) 'A "Beautiful Death" and the Disfigured Corpse in Homeric Epic', in *Jean-Pierre Vernant: Mortals and Immortals. Collected Essays*, ed. F. I. Zeitlin. Princeton: 50–74.

(1991b) 'Mortals and Immortals: the Body of the Divine', in *Jean-Pierre Vernant: Mortals and Immortals. Collected Essays*, ed. F. I. Zeitlin. Princeton: 28–49.

Vernant, J.-P. and Vidal-Naquet, P. (1988) *Myth and Tragedy in Ancient Greece*, trans. J. Lloyd. New York. [2 vols., Paris 1972 and 1986.]

Verrall, A. W. (1905) *Essays on Four Plays of Euripides*. Cambridge.

Versnel, H. S. (1990) *Inconsistencies in Greek and Roman Religion I. Ter Unus: Isis, Dionysos, Hermes. Three Studies in Henotheism*. Leiden.

Vickers, M. (1995) 'Heracles Lacedaemonius: The Political Dimensions of Sophocles' *Trachiniae* and Euripides' *Heracles'*, *DHA* 21 (2): 41–69.

Vidal-Naquet, P. (1988) 'Hunting and Sacrifice in Aeschylus' *Oresteia'*, in Vernant and Vidal-Naquet (1988): 141–59.

Vollkommer, R. (1988) *Herakles in the Art of Classical Greece*. Oxford.

Waldmann, H. (1962) *Der Wahnsinn im griechischen Mythos*. Diss. Munich.

Walker, H. J. (1995) *Theseus and Athens*. New York.

Walton, J. M. (1997) 'Introduction', in *Euripides Plays: Five. Andromache, Herakles' Children, Herakles*, eds. J. M. Walton and K. McLeish: vii–xxiii. London.

Ward, A. G. (ed.) (1970) *The Quest for Theseus*. London.

Webster, T. B. L. (1967) *The Tragedies of Euripides*. London.

(ed.) (1970) *Sophocles: Philoctetes*. Cambridge.

Wees, H. van (1992) *Status Warriors: War, Violence and Society in Homer and History*. Amsterdam.

West, M. L. (ed.) (1966) *Hesiod: Theogony*. Oxford.

(ed.) (1987) *Euripides: Orestes*. Warminster.

Whallon, W. (1995) 'The Furies in *Choe.* and *Ag.*', *CQ* 45: 231–2.

Wilamowitz-Moellendorff, U. von (ed.) (^{2}1895) *Euripides: Herakles*. Berlin. [1st edn, Berlin 1889.]

Wildberg, C. (2000) 'Piety as Service, Epiphany as Reciprocity: Two Observations on the Religious Meaning of the Gods in Euripides', in Cropp et al. (2000): 235–56.

Wilkins, J. (ed.) (1993) *Euripides: Heraclidae*. Oxford.

Williams, D. (1986) 'Dolon', in *LIMC* III.1. Zurich: 660–4.

Willink, C. W. (1988) 'Sleep after Labour in Euripides' *Heracles*', *CQ* 38: 86–97.

Wilson, P. (2000) 'Euripides' Tragic Muse', in Cropp et al. (2000): 427–49.

Winkler, J. J. and Zeitlin, F. I. (eds.) (1990) *Nothing to do with Dionysos? Athenian Drama in its Social Context*. Princeton.

Winnington-Ingram, R. P. (1980) *Sophocles: An Interpretation*. Cambridge.

Wolff, C. (2001) 'Introduction', in *Euripides: Herakles*, trans. T. Sleigh. Oxford.

Woodford, S. (1966) *Exemplum Virtutis: A Study of Heracles in Athens in the Second Half of the Fifth Century B.C.* Diss. Columbia.

(1971) 'Cults of Heracles in Attica', in *Studies Presented to George M. A. Haufmann*, eds. D. G. Mitten et al. Mainz: 211–25.

Worman, N. (1999) 'The Ties that Bind: Transformations of Costume and Connection in Euripides' *Heracles*', *Ramus* 28: 89–107.

Xanthakis-Karamanos, G. (1980) *Studies in Fourth-Century Tragedy*. Athens.

Yoshitake, S. (1994) 'Disgrace, Grief and other Ills: Heracles' Rejection of Suicide', *JHS* 114: 135–53.

Yunis, H. (1988) *A New Creed: Fundamental Religious Beliefs in the Athenian Polis and Euripidean Drama*. Göttingen.

Zeitlin, F. I. (1965) 'The Motif of the Corrupted Sacrifice in Aeschylus' *Oresteia*', *TAPhA* 96: 463–508.

(1966) 'Postscript to the Sacrificial Imagery in the *Oresteia* (*Ag.* 1235–37)', *TAPhA* 97: 645–53.

(1970) 'The Argive Festival of Hera and Euripides' *Electra*', *TAPhA* 101: 645–69.

(1990) 'Thebes: Theater of Self and Society in Athenian Drama', in Winkler and Zeitlin (1990): 130–67.

(1996) 'The Body's Revenge: Dionysos and Tragic Action in Euripides' *Hekabe*', in F. I. Zeitlin, *Playing the Other: Gender and Society in Classical Greek Literature*. Chicago: 172–216.

Zelenak, M. X. (1998) *Gender and Politics in Greek Tragedy*. New York.

Zuntz, G. (1955) *The Political Plays of Euripides*. Manchester.

INDEX OF PASSAGES CITED

1424: 179
Hipp. 5–6: 117
7–8: 97
120: 117
442–50: 98
451–2: 99
451–61: 99
887–90: 113
895–6: 113
1166–8: 113
1169–70: 113
1328–30: 77
1420–2: 117
IA 794–800: 107
1375–86: 134
Ion 589–606: 153
916: 105
1074: 51
IT 72–6: 38
267–8: 48
282–308: 65
283–4: 65
282: 65
285–300: 69
297: 48
308: 64, 65
310–11: 64
380–91: 104
388: 105, 106
389–91: 15
1428–30: 38
Med. 24–36: 62
89–95: 62
92: 63, 65
187: 48
187–8: 63
1173–4: 64
1174–5: 63
1175: 64
1183: 63
1197: 63
1279–84: 62
1281: 62
1284: 62
1342: 48
1407: 48
Or. 36: 66
166–86: 68
215–16: 68

219–20: 63, 64
224: 63
253: 63
259: 63
268–72: 65
270: 67
277: 65
277–9: 68
415: 167
418: 94
546: 29
792–4: 165
1022: 187
1031–2: 157, 187
1060–4: 134
Rhes. 209: 26
Supp. 111: 160
176–9: 156
286: 160
293: 154
301–13: 154
314–19: 136
320–5: 154
467–75: 155
518–21: 155
524–7: 38, 155
542: 155
576: 155
577: 155
839–40: 187
1059–63: 133
1165–73: 155
Tro. 23–34: 103
67–8: 104
208–9: 153
218–19: 153
307: 65
467: 116
469: 96
608–9: 186
698: 186
764–5: 15
766–73: 110
770: 109, 110
884–8: 88
885: 94
889: 89
924–31: 103
948–50: 98

INDEX OF PASSAGES CITED

HYGINUS
Fab. 32: 75

ILIU PERSIS
fr. 1.8 Davies: 63
ISOCRATES
5.109–14: 6

LUCIAN
JTr. 41: 90
LYCOPHRON
Schol. on *Alex.* 38: 75

MELANIPPIDES
fr. 758. 1–2 *PMG*: 127

NICOLAUS DAMASCENUS
FGrH 90 F 13: 74

PANYASSIS
fr. 1, Bernabé, *PEG*: 72
PAUSANIAS
1.15.3: 75, 182
5.2.1–2: 149
9.11.2: 72, 126
32.4: 75, 182
PHERECYDES HISTORICUS
FGrH 3 F 14: 73
PHILOSTRATUS
Her. 35. 14–15: 167
Imag. II 23.4 (378 K.): 122
PINDAR
Isthm. 4.41–3: 102
4.67–70: 74
4.70 Snell: 39
Nem. 1.62–6: 6
3.22: 5
7.20–30: 102
7.96–7: 157
Ol. 1.28–9: 101
1.30: 101
1.35: 101
1.37–51: 105
1.53: 101
3.28: 76
9.30–41: 6
9.35–41: 102
10.27–34: 149
10.34: 6

Schol. on *Isthm.* 4.104g: 5, 73
Schol. on *Ol.* 10.19b: 38
PISANDER
fr. 10, Bernabé, *PEG*: 6, 20
PLATO
Ap. 37c6: 132
Leg. 9, 873c–d: 166
Phd. 62b–c: 166
PLUTARCH
Lys. VII.4: 41
Mor. 756 c: 90
1052 E 40: 91
Vit. Thes. 29.3: 160
POxy.
2400, vol. 24, 107–9, 11. 10–14: 71
PROCLUS
Chr. p. 40, 28: 72

SENECA
HF 483–4: 39
SOLON
13, 63–70: 118
SEXTUS EMPIRICUS
Adv. Gramm. 253: 108
264: 108
Math. I 288: 89
SOPHOCLES
Aj. 44: 170
46: 170
51–8: 69
69–70: 64
74–80: 172
91–3: 169
108–10: 66
111: 169
112–13: 169
127–33: 169
134–200: 168
205: 171
239–42: 66
274: 65
287: 65
290: 65
301: 65
303: 67
317–20: 187
322: 45, 65
371: 172
372–91: 171

225

GENERAL INDEX

Amphitryon:
    criticism of Zeus: 95–6, 112
    debate with Lycus: 135–42
    on Heracles' uncontrollable character:
        19, 44–5
Athena: 44, 64, 123–7, 161, 192

Chorus:
    and hoplite formation: 145–6
    on Heracles and Apollo: 46–7
    on Heracles' contests: 31, 137, 146,
        161–2
    on Heracles' madness: 61–2
    on the reward of virtue: 32–4, 119
    reaction at the murder of Lycus: 42,
        119, 149

Euripides' *HF*:
    approaches to the play: 1–3, 13, 21–2,
        32, 54, 55–6, 82–4
    Dionysiac metaphor: 48–51, 66–7
    hunt-imagery: 31, 66, 148–9
    interplay between dramatic past and
        dramatic present: 24–35 *passim*,
        79–80, 146–7, 149–50
    mystic overtones: 51–4
    openness: 43, 56
    overdetermination and ambiguity:
        22–3
    reversal of polarity between Heracles
        and Lycus: 24–8, 35
    second stasimon: 32–4, 46–7, 50–1
    unity: 1, 25
    Wilamowitz's view: 1–2, 40, 83, 180

gods:
    incomprehensibility: 117–27, 190–1

Heracles:
    ambivalence: 3–4, 5, 9

arete: 5, 6
assimilation of opponents' traits:
    38–40, 45
averter of evils (*alexikakos*): 24, 56
civilizer of mankind: 5, 9, 24, 38
his labours as purification: 24
panhellenic status: 83, 161, 162
in tradition: 4–8
transgressive: 5, 6, 7
Heracles in *HF*:
    ambivalence (interplay between virtue
        and excess): 9, 21, 32, 35, 47, 48–9,
        51, 53, 54, 55, 56
    ambivalence and Dionysiac context:
        48–51
    ambivalence and mystic allusions:
        51–4
    and Achilles: 41–2
    and Ajax: 167–73, 178
    and Apollo: 46, 47
    and Athena: 125, 161
    and Oedipus in Soph. *OC*: 93–4, 164–5
    and Prometheus: 121, 157–8
    arete: 8, 9, 14, 54, 55, 81, c4.3 *passim*,
        190
    aristos: 131–2, 135
    as an archer: 137–51
    change of attitude towards gods:
        176–8, 182
    confusion between good and bad
        violence: 31–4, 45, 47, 54
    development of his notion of divinity:
        85–100, 114–16, 192–3
    duality: 25, 47, 54, 55
    enlarged knowledge of life: 178
    family-man: 78–80, 131
    idealized, 21, 22
    identification with virtue: 24
    impure: 13, 21–2
    kallinikos: 79, 147